PATTERN CUT TECHNIQUES FOR LADIES' JACKETS

PATTERN CUTTING TECHNIQUES FOR LADIES' JACKETS

Jo Baker-Waters

THE CROWOOD PRESS

First published in 2017 by
The Crowood Press Ltd
Ramsbury, Marlborough
Wiltshire SN8 2HR

www.crowood.com

British Library Cataloguing-in-Publication Data
A catalogue record for this book is available from the British Library.

ISBN 978 1 78500 177 2

Dedicated to the true Gentleman of Fashion:
Richard Nicoll 1977-2016

Typeset by Kelly-Anne Levey.
Printed and bound in India by Replika Press Pvt Ltd

Contents

Acknowledgements

I am incredibly grateful to many people for their support and assistance during the years it took to write this book.

Thank you to all of the designers I have had the pleasure to work with who have contributed their work so generously: Richard Nicoll and Nicholas Oakwell. It would not have been possible to demonstrate the diversity of jacket styles in this book without their participation.

I am extremely fortunate to have constructive reviewers, support, and photographic input from colleagues in the industry – Anthony Brotheride, head of menswear at University of Northumbria, in Newcastle, UK; Lee Marsh, Savile Row bespoke men's tailor, 'Lee Marsh Bespoke'; Alexandra Glibbery, Director of womenswear at Calvin Klein Platinum; Katherine Brotheridge, Women's Design Lecturer at the University of Northumbria, in Newcastle; Anthony Martin of Benson and Clegg; and Richard Waters Photography for all photographic images included throughout the book.

A special thanks to the beautiful Jessica Lamb, for allowing me to photograph the process while taking her body measurements. Endless thanks to my parents for their encouragement to enter into the arts, and Richard Waters for sacrificing his downtime to assist me throughout the process.

A final thank you to the legendary Andreas Gomez of Gieves & Hawkes – master craftsman, my mentor and friend – for sharing your knowledge of tailoring during my apprenticeship.

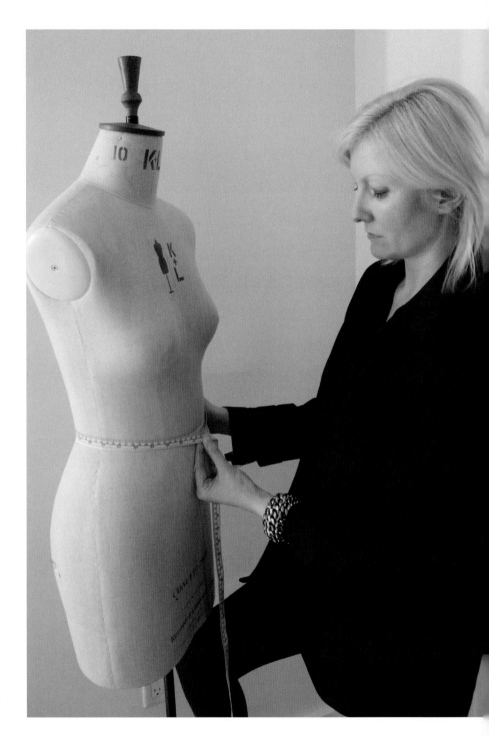

Preface

The fashion industry relies on the skill of artisans – drapers, pattern cutters, tailors, and dressmakers; all of these skills are essential in realizing the vision of the designer.

Whether it is cheap, fast fashion designed for the throwaway generation, with its ever-changing demands of fashion trends, or haute couture – handcrafted clothes created over time for longevity – both require the same foundation of skills in pattern cutting to create a first draft, but require slight variances to finish the pattern, depending on the level of garment construction, and whether it is handcrafted or machine sewn.

I am fortunate to have had what I consider to be two educations in pattern cutting within the apparel industry: one in traditional handcrafted techniques for haute couture and bespoke tailored clothing; the other in ready-to-wear fashions, for runway collections. Both these aspects form intelligent parts of a great industry. Each can learn from the other – the bespoke trade teaching traditional style, and ready-to-wear teaching fashion creativity. I have set out to combine techniques and teach a cross-section of methods that can be used to obtain a pattern personal to the style of the cutter, promoting individuality in patterns, and precision in style lines.

The task of condensing pattern-cutting techniques for ladies' jackets into a single volume has been a considerable undertaking. In attempting it, I wanted to document an extensive view of haute couture, bespoke tailoring and ready-to-wear. The clothing industry as a whole is explored, utilizing flat drafting techniques and dress modelling on the mannequin for traditional and fashion-forward styles of jacket.

I am grateful to everyone in every section of the trade who has collaborated with me over the years to contribute to the knowledge presented throughout this book.

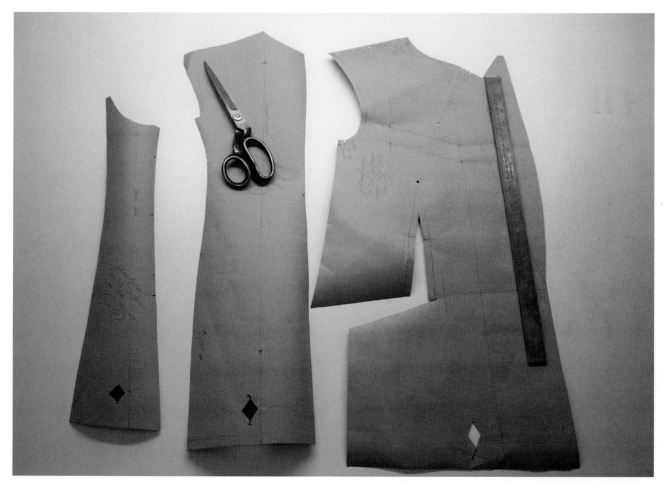

Introduction

In modern couture, bespoke tailoring, and ready-to-wear, a pattern is used as a template to transfer the parts of a garment into cloth. The patterns are drafted onto paper or card, and are kept as a record, which can be used again and again to adapt into new styles – a process known as pattern making in the US, or pattern cutting in the UK. This book focuses entirely on pattern making for ladies' jackets.

The ladies' jacket is a garment cut in cloth, which is worn as an outer layer, traditionally as part of a suit, or as a sports jacket. Cloth has a two-dimensional form, and as a covering for the body, the fabric must conform to the three-dimensional curves of the body and its prominent parts – the neck, arms, shoulders, bust, waist and hips. The jacket is comprised of several panels joined by seams and darts, and the shape of each panel must relate to the particular area that it will cover. This relationship between the cloth and body is called 'the fit'.

The jacket will suspend naturally across the form, to the pull of gravity. The relationship between the cloth and the pull of gravity is called 'the hang'. If the jacket hangs badly, the lack of alignment with the body and vertical pull of gravity can offend the eye, but when the hang is arranged correctly, it appears in harmonious order and 'in balance' to the wearer. To achieve perfection in tailored jackets can take years of experience, and a lot of patience, but with a little common sense and hard work, the basic groundwork starts here.

There are two main sectors of the clothing industry that will be discussed throughout the book: traditional bespoke tailoring, and the ready-to-wear market. The same principles of pattern making apply to both systems. Cutting a pattern for a ladies' jacket can seem a daunting puzzle at first with its complex anatomical lines and formulae. This book introduces the process of drafting a pattern, and breaks it down into two methods: flat pattern cutting and the art form known as draping.

The objective is to draft a pattern for a jacket using a flat pattern cutting system, drape techniques, or a combination of the two.

Flat pattern cutting

The first system begins with drafting a master pattern known as a basic block, in the form of grids divided by anatomical landmark levels. This is retained as a master copy, and a first

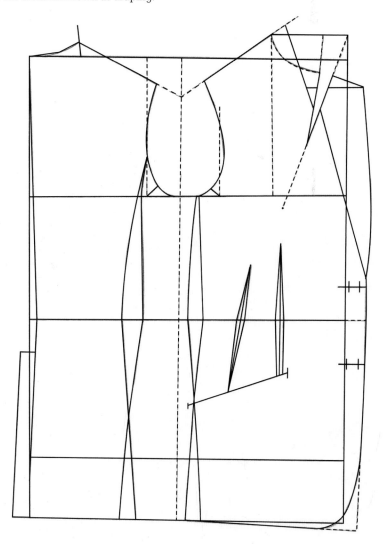

Opposite page: Author's jacket on the dress form for Richard Nicoll show.

The divisional grid system of a single-breasted blazer.

9

pattern is traced with added seam allowances and inlays. The method uses a flat divisional system, drafted by hand, on paper, applying geometry to the various measurements of the draft. The first draft is labelled as the basic block, comprising of one half pattern, with the intention to cut one pair in cloth. It will include a forepart, side panel, and back. Darts and seams are outlined to fit the neck, bust, hips, waist and shoulders. A two-piece tailored sleeve is also documented, separated as an under sleeve and a top sleeve.

The basic block can then be used and adapted for design variations, adjusting style lines by moving seams and darts to alter the fit, shoulder lines, lapel proportion, and silhouette.

Style in cutting is explored in the form of the single-breasted blazer with one-, two- and three-button fastenings, and the double-breasted blazer with its various rows of show and functioning buttons. The iconic tuxedo is studied, introducing the traditional design details and its history, documenting modern updates

to the jacket. Fashion in shoulder lines and sleeve heads is also considered, describing adjustments to the shoulder pad and pattern; style lines in collars and lapels are explained. An overview is given of the many design details that can be incorporated within the style of a jacket pattern.

The block is then transferred into a working flat pattern, by tracing a second copy from the master draft, separating the panels and adding seam allowance and inlays onto the net edges of the pattern. All balance notches are marked to indicate the landmark levels on the pattern. A facing, lining and all its internal structures can be plotted from the master draft, and pocket details are selected; and accompanying pattern pieces can be drafted.

The pattern can be made up in a test fabric, usually calico or muslin, and a first fitting can be done on a dress-maker's mannequin, customer, or fit model, with the exact body measurements of the pattern. After the fitting, changes will be made, the

pattern will be altered and a new toile re-cut until the designer and pattern maker are happy that the design is correct. This method is based around flat pattern making, and is called 'flat' because it is primarily done to the 2D pattern, on the pattern-making table, using blocks and measurements.

Flat-pattern drafting systems evolved in the 1800s and progressed essentially into two methods: the direct method and the proportional method. Both methods use measurements that are taken on the body, the form, or from an existing garment.

The direct method is used in ready-to-wear, taking body measurements and converting them into a standard size code, which can be used to manufacture multiple garments, from a sample size pattern, which is graded up to bigger sizes for retail.

The proportional method is a way of drafting blocks using proportional body measurements; the rest of the measurements are calculated based on the height, or working scale. It is an older system and has been well

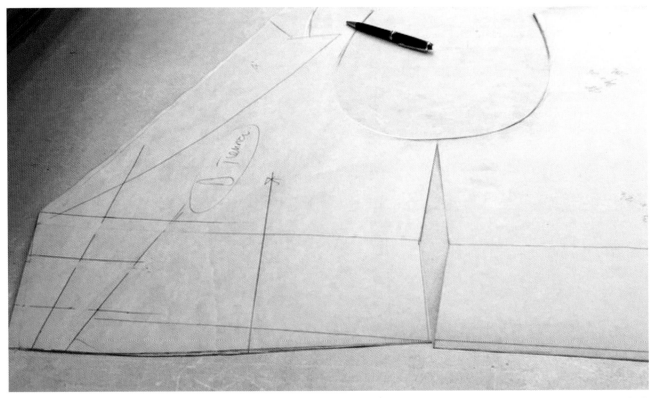

Benson & Clegg bespoke tailors' waistcoat pattern drafted onto card, using customer measurements and the proportional cutting method.

documented in historical tailoring literature. Traditional bespoke tailors on Savile Row, London (the home of British men's tailoring) use the proportional method, and take a set of personalized measurements and make anatomical observations, respective to the client. Each cutter will have devised their own system, and working scale based on the basic principles of flat pattern cutting, advanced with experience of the fitting process. For several hundred years, uniforms and bespoke men's suits have been crafted with a single set of measurements, and a series of fittings to perfect the shape. The outcome is then recorded as a final flat paper pattern, so that the client can return and order other garments.

The system introduced in this book uses a combination of proportional and direct pattern drafting methods. A comparative size chart has been included for the purposes of converting measurements into a size code; but also a comparable working scale has been applied using the bust size to apply widths and depths on some of the calculations. The size code that has been applied to all drafts is a US size 6, UK size 10. The working scale for a 36" bust and under is half the bust size.

The practice uses proportional measures, with the option to apply bespoke direct measurements to cross-reference while drafting the pattern; and measures from a jacket can also be applied into some of the instructions. The measurements required to plot the draft have been divided into proportional measures, direct measures and jacket measures.

Some of the measures are fixed; others are taken in motion. This is because we move: we don't have fixed design lines like a dress form and therefore the numbers might easily differ when transferred into a flat pattern. Therefore the process has been divided into three stages of taking measurements, to incorporate stationary measurements (attained in a static straight line) and those in motion (captured in the action of bending the elbow joint to obtain the

movement in the final measurement of the arm length). The final stage is to take dimensions from a jacket; it is advantageous to reference an existing garment with its already included increments. This three-stage system will advise where to increase the value of the measures to add ease into the pattern, at the correct pivotal points of movement.

It is widely recognized that taking body measurements and using those to create a pattern is the first step to obtaining a well-fitted jacket, but if all measurements are taken directly without carefully comparing them to a standard chart, then the block can turn out inaccurate, as our bodies can never be measured exactly. A comparative size chart and working scale will help the cutter to identify figure abnormalities, which may have been missed while obtaining the measures and observing the client. The working scale and size chart is an essential companion to evaluate the subject appropriately and allocate a size code.

To construct a jacket block, the reader can select a set of standard measurements from the size chart (which uses standard US, EU and UK sizing in metric and imperial), or insert a set of measures from the body or mannequin. Flat pattern cutting teaches a divisional grid system, by applying measurements, but this forms only the basic groundwork of the knowledge in the system. Experience in fit, and training the eye to observe, are essential to developing skill in pattern cutting.

It should be noted that all patterns have been drafted by hand, drawn in pencil, at a quarter scale of a full-size pattern. To obtain a quarter-size pattern the full size measures are divided by four. Should the reader wish to enlarge the patterns to their full size, this can be done using a photocopier or Photoshop.

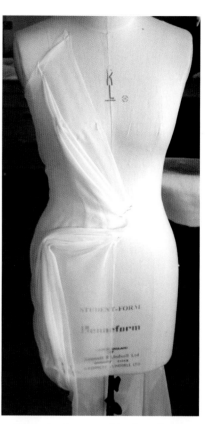

When draping a combination of cuts, folds and tucks can transform a blank textile into a piece of artwork.

Author's toile: a fold has been intricately draped into the lapel of a jacket.

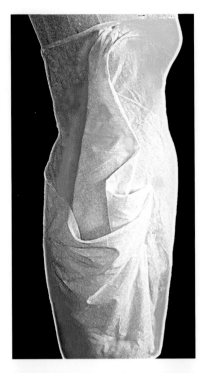

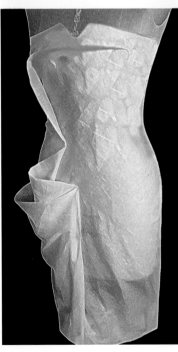

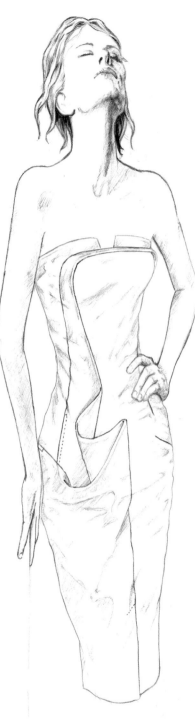

Draping can be captured in illustrations on the figure or mannequin.

Draping

Draping is another way to obtain a pattern. An atelier will use the art of French modelling techniques (first mastered by artisans in Paris) to obtain innovative silhouettes. The atelier drapes onto the three-dimensional form a two-dimensional fabric, using gravity to aid the craft, with a combination of cuts, folds, and tucks to transform a blank textile into a piece of artwork. A pioneer in draping was Madeleine Vionnet, who revolutionized the art form using expanses of uncut fabric, ordered in geometric and curvilinear shapes, which when sewn and left to hang on the body would drape beautifully. Draping is reserved predominantly for bias draped gowns and dresses.

This technique can also be translated into tailored jackets, however: it is applied when the design is so complex that it cannot translate immediately to a flat pattern.

A design sketch can be illustrated after a muslin toile (or similar fabric in keeping with the desired cloth from the finished article) has been pinned or tucked to a desired style on the mannequin, to aid the design process.

The dimensions of the form must match the dimensions of the wearer, or intended size, and the form can be padded out with wadding or foam to achieve this. After the fabric is modelled in the desired fashion on the form, markings are made all over the muslin to help transfer the shape, as well as seam intersections, darts, pleats, and other details onto paper; this is so that when the muslin is flattened out on to paper, there is no later confusion. The markings are then transferred to a piece of pattern paper. It is from this drape that a first pattern can then be traced and the lines and measurements smoothed and checked, before a new first toile is sewn and ready for a fitting on a model.

Flat pattern cutting versus draping techniques

It has been established that there are two main approaches that can be taken when converting a design into a 3-dimensional object for the first time. The chosen method very much depends on the design that needs to be achieved, and the particular working styles of the designer and/or the pattern maker.

The two processes can be used side by side: neither is more correct, and there are times when one will be more effective than the other depending on the design and personal preference. Flat pattern making will be quicker for designs that are more traditional in style, or closer to existing pattern blocks previously developed, for designs that are closer to the body or more classic in nature, or for those pattern makers who feel more comfortable working in this method. However, flat pattern cutting can be restrictive in two dimension, which is why draping is sometimes preferred for more creative projects; points and seam lines can be plotted with ease on the mannequin, as it achieves a more three-dimensional perspective.

For designs that are more organic in nature, have more unusual proportions, seam lines, darts, lapels and collars, then drape is going to be the informed choice, especially for those who like to see and experiment with the design as they go along, rather than committing to one pattern straight off. It can also greatly influence the design process as the results can be sketched. There are also times when designers will work directly on the stand using real fabrics and apply embellishment or build up texture while the design is holding the shape of the human body. But in most cases the designer will want to be able to reproduce the design and will need to have a flat pattern for production.

It is my opinion that the most successful pattern drafting systems have been devised by using a combination of both flat pattern cutting and draping techniques, combining the proportional and direct pattern drafting methods with modelling on the mannequin. These pioneering new hybrid techniques for haute couture have made it possible to create innovative proportions, silhouettes, and details, which have influenced the new generation of fashion designers across the garment-making industry.

Who this book is for

This is a textbook for aspiring designers, fashion students, apprentice tailors, home dressmakers, or for pattern makers who want to further their pattern knowledge by means of visualizing techniques and systems. Many books available on the subject present strict points of view, with vague directives and no instructions on how to finish a pattern in its entirety. This book combines step-by-step teachings and tips, with a series of diagrams, photography and exemplary garments from international runway shows and the author's own work. Instruction is supported with a basic teaching structure to understand the principles of pattern making, and includes studies of the broad array of style variations in jackets.

The goal is to develop a unique cutting language of your own, which is not discouraged with judgment and preconceived notions. Rigid, archaic tailoring systems can inhibit truly creative expression in pattern cutting. The key message of this book is that pattern cutting evolves constantly, and you will never stop learning; whether it is conducting challenging fittings or developing innovative shapes that require combinations of systems to achieve the desired results, a pattern maker has to be open to breaking the rules occasionally. But in order to break the rules a discipline must firstly be learned, one that requires constant observation, and practice. You should expect the results to be gradual and cumulative. However, once these skills are acquired they can be used to create beautiful jacket patterns.

Using this book

The ten chapters in this book can be followed in any desired order, depending on experience.

Students or apprentice cutters should start with flat pattern cutting techniques, using a size code; the suggested size for the blocks is a US 6, UK 10. The formulae in the step-by-step instructions are all calculated with the measurements for this size and give the correct value to be applied into the paper pattern. Practise drafting the blocks using the supplied measurements, with the included templates to assist with the drawing of true lines; and experiment with the style variations in later chapters. As soon as skills start to grow, take a set of your own measurements of a subject and try inserting them into the formulae to make bespoke patterns.

All patterns incorporate design elements into the process by considering details and silhouettes that will flatter the subject, for further exploration and development of skills. Photographs throughout the book will help to build a broad knowledge of details and silhouettes for designing the jacket, its lines, details, proportion and making a working pattern, acquired through flat paper techniques or draping on the form.

It is my hope that working with this book the reader will develop a jacket cutting style that is unique as their signature. Only through ongoing practice and experimentation will you be prepared to work with the spontaneity and imagination required to create stylish pattern cutting for ladies' jackets.

Chapter 1
Designing the Style of a Jacket

What you wear is how you present yourself to the world, especially today, when human contacts are so quick. Style is instant language.

Miuccia Prada

This chapter deals with designing a jacket, by planning the pattern in the form of a two-dimensional sketch, as a figure illustration. It is important to resolve design at this stage: to decide fit, details, and proportion before drafting the flat pattern. Ideas can be draped on the form and photographed, then sketched from, but regardless of the preferred system to obtain a design, the process begins with designing the style of a jacket in the form of a sketch. The style considerations that must be studied before putting pencil to paper are explored below, as are techniques to hand draw an example jacket on the figure, using illustrative shading techniques step-by-step.

It is important to understand different styles in design and cutting for tailored jackets; it can take years of study to master the cutting techniques required to realize complex design silhouettes in patterns. It is advisable to start from the beginning, to explore the differences between style and fashion in tailoring, its history, and the design elements to incorporate into a jacket.

Style

Style is quite simply a way of expressing a look in a particular way, with a distinctive appearance. It defines who we are and what we wear. There are no limits to how fashion can be communicated, designed, or presented. Style cannot be avoided, as it is impossible to do something without articulating an idea in a certain way. Even the labels or hanging tags inside jackets are written in a certain font type, to be in-line with the designer branding.

Every style amplifies an outlook on life, setting the mood, philosophy or aesthetic. In the Nicholas Oakwell look book images shown in Fig. 1.2, the suit presents chic luxury, with sharp tailoring, accoutrements, and styling.

Style versus fashion

There is a slight difference between 'fashion' and 'style', even if their dictionary definitions are nearly identical. Today, the term 'fashion' is always used to describe clothing, especially clothing trends; the fashion industry refers to retailers, designers, and fashion media (journalists, models, photographers) who sell or promote ready-to-wear fashion, or 'fast fashion'. The term 'style' can be used to describe clothing from bespoke tailors or haute couture, custom-made to an individual's style, not necessarily fashion- or trend-led; it may also refer to the pattern maker's 'cut', or signature style of cutting.

Opposite page: Fig. 1.1 Author's jacket on the dress form, for Nicholas Oakwell Couture Show.

Fig. 1.2 Nicholas Oakwell, Autumn/Winter 2012. Couture suit, hand woven tweed in gold and black.

Fashion also means the prevalent style at a certain place and time. Something 'fashionable' conforms to one or more popular trends; something 'stylish' has a nice composition and flair. Though fashion may be used as a synonym for style, it implies popularity or trendiness.

Ladies' tailoring silhouettes: A brief history

It did not become fashionable for women to wear finely tailored suits until the later part of the nineteenth century; before then these were reserved exclusively for men. From around 1870, women adopted tailor-made shirts and jackets designed for outdoor pursuits, sports activities and equestrian styles of dress, worn with flowing dresses underneath, floor-length skirts, or – more notably – the riding skirt, designed to allow women to sit side-saddle on horseback. The pattern technique for this cleverly had the angle of an inclined leg incorporated into the draft. The influence of sport was prevalent for this period and influenced greatly the transition away from the strict dress codes inflicted on women from the early nineteenth century.

By the late 1890s, formal coats like the tailcoat, tuxedo, and smoking jacket were still reserved exclusively for men's evening dress; however, when ladies retired, it was acceptable for them to wear a smoking jacket. A smoking jacket is similar in form to a dinner tuxedo jacket, but quilted for warmth, as a lounge coat. The edges also were trimmed with cord known as 'frogging', which was hand-applied into inventive patterns. All bodices and jackets worn by women at this time were tight-fitting to resemble the undergarment of the corset; the pattern was cut with several panels and princess seams, to achieve this silhouette. The sleeves were always tight to match the bodice, and the famous 'leg-of-mutton' sleeve was

1890s   **1930s**

Fig. 1.3 Ladies' tailored silhouettes: 1890s, 1930s, and 1950s.

popular. This had huge volume in the sleeve head, created with darts or tucks and filled out with sponge, and tapered into a slim cuff.

The turn of the century in Europe was a period of extravagance and great flamboyance. Women's silhouettes were very heavy in the bust, and dress was lavishly adorned with lace, floral embroidery, sequins, and ribbon. The age was dominated by flowing gowns made in *crêpe de Chine*, chiffon, tulle and silk; the amount of sheer labour that went into making one of these gowns was immeasurable. Bolero jackets were the only significant women's tailored style; these were cropped, with tight sleeves.

From 1910, there was a remarkable change in women's silhouettes, as loose-fitting, longer jackets were being worn. After the First World War, Chanel presented unstructured suit jackets, straight and square in cut, preparing the way for the 1920s. Jackets were straight and collarless, and the bust was entirely boyish: women were desperate to flatten their bust lines to conform to the prevailing mode of androgyny. The waist disappeared altogether, and was positioned low into the lower hip, with a dramatic lengthening effect.

The 1920s gave birth to a new kind of woman, frivolous and free from restrictive dress. Chanel's 'Flappers' were the new androgynous ideal: girls were determined to look as much like boys as possible, even chopping off their hair into bob haircuts. The roots of this movement originated in the underground 'Weimar' cabaret clubs, in Berlin. All the female performers – Margo Lion and Marlene Dietrich, to name but two – dressed as boys, wearing tuxedo suits.

Throughout the 1920s and '30s, Marlene Dietrich (inspired by Margo Lion) famously had her suits made at traditional men's tailors in Paris and London, including Savile Row's Anderson & Sheppard. This was viewed by the rigid traditional tailors as outlandish, and perversely eccentric, but paved the way for other women to follow suit, and fashionable high society women did.

Fig. 1.4 Margo Lion (with Wilhelm Bendow, right) in 'Was Ihr wollt. Nachtrevue in neunzehn Bildern', in Berlin, 1927. A famous icon of the 'Weimar' German cabaret scene.

But the outstanding revolutionary design talent of the era belonged to Coco Chanel, Elsa Schiaparelli, Madame Grès, and Madeleine Vionnet, with softer, more comfortable fits and fabrics that remained popular through to the late 1930s.

The Second World War had a profound effect on women's tailoring.

Jackets became more structured and fitted again, with the styling of collars and lapels resembling men's jackets. The look was simple but stylish, militarized with strong shoulders, heavily padded and a nipped-in waist. This uniform silhouette prevailed throughout the 1940s.

Many of the Parisian couture houses closed during the war, but afterwards, Balmain, Balenciaga and Dior emerged, putting Paris firmly back on the map. In 1947, Dior presented a collection that was immediately called the 'New Look': its return to femininity, corseted waist, defined bust, and rounded shoulders were the opposite of what had gone before. High fashion remained mature and elegant, demanding special clothes. Dior went on to introduce new silhouettes every season, producing two collections a year.

The 1950s were an intensely creative period in design activity. Couture was both architectural and structured, and implemented the return to using stiff canvases, padding and even boning (used to structure the internal canvas of corsets). In 1954, Chanel re-opened her house, and in direct contrast to Dior, she re-introduced her relaxed, unstructured, soft suit, rebelling against the 'New Look', showing straight silhouettes and soft suits.

Women started wearing trouser suits as an alternative to the skirt suit in the mid-1960s and through the 1970s; in 1966 Yves Saint Laurent's iconic Le Smoking suit, a tuxedo, was the first of its kind to be documented by the fashion press. Celebrity Savile Row tailor, Tommy Nutter, famously tailored tight-fitting jackets, with wide lapels and pagoda shoulder line proportions, and wide-leg pants. This trend continued into the 1980s, when 'power dressing' emerged, and heavily padded shoulders and oversize proportions dominated ladies' suits. Designers like Gianni Versace, Giorgio Armani, Chanel, and Calvin Klein reigned during this period. This is where ready-to-wear fashion really took off and the decline in handmade clothes began.

The 1990s saw the arrival of British design talent, John Galliano and Alexander McQueen, with their inventive theatrical fashion shows. Alexander McQueen trained as a tailoring apprentice on Savile Row, working also at Gieves & Hawkes

and Anderson and Sheppard; as a result, an emergence of exquisite art tailoring appeared.

Since the turn of the century, the fashion industry has grown, with a multitude of designers, brands and retailers, but sadly only a handful of traditional tailors and couturiers remain. Currently, no single look is able to dictate the way we dress, the way it did historically. This is due to the sheer number of providers of fashion and the constant re-interpretation of fashion. While these fashion phases come and go, traditional tailoring has never really faded. Women have always had the tailored jacket, either combined with the pant or skirt, or worn as a sports jacket. What remains are the considerations to design the style of a jacket; whether bespoke or ready-to-wear.

Style considerations – planning the design

The style of a jacket is determined by the details: the length, lapel proportion, style, fit, pockets, shoulder line, body vents, the number of buttons and the button wrap.

All styles of jacket are identified as single-breasted or double-breasted, or recognized as an evening tuxedo, which is reserved exclusively for formal styles. Each style has detail differences, which will alter the design and proportion in fit.

These all need to be considered before recording the idea in the form of a sketch, and before planning the pattern.

Fit

The female body has shape in the form of the bust, waist and hip line; it poses a challenge to flatter the female form and innovate shapes in ladies' jackets, as the fit is more complicated than in men's jackets.

If the jacket is intended to fit closely to the body, then the design should have construction details such as darts and seams, to achieve the shaping in the garment. A fitted ladies' jacket should taper in at the

waist. The addition of a princess seam over the bust, or additional darts, will accentuate the bust, waist and hip silhouette, and creates the illusion of an hourglass fit. This kind of fit looks feminine; the seams follow the contours of the body, nipped in to closely fit the panels and darts in the pattern. The addition of flare at the hip, or a peplum can also significantly change the look of the jacket, varying the lines.

By comparison, androgynous fits are straighter in appearance and are cut like a man's jacket – square and boxy, with very little shaping at the waist. The shoulders drop slightly, as they are wider, and the fit is generally loose, giving a masculine silhouette, with only slight shaping at the waist, and a neck dart. It still clings to the wearer, but the fit is subtle and understated; less shaped.

The jacket sets the proportion for an entire look and, as such, the scale and fit should be the first design consideration.

Length

The length of a jacket will be pre-determined in the sketch and translated into a flat pattern draft; or calico will be hand cut to the desired length, when draped and pinned on the form. The length drawn onto the design sketch should reflect what is translated proportionally into three-dimensional form. The measurement to determine the length of a jacket is taken at the centre back seam, measured vertically from the back nape of the neck to the finished hem on the jacket. The run of the hemline through to the side panel and front forepart is determined from the back length. This length depends greatly on the desired style.

In fashion, new lengths are deliberated every season – classic, cropped, hip length, knee length, and sometimes floor length. When designing a jacket pattern, a measurement can be taken from an existing garment or vintage piece that you love the length of.

Certain traditional styles of jacket will need to be cut in keeping with its established legacy. The skirt of the tails on a formal tailcoat for example, will traditionally be cut to sit at the back of the knee point; it will never deviate too far from that. A cropped Chanel tweed jacket will be precision cut to the true waist. The classic overcoat will be cut to sit just above the knee point, or to the upper hip in a pea coat, traditionally a long reaching garment, which progressed to a shorter length throughout the twentieth century.

In bespoke tailoring, the length will depend on the wearer and their height. A standard centre back length will be calculated when creating the first pattern, but during the fitting process the length will be altered in balance to the height and wishes of the client.

In ready-to-wear, there will be two types of fit model. For the runway shows a taller, slimmer model is preferred, from 6ft/72"/182.9cm height and upwards, so the proportion in length will be significantly longer. After the show, a new fit model will be selected, generally a size bigger, with a height of 5ft 6"/65 "/167.6cm. The garments are put into production and a revised length and fit are calculated for the new height of the fit model, adapting for retail.

The button wrap and number of buttons

The wrap at the front of a jacket will either be single-breasted (S.B.) or double-breasted (D.B.). It refers to the size of the extension added on to the centre line. The wrap itself will be calculated to include the size of the button, and the width of the wrap can be cut wider or narrower, depending on the style and design. The number of buttons at the centre front will vary: one, two or three buttons. Button closures are also traditional details at the cuff of the sleeve.

The lapel

There are three basic forms of lapels: notched lapels, peaked lapels and shawl lapels. The classic notch lapel

Fig. 1.5 Author's bespoke ladies' tailcoat.

is standard on S.B. suits and is cut at an angle, with a stepping effect. It is used on all styles of S.B. suit jacket, including the blazer, and the overcoat, but rarely on a D.B. jacket. The notch lapel is ideal for classic tailoring and will look timeless. The line of the

lapel edge can be shaped to a desired line; as a general guideline, the more curved the line, the more feminine it will appear. A straighter line is more masculine, and a subtle curve is softer on the eye. The height can be cut low or high, depending on the style.

Fig. 1.6 Notch lapel.

Fig. 1.7 Shawl lapel.

The peak lapel is the most formal, featuring on D.B. jackets, which is why it can also be named the D.B. lapel. It will also feature on the tuxedo dinner jacket, tail and morning coats, on blazers, and on overcoats, both D.B. and S.B.

The width and proportion of the peak lapel have been modified through the decades. The 1970s pushed the boundaries for lapels with ever increasing widths pioneered by Tommy Nutter. This iconic lapel became indicative of the decade.

The shawl lapel, or roll lapel, was originally seen on men's smoking jackets in the early 1900s, but today is more commonly seen on tuxedo jackets. It is a continuous curve, which is 'grown-on' into the top collar. Its shape determines whether it is a shawl or roll collar: the shawl has an exaggerated rounded curve above the buttonhole position. The roll lapel is subtle in shape.

Versions of the shawl and roll lapel have also been carried over into daywear and can be seen on the runway in various styles of jackets.

Pockets

Traditional tailoring pockets originated in menswear and were designed to be functional and appear on the hip in the form of a double-jet pocket, a jet with a flap, or patch pockets. Sometimes a ticket pocket can be added above the right hip pocket. It is also customary for an outer breast welt to be positioned above the left chest. Classic inner pockets machined onto the inside facing and front lining are two in-breast jet pockets, pen pockets, mobile phone pockets and ticket pockets.

These exact pocket details cross over into ladies' tailored jackets, but on a smaller scale, with the intention of looking decorative, rather than being functional. It is highly unattractive to fill out pocket bags with items that add unnecessary bulk to certain parts of the female figure. Typically ladies' jackets will still have classic hip pockets: double jets, jet and flap, or patches, positioned straight or slanted. However, on extremely fitted jackets it is aesthetically displeasing to add the outer welt to the chest, as it can distort the bust line. The inside pockets will be replaced with a single ticket pocket or no pockets, due to the excess bulk caused through the silesia pocket bags, which can create an unflattering silhouette.

For androgynous styles of jacket, there is flexibility to add pockets, as the cutting is straighter, less tapered at the waist point. These are the only styles that could accommodate a chest welt, or a selection of inner pockets, akin to a man's jacket.

The choice of pocket selection is dependent on the style of jacket. Whether practical or decorative, pockets are another necessary consideration for the design.

Fig. 1.8 Peak lapel.

Fig. 1.9 Nicholas Oakwell jacket on the mannequin showing wide peak lapel.

Fig. 1.10 The peak lapel will also be used on the tuxedo jacket and covered with silk.

Body vents

The vent in a jacket is a rear split positioned below the waist line, either at the centre back or on the side panel seams. Traditionally vents were applied into outerwear, for outdoor pursuits – riding attire, shooting jackets, fox hunting coats, or overcoats. A single vent would also appear on formal morning or tail coats. Vents are appropriate, particularly when using pockets, and sitting down, to improve the hang of the jacket. For reasons of practicality, vents are still considered a classic addition to jackets, in men's and ladies' wear, and are frequently designed into the modern jacket today.

There are three styles of vent: the centre vent (single vent) placed in the centre back seam; side vents (double vents) placed in the side panel seams; or no vents, commonly seen in ladies' jackets.

The shoulder line

The shoulder line can transform the wearer. A classic tailored jacket will have a lightly padded shoulder line, created with the addition of a shoulder pad. The thickness of the pad is measured and the pad allowance is incorporated into the pattern of the sleeves and the front and back shoulder.

The pattern and pads can also be customized to develop new shoulder styles; the raised shoulder, known as a 'pagoda' shoulder line is marked in the pattern to rise at the shoulder ends. In the 1990s, the pagoda was pushed to new extremes with the beautiful craftsmanship of the late Alexander McQueen; he was pushing boundaries to create art fashion in his beautifully violent shows. McQueen re-invented Tommy Nutter's pagoda shoulder line, and inspired a new generation of innovation in tailoring techniques and proportions.

The height at the shoulder ends and sleeve cap would need to be raised by several inches, and built up with a shoulder pad, with inner solid structure to support the vast height. The pad is built up with layers of sponge, and ply wadding, tacked and moulded by hand to sculpt the shape, which radically transforms the silhouette of the shoulder line.

The sleeve

The classic jacket will have a two-piece sleeve: an under sleeve and top sleeve with a functioning cuff vent with four buttons. Ease and fullness at the crown is incorporated into the pattern, so that the sleeve will roll at the sleeve head. The fullness should be 1"–2½", depending on the jacket size and the cloth weight.

Drawing a jacket design on the figure

Designers will choose to record their initial design ideas hand drawn as roughs, then transfer to full figure illustrations. In the style of Madelaine Vionnet, an atelier will drape ideas on the mannequin for inspiration, and sketch from the desired results. If the jacket has an unusual shape or lapel, it will be useful to drape the idea and test it on the stand, before committing to a design.

The design in Fig. 1.13 was developed entirely on the mannequin during the design process, and the outcome recorded and sketched into illustrations.

Prior to commencing the pattern for a jacket a sketch should be illustrated on a full figure; this is where all the elements of the design will be captured, and should be referenced while drafting a pattern. Think about the proportion, fit, details and what it will be worn with; and consider the style of bottoms.

Research should be undertaken before starting the design of a ladies'

Fig. 1.11 A model wearing a pinstriped trouser suit by Yves St-Laurent. This suit for evening wear, known as 'Le Smoking' became his signature piece. Photo: Reg Lancaster/ Hulton Archive/Getty Images)

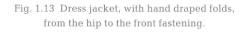

Fig. 1.12 Pencil-drawn fashion illustration
of Trench with faux lapels.

Fig. 1.13 Dress jacket, with hand draped folds,
from the hip to the front fastening.

jacket, or suit. This can be compiled from current designer runway shows for fashion-inspired styles; inspiration can also be drawn from conceptual art and photography, *film noir*, antique clothes, vintage *Vogue* publications and historical source pieces.

To draw fashion illustrations with a pencil in a realistic and convincing way is a useful skill to acquire, and takes a lot of practice, even for the fashion designer or artist. Here are some useful drawing principles that can be applied to the tailored jacket, when rendering a design and its fabric.

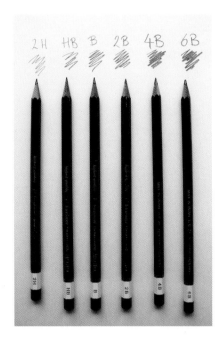

Fig. 1.14 Pencils with shading next to the tip.

Pencils

The right pencils are essential drawing tools, and there is a wide selection of different types to choose from, all coded. A drawing can easily be made with one graphite pencil – HB or 2B would be perfect for this, as they can be used to draw any subject, and render shadows with shading. Or a selection of three pencils can be used to create different effects, as they will provide a wider range of dark values, adding more depth to the illustration. The most commonly used are:

- HB for outline sketching
- 2B for all the sketching, and shading immediate values
- 4B for darker shadows
- 2H for lighter shadows

It is advisable to try out all graphite pencils, to see what type is preferable for your own personal drawing style.

Shading

Shading is a significant element when trying to draw fabric in a realistic way. However, do not start adding shadows until the right shapes and folds of the fabric have been added in the initial sketch.

Consider this sketch as the foundation of the drawing. Take time with the drawing, making sure that all the major components of the subject are in place before focusing on the smaller details. Going about it this way will save a lot of time erasing darker pencil strokes later on. Begin by focusing on things like proportions, shapes and the way in which the fabric drapes. Pay attention to the direction of the folds and think about how the fabric is draped over the shape that lies underneath, be it a surface, object or human body.

As soon as the designer is happy with the line drawing, start shading shadows. Doing so will begin to give the drawing dimension and the appearance of volume. It is tempting to reach for the dark 4B pencil and start drawing the darkest areas, but it is better to block out general areas with a 2H (or lightly shading with a 2B) pencil first.

Fabric textures

Fabrics come in a variety of textures, such as tweed, bouclé, satin, velvet, or lace. They all have their own distinctive look and feel because of their texture. This is an important element to focus on when drawing, whether you are using markers, acrylic, watercolour, or colouring pencils. The best way to render textures in a realistic way is through observation, looking at the way that the light hits the fabric. Ask questions to decide what shade of pencil to use, where to draw shadows and what to leave plain:

- Does the fabric look flat like gabardine? Study the twill weave pattern, and practise rendering its appearance.
- Does it have a pile like velvet? Add fur texture to give the appearance of the pile on velvet fabrics.
- Does it shine like satin? If so, draw the strong contrast between light and shadow.

When it comes to fashion design, ideas need to be laid to paper quickly before the idea is lost. It is better to create a convincing yet loose and fast representation of the fabric desired without wasting too much time on details; these can be re-drawn later. These illustrations serve the purpose of representing the designer's idea, based solely on the image in the mind. Therefore, factors like the texture of the fabric and its weight are very important and will determine how it will drape over the body. Consideration of these factors and visualizing certain types of fabric draped over a body will assist the designer to draw believable illustrations, in a clear and accurate manner.

Some important considerations when drawing a tailored jacket:

- Balance – details on both sides of the centre line should be symmetrical and balanced, and in harmonious arrangement with the figure it is to be drawn on.
- Accuracy – depending on the style of the drawing, lines for a technical drawing should be precise, and lines for fashion illustrations can be what are considered to be free, and unrestricting. Drawing lines should not be stiff: adding movement lines can help this.
- Perspective – draw in one of two perspectives: two-dimensional, which offers a fully symmetrical front view that appears to be still; or three-dimensional, where the garment tilts slightly to offer a 3-D view of the front, including the side, giving the appearance that the drawing has movement. Whichever pose is selected, the balance of the jacket should not be distorted.
- Process – when one part of the garment is drawn, sketch the corresponding part straight away: draw the left lapel, then the right lapel, the left shoulder, then the right shoulder, and so forth. This way the flow will not be broken, and errors will not occur.

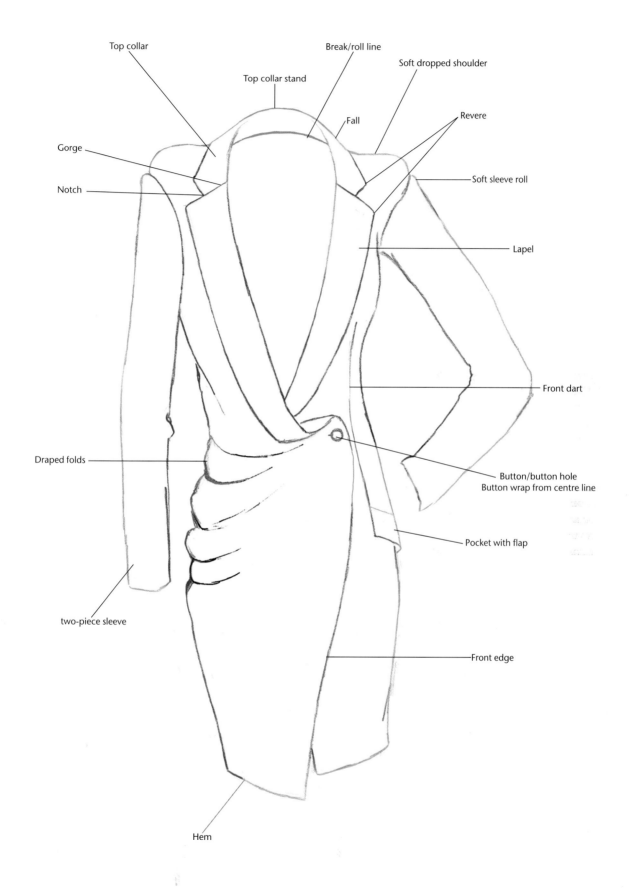

Top collar

Break/roll line

Soft dropped shoulder

Top collar stand

Revere

Fall

Gorge

Soft sleeve roll

Notch

Lapel

Front dart

Draped folds

Button/button hole
Button wrap from centre line

Pocket with flap

two-piece sleeve

Front edge

Hem

Fig. 1.15 The design elements to consider when drawing a tailored jacket.

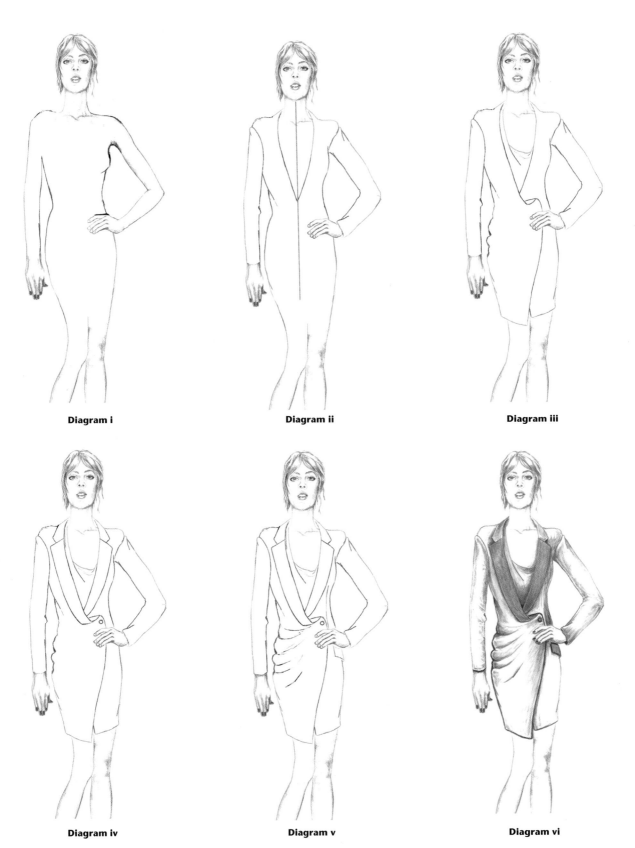

Diagram i Diagram ii Diagram iii

Diagram iv Diagram v Diagram vi

Fig. 1.16 Stages of drawing a drapey tailored jacket on a figure.

1. Select and trace the appropriate figure for illustration, and section parts of the body where the jacket will be drawn. These parts should be left blank. The head, neck, hands, legs and feet can be left shaded, as desired (Diagram i).

2. Draw the centre line placement – If this is not exact in position, the drawing will appear incorrect. Plot the roll/break line from the neckline to the crossover point, which can be identified, and drawn as the letter 'V'. This is the

location the lapels will be drawn from. The size of the opening is dependent on the design, and can be cut high above the waist line, lower, or directly on the true waist. Add the fall of the top collar from the collarbone into the neck. Draw the outline of the shoulders; raise them above the figure outline if they are padded, or shape them depending on the style, then render the armhole, sleeves, and cuff length (Diagram ii).

3. Draw in the general outline of the jacket – fitted, boxy, square, semi-fitted. Add in the allocated button wrap, and its spring from the button point, which can be faintly indicated with a small mark for now. In this example, the wrap has a wider extension, due to its particular style. It is not a traditional single-breasted fastening, but a double-breasted extension with a single button, hence the wider wrap. Draw in the front edge, and the length of the jacket. Indicate some folds at the right hip, as this particular style was intended to combine drape and tailoring (Diagram iii).

4. Indicate the first top button. Attempt the revere, but concentrate on the lapel; mark the width from the armhole, the gorge line will be slanted, but straight, and consider the extension of the lapel notch. Draw in the top collar next; decide how high the revere will sit from the waist, below the shoulder line. The collar will join the fall line, which sits higher around the circumference of the neck, due to the collar stand (Diagram iv).

5. Sketch the front darts, pockets and seams. Due to the individuality of the design, only the left side has a front dart and a pocket; traditional jackets will always have them on both sides. The right side has cascades of folds from the side seam draped into the front button; draw these folds (Diagram v).

6. Shade, or colour the illustration as desired. Start with lighter shadows, then add darker tones to add depth and movement to the drawing (Diagram vi).

Fig. 1.17 Traditional wool suiting cloths.

Choosing the right fabrics for the design

Choose a jacket fabric that suits the style that has been sketched; in other words, the fabric's properties – the weave and pattern – need to complement the design. As an example, a large check cloth would not be suited to jackets with lots of darts and seams, which would break up the pattern into a mis-matched mess, but might look ideal in less fitted cuts, with fewer panels, where the check pattern can be matched and flow over the body in an appealing manner. A linen or cotton jacket will not be able to support structured styles, and will show every discrepancy in make, but will favour a lightweight construction, and dictate the choice of internal linings.

Wool is the 'no-brainer' choice for structured tailored jackets. It will help build structure into the bodice and it fits close to the body, moulding over curves with ease. Wools come in several different weights:

*   Lightweight cloths: 7oz/198g, 8oz/227g
*   Mid-weight cloths: 9oz/255g, 10oz/280g
*   Heavy weight cloths: 12oz/340g, 13oz/370g, 14oz/396g, 15oz/425g

The lighter the weight of cloth, yarn blend and tightness of twill weave, the more difficult it is to hand tailor, as it shows up every stitch and internal interlinings that build structure into the jacket. They also do not press as well, so they are more suited to machine techniques, with minimal design details. The heavier the cloth, the easier it will be to hand tailor, press and fit the jacket.

The fit of the jacket should also depend on the fabric choice. A fitted jacket with a nipped in waist (hourglass silhouette) will suit mid-weight wools. In contrast, a boxy shape, French in style, will be more suited to bouclé or tweeds, synonymous with a Chanel ladies' suit.

Chapter 2
Tools and Materials

To make a pattern for a jacket, it is important to have the right tools and materials to work effectively; without them, cutting a pattern is strenuous. This chapter introduces essential supplies and tools of the trade, with explanations of how they can be used throughout the pattern-making process. The information is presented by category, and both vintage and modern pattern making rulers and tools are discussed.

As with any skilled craft, having the right equipment is vital in order to achieve the appropriate level of expertise. This can be expensive initially when starting out, but, if they are well looked after, tools will last several lifetimes. Tailoring apprentices will inherit rulers, sticks and curves from their masters; I too still use the implements inherited as an apprentice on Savile Row, many of which are not manufactured any more. Some of these have been included in the directory, and are now so specialized that they may be hard to obtain if you are not working directly within the industry. Enthusiasts can search at online auction sites (ebay, for example), which have proven to be effective to find antique tools and vintage technical publications, or at antique shops. For all other equipment, a list of stockists is included at the end of the book.

Opposite page: Fig. 2.1
A Gieves & Hawkes Savile Row workshop. Rows of finished patterns are stored and hung on pattern rails, using pattern hooks. The styles will be kept as a record, and used for new pattern variations.

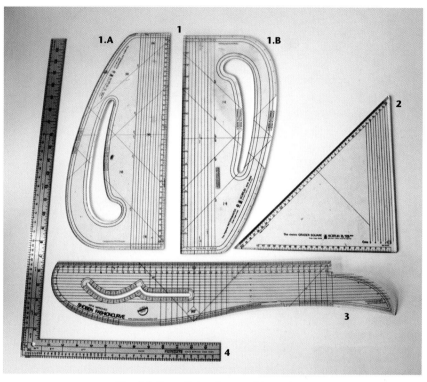

Fig. 2.2 Essential pattern-making rulers.

Essential pattern-making rulers (Fig. 2.2)

1. The pattern master – a ruler with a curve, used for marking straight lines, the straight grain and bias lines and seam allowances. Can be purchased in metric (1.A) or imperial (1.B) for adding allowances, inlays and seam allowance onto the paper pattern.

2. The pattern triangle – a triangle with measurements to square lines. It is used for marking straight lines, the straight grain and bias lines and seam allowances. It can be purchased in metric or imperial for adding allowances, inlays and seam allowance, and may be used instead of, or in addition to, the pattern master or Shoben curve.

Fig. 2.3 The pattern master is used to rule straight lines on the pattern.

3. The Shoben curve – a ruler with a form curve, is an excellent addition to the pattern master. Designed by Martin Shoben, it is used for marking straight lines, the straight grain and bias lines and seam allowances. It can be purchased in metric or imperial for adding allowances, inlays and seam allowance, and may be used instead of, or in addition to, the pattern master or pattern triangle.

4. Tailors' square (24"/61cm × 14"/36cm) – a metal ruler with two arms forming a 90° angle, that measures, rules and squares simultaneously. Traditional tailoring squares are wooden, and rare, but are still in use, especially by traditional tailors on Savile Row, London. Most of them have been passed down through generations, from cutter to apprentice.

Additional pattern-making rulers: the curve sticks and yard stick (Fig. 2.4)

1. Hip curve ruler – blends and shapes seams, hip lines, armholes, necklines and lapels. It has an exaggerated curve.

2. Vary form curve – shapes hip line, seams and lapels. This is a more subtle curve shape, when compared to the vary form curve.

3. General tailors' ruler – general ruler for marking straight lines, 20"/50.8cm.

4. The metre ruler (39 "/100cm, mostly used in the UK to measure longer lengths) and the yard stick (36"/91.44cm, mostly used in the US).

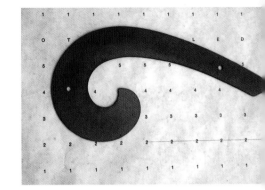

Fig. 2.6 The French curve.

5. The French curve – a traditional curve stick, more suited for ladies' cutting, and drawing shaped seam lines, used predominantly in haute couture. The curve is rare to find, but can sometimes be found and purchased through ebay, or second-hand/vintage sewing suppliers. A quarter-scale diagram has been provided, which can be enlarged to full scale using Photoshop, or a photocopier, as these rulers are hard to obtain. Transfer onto card and the shape can be used as a template for pattern cutting, as shown in the photograph at the beginning of this chapter.

Pattern-drafting tools (Fig. 2.7)

1. Tailors' straight pins – long, sharp tailors' pins for use in fittings, draping and during the sewing process; about 2.8cm/1 " is a good length. They should be fine so as to not to damage the cloth, and be thrown away if the end is blunt. A pincushion for the worktable, or a cushion attached onto a sewing machine, will avoid the loss of pins. Also, a pin holder can be fastened around the wrist, which is also helpful for use during fittings, and when draping on the form.

2. Paper scissors – scissors for paper cutting can vary in length, according to the comfort of the pattern maker. For cutting out

Fig. 2.4 Additional pattern-making rulers.

Fig. 2.5 The vary form curve is used to draw curved lines on the pattern.

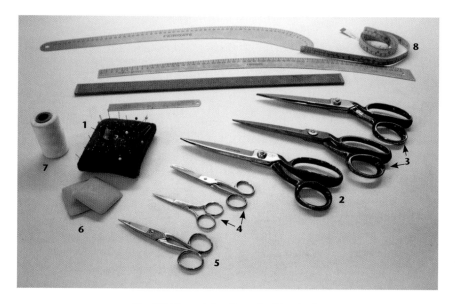

Fig. 2.7 Essential pattern drafting tools.

Fig. 2.8 The tape measure is used to check measurements on a pattern.

the paper pattern, use a pair up to 6"/15.2cm length. Card shears can also vary in length; 8–10"/20.3–25.4cm is advised. Keep paper scissors specifically for paper and card shears for card. Try not to drop your scissors or shears, as this can permanently damage the blade and pivot point.

3. Tailors' cloth shears – used for cloth cutting and chopping out sample toiles or garments in fabric. Lengths can vary: 10–14"/25.4–35.6cm. A decent size to use is 11"/27.9cm, as they are not too heavy. They should be kept specifically for cutting fabric, as card/paper will blunt the blades quickly, causing them to 'bite' when cutting out. Keep a pair of less good shears for cutting heavier fabrics like canvas, horsehair, tougher cottons, and calico. Clean the blades regularly with a drop of oil and scrap cloth to maintain their longevity.

4. General purpose scissors – 4"/10.2cm length, to snip threads when sewing first toiles of the pattern, or for jacket bastes, or for use while draping.

5. General buttonhole scissors – a good quality pair of sharp scissors around 5¼"/13.3cm long. They are useful for cutting thread and general duties while sewing, as well as cutting buttonholes. They are sharper and stronger than general thread scissors, for more precision work.

6. White tailors' chalk – this is the traditional medium for marking the outline of the flat pattern onto suiting, when chopping out a jacket, as well as during fittings and construction. Use white only as it brushes out more easily than coloured chalk (blue, red, yellow, black). Coloured chalk can be useful for marking on to calico toiles or onto internal chest canvases, provided the cloth is dark enough so that the chalk will not show through.

7. Basting thread – this cotton is used for temporary mark stitching and basting seams for a first fitting, to check the fit of the pattern. It will break very easily, so it cannot damage seams when the jacket is ripped apart. It is used for all temporary basting on jackets and for tacking in shoulder pads for fittings, and for loose stiches in draping.

8. Tape measure – an essential tool for recording measurements on the pattern, on the form, and in fittings. Metal-tipped plastic tapes are not very accurate, as it is difficult to see the measures. These are commonly obtained from suppliers, and can be effective if the metal tip is removed from the beginning of the tape. Metal tape in a dispenser, usually ¼" wide, is also very accurate, and flexible, for taking measurements.

Pattern-drafting tools (Fig. 2.9)

1. Pencil case, to include:

• Drawing pencil – an HB pencil is useful for drawing onto calico/muslin toiles during the fitting process, for marking lines or pocket positions, and for marking balance notches, and bust position while draping a shape. It needs to be soft to mark the fabric with ease.

• Sharpener – although it is preferable to have a softer lead for marking onto muslin/calico toiles, the tip should still be kept sharp.

• Eraser – to rub away unwanted pencil lines on the pattern.

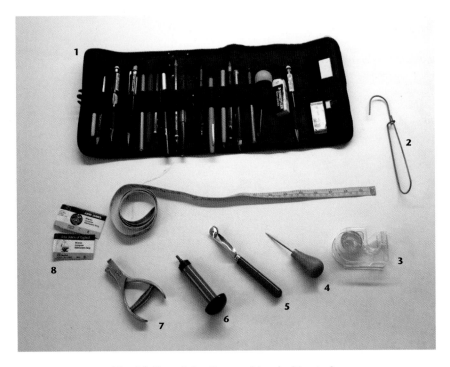

Fig. 2.9 Essential pattern-making drafting tools.

- Mechanical pencil – for all paper pattern work use a 2H or 4H (as preferred) to plot all lines in the divisional grid system, and any amendments to the pattern pieces. If the pencil is too soft, the lines on the pattern will smudge and look untidy; if the pencil is too hard it will deface and cut the paper when lines are marked, so match the pencil with the paper medium. A 2H pencil is good for spot and cross paper; chalk is useful on brown paper; a pen can be used on card to trace a finished pattern.
- Coloured pencils/pens – red and blue pencils to identify pattern changes; coloured pens to write fabric information; red pens to indicate that it is the lining; black to label the written information; and green to label fusing pattern pieces.
- Tailors' thimble – this is traditionally used by tailors. Choose a steel thimble, one that is the correct size to your middle finger, with indentations that accommodate the needle.

It should be worn only on the middle finger, and to help it stay in place when sewing, lick your finger – the saliva will help it to stick in place!

Fig. 2.10 The magic tape is used to help fix pattern issues, while altering the proportions.

2. Pattern hooks – to hold patterns together for hanging on a rail, so that all the pieces do not get separated and lost.

3. Magic tape/Scotch tape – fixes mistakes, allowing the cutter to stick paper onto the pattern to adjust corrections. Unlike regular sticky tape, it can also be drawn onto. (Fig. 2.10)

4. Bodkin/awl – can be used instead of the tracing wheel to trace off lines onto paper, by piercing faint dots. It is more accurate than the tracing wheel, as the wheel has a tendency to slip, and sometimes stretch the pattern when rolled over the lines. It is more time consuming to plot lines than to use the wheel, but the inexperienced beginner can produce more precise tracing results.

5. Tracing wheel – this is a pointed wheel, used for tracing new patterns from existing patterns. It transfers the shape onto paper with a series of dotted lines. It can take some years to master effective use of the wheel, adding the right pressure with your hand, to trace accurately without stretching the existing pattern or moving the pieces.

6. Pattern drill – a tool for piercing a hole in the pattern. It indicates pocket placement, buttonhole placements and the ending of a dart.

7. Pattern notcher – this has a blade that cuts out ⅛"–¼" into the pattern's edge to indicate balance notches. As the patterns are traced, the notch cut outs are marked into the fabric with tailor's chalk or a small cut, for the tailor or dressmaker to follow. The notch is used to indicate seam allowance, identification of front and back patterns, waist and hip balance points, front and back sleeve pitch points, ease and fullness control, dart positions, and placement for inserts.

Fig. 2.11 Showing the use of tape on a calico toile to acquire a style line.

8. Hand sewing needles – these are available in different lengths. For general hand sewing a #7 sharp is suitable, which is longer and great for tacking in baste fittings, toiles and draping. A shorter needle, #9, is better for all finishing work and pad stitching. Avoid purchasing needles where the end with the eye is thicker than the needle itself, as it can rip the surface of the fabric as it goes through the cloth.

9. Design tape (Fig. 2.11) – this can be used instead of black twill tape, and without the use of pins, as it has one side that sticks to the form or garment. It is ideal for plotting design lines to transfer onto the pattern. On Fig. 2.11, the front edge of a jacket has been re-shaped into a new line during a fitting on a calico toile. Black twill tape can be used instead of design tape for placement of style lines on the form or garment; however, the tape needs to be pinned into the preferred position, which is how it differs to design tape. Twill tape can also be used when taking measurements on a female client.

The true waist can be identified quickly, once tape has been tied around the circumference.

Pattern-making paper/card

Plain or 'spot and cross' rolls of pattern paper are used for making the first patterns for a new block. The master draft is plotted onto paper, and traced off as a first pattern copy, and separated into pattern pieces with seam allowance.

A toile is cut and sewn for a fitting in calico, to check the balance and fit of the block, on the form or a fit model. The adjustments from the fitting are altered on the first copy of the pattern, and traced again onto paper to make a second pattern, in preparation for another fitting. The process of 'fit' and 'alter' of the pattern continues, and is recorded at each stage, until the fit is flawless. The pattern is then finished, and collars, lining, fusing and pocket patterns are traced.

Plain paper is ideal for a beginner or student to practise on. It is a thinner weight, good for tracing, and cheaper for practising flat pattern cutting systems.

Blue spot and cross paper is better for the more experienced pattern maker. 90-degree grain lines can be marked with ease, due to the rows of perpendicular columns. It is more durable than plain paper and does not tear as easily. It is a little more expensive, but worth the extra cost, as it is a delight to draw on. The paper patterns are usually kept and stored in an envelope, for reference. They record all the stages of fit and adjustment, throughout the process.

The finished pattern can be transferred onto heavy card, to retain its longevity, as over time the paper will become torn and creased.

Heavyweight pattern paper is called Manila card, or hard paper, and is primarily used for 'production patterns', in ready-to-wear. Once the fitting stages are concluded, the amendments have been updated, and the rest of the pattern finalized, the finished pattern can be transferred onto card. In bespoke tailoring a medium-weight brown card is used.

Brown medium-weight paper is largely used in haute couture or for bespoke tailoring patterns on Savile Row. It is for classic, made-to-measure/

Fig. 2.12 Rolls of lightweight paper are used to draft first patterns.

Fig. 2.13 A first pattern is traced from the master draft of the divisional grid system, and seam allowance added to the net sewing seams.

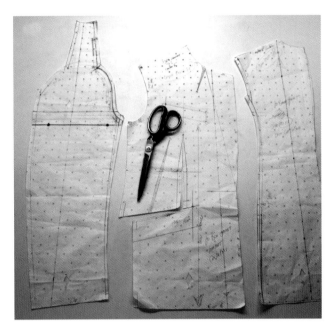

Fig. 2.14 Pattern pieces in paper will become worn and creased over time, from alterations and use.

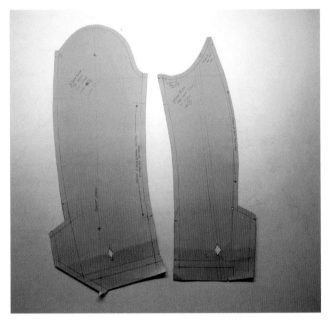

Fig. 2.15 Heavyweight paper/card is used to transfer the finished paper pattern into a durable weight, to retain the longevity of the pattern.

Fig. 2.16 Finished card patterns.

Fig. 2.17 Paper patterns transferred onto card: the hard pattern can be used to grade up to multiple sized patterns for retail, and for the development of new blocks in forthcoming projects.

bespoke garments. Patterns are marked in chalk or pencil onto the brown paper, as a guideline, from a set of proportional measurements, or from existing pattern blocks from the pattern archive, which are adjusted to fit the customer.

The new pattern is then used to strike tailored suits into the selected wool or suiting, with seam allowances and inlays added directly onto the cloth.

In tailoring, the plain baste is used as a first fitting. It is the outer shell of the jacket with inches of inlay left inside, which will allow the jacket to be altered as required. The pieces are hand tacked together and tried on the customer. The plain baste is ripped down and the changes re-marked directly onto the cloth pieces in chalk, ready for a second fitting called a 'pocket baste', which

is basically another shell fitting with the pockets machined in. Notes are made to the existing brown paper pattern throughout the process, but are principally marked directly onto the baste, as the fit decisions are dependent on the individual properties of the suiting and style choices discussed in the fitting room.

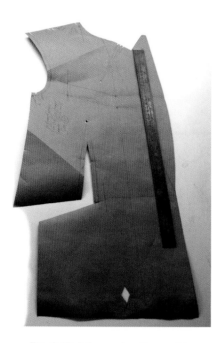

Fig. 2.18 A forepart pattern cut in medium-weight card.

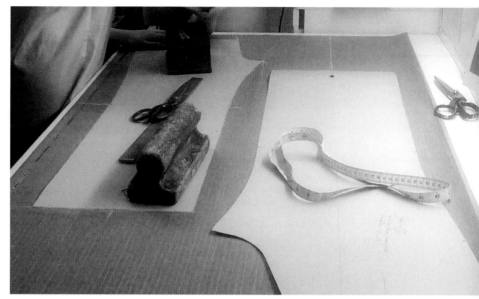

Fig. 2.19 A bespoke pattern is laid directly onto suiting, and marked in chalk. Inlays and seam allowances are marked directly onto the cloth, and then the pieces are chopped with shears.

Weights and blocks

Weights are useful for holding patterns securely, when tracing and marking onto a clean sheet of paper.

Fig. 2.20 Weights – the use of a wooden block or metal weight is effective to hold a pattern in place.

The tailor's mannequin

The dress stand, or form, as it is also known, is used to drape on, to check and scrutinize the fit and balance of a jacket, the sleeve pitch, proportion, pocket positions and buttonhole location. The form can also act as a replica of the customer the garment is being made for. As the form comes in a standard size true to the specifications of the manufacturer, it would need to be adjusted using padding, to imitate the figure of the wearer.

A professional tailor's stand is an expensive but necessary investment, and should not be a display stand or vintage mannequin. There are a few manufacturers in the UK, Europe and the US: Kennet & Lindsell are British established and have a heritage and good reputation. Siegal & Stockman operate in the US and UK and are the most renowned. There are also some bespoke makers in Europe who will custom-build mannequins to your desired sizing.

In the list of suppliers featured at the end of the book you can find names and contact details for stockists of the tools and materials mentioned in this chapter.

Fig. 2.21 The tailor's mannequin. The male torso and female dress stand.

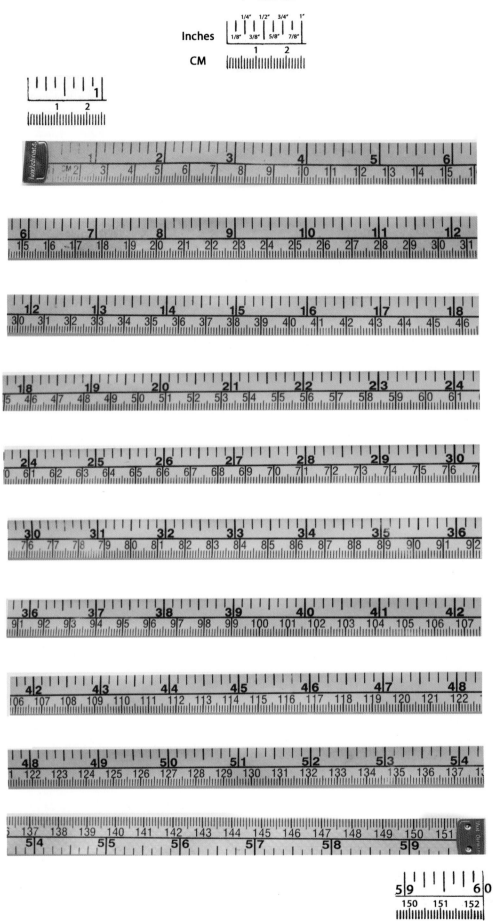

Fig. 3.1 The tape measure counting chart, for the purpose of recording measurements, and imperial/metric comparison.

Chapter 3
Measurements and Size Codes

Flat pattern cutting uses a scientific method, applying calculations derived from taking a set of measurements of the body. The measurements will be applied into a personalized paper pattern for the intended wearer, and will be used to allocate a size code, in consideration of the proportional dimensions. The numbers recorded are the first requirement towards drafting a correct pattern.

This chapter teaches the skill of taking measurements accurately, by introducing three separate ways to obtain values for the key measurements needed to draft a jacket. The first is 'proportional', to obtain a set of the key landmark measurements; the second is 'direct', capturing specific personalized measures; the third is to measure the proportions of a jacket, and recording the values. A size chart is included, to help review proportional sizing, in both imperial and metric.

It is important to master the skill of taking accurate measurements on the figure: even an outstanding cutting system will fail if the combined measures are incorrect. As always, constant practice will provide proficiency in the results.

As the focus of this book is on tailored jackets, measurements for just the upper body are discussed throughout chapter.

Anatomy for tailors

Identifying the location of anatomical points on the body will improve accuracy when taking a full set of body measurements.

Before taking a set of measurements the wearer or fit model should be prepared by marking certain balance levels on the body, aided by the understanding of human anatomy and skeletal points. These points can be fixed by eye (good observation is essential for a pattern cutter), and balance levels can be marked with twill tape, pins, tape, or chalk; or realized by prodding with fingertips, for landmark bones.

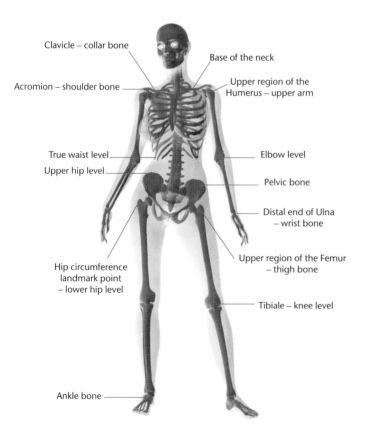

Fig. 3.2 Skeletal diagram to show anatomical points on the front body.

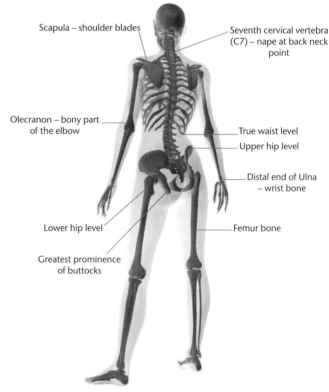

Fig. 3.3 Skeletal diagram to show anatomical points on the back body.

To locate the true waist level a waist belt, cord, or black twill tape can be used, and should be placed around the waist, for the purpose of establishing the balance level (Figs. 3.4 & 3.5).

The upper hip circumference level can be marked in the same way, with a second row of tied tape fixed to correspond with the widest prominence of the stomach, located from the side on the hip bones of the pelvic skeleton (Fig. 3.6).

The position of the hip circumference level (lower hip) is located about 8″ below the true waist, and is positioned at the lower region of the pelvic bone, where it joins the top of the femur, at the thighbone (Fig. 3.7).

To locate the correct bust position, vertical pins can be placed over the exact nipples on the outer garment the subject is wearing (take care not to prick the wearer with the pin; the sharpest point of the pin must face downwards). Chalk marks can also be used instead of pins (Fig. 3.8).

The neckline is identified by the collarbone at the front, where it joins the clavicle bone running to the shoulder. The curve in the front can be measured to the shoulder point, where it continues into the nape at the centre of the back neck.

At the underarm a triangle pattern ruler can be placed horizontally into the wearer's armpit; this will allow a mark to be made on the lower side for the depth of armhole and the height of the underarm midpoint.

Locating landmarks on the wrist can assist to determine the sleeve length. The ulna and radius are the two long bones in the forearm, and it is at the end of these bones that the sleeve length is decided.

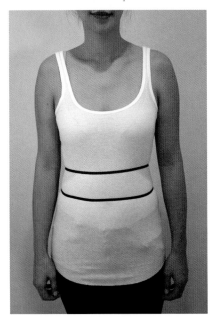

Fig. 3.4 The model is prepared by using twill tape, placing at anatomical levels on the body.

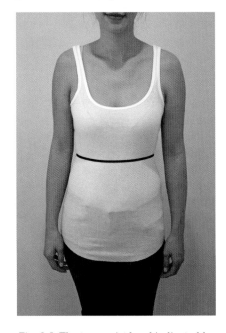

Fig. 3.5 The true waist level indicated by twill tape tied around the waist.

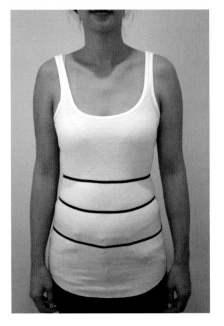

Fig. 3.6 The upper hip level indicated with tied twill tape, to correspond with the widest prominence of the stomach.

Fig. 3.7 The hip circumference (lower hip) indicated with tied twill tape positioned at the lower region of the pelvic bone.

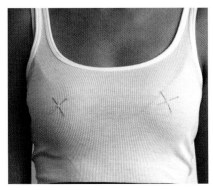

Fig. 3.8 The bust points can be indicated with pins or by making chalk marks.

Taking measurements for a tailored jacket

After all the location points have been verified on the body, a set of direct and proportional body measurements can be taken using the tape measure (see Fig. 3.1) for comparative imperial and metric measurements; this chart can also be used for the purpose of counting during the process).

The tape measure is used to record all measurements obtained from the fitting, and can be purchased in both imperial and metric; this helps to compare the values and work in both inches and centimetres.

Choose a subject model to measure, and perform the procedure of taking measurements. Practise observation: the art of recognizing small abnormalities requires practice and perseverance. Pattern cutting jackets to specific measurements can be challenging, when

IRREGULARITIES IN THE FIGURE

- Postural stance – upright erection
- Postural stance – forward erection
- Long neck
- Short neck
- Down right shoulder (abbreviated to D.R.)
- Down left shoulder (abbreviated to D.L.)
- Sloping shoulders
- Square shoulders
- Prominent right shoulder blade
- Prominent left shoulder blade
- Prominent shoulder blades
- Round back
- Prominent bust
- Hollow back waist
- Protruding belly
- Prominent seat or hip increase to bust proportion
- High left hip
- High right hip

considering variations of figure, and disproportionate shapes. Even when cutting standard size codes the figure disproportions of the fit model should be noted. Keep in mind the dimensions for a proportionate figure, and when the tape registers a difference from the norm, the increase or decrease should be recorded. Tailors will have their own system for recording the peculiarities. The checklist below includes many of the possible irregularities to look out for.

Taking a full set of proportional measurements will assist the pattern cutter to allocate a size code from the size chart (see page Fig. 3.56). In addition, a full set of direct measurements that are personal to the subject should also be taken for cross-reference while drafting the master pattern. It can also be helpful to try a jacket on the model, or ask the subject to bring with them a jacket they love the fit of, and record a set of jacket dimensions.

Ask the subject questions during the process about the jacket: Is this the shoulder length you like? Do you like shoulder pads? Is this lapel too wide for you? Do you like the fact that it is nipped in at the waist? Suggest modifications, if you feel there are elements that could improve the style, or fit. Listen to the responses and record the comments, to make the necessary adjustments when drafting the pattern. Verifying as much information as possible will only aid the process.

Take the measurements in a definite sequence order, as described below. An equal degree of closeness or looseness should be applied to the tape measure and maintained as much as possible, throughout the process.

Proportional measurements

The height is recorded and the postural stance of the wearer/fit model should be scrutinized immediately (*see* Figs. 3.9, 3.10 & 3.11).

1. *Bust (Fig. 3.12)*
    Anatomical location point: the widest level over the bust points.

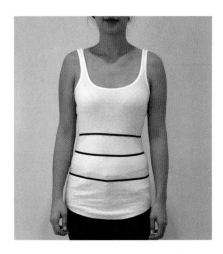

Fig. 3.9 The front postural stance of the subject.

Fig. 3.10 The side postural stance of the subject.

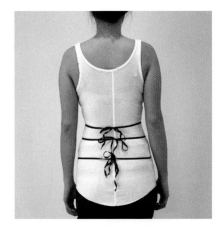

Fig. 3.11 The back postural stance of the subject.

Fig. 3.12 The bust measure.

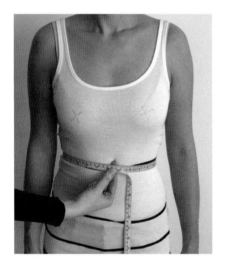

Fig. 3.13 The true waist measure.

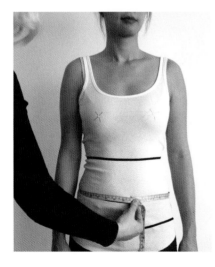

Fig. 3.14 The upper hip measure, front view and side view.

Facing the model, fix the tape from the same level in the back at the lowest point of the shoulder blades and under the wearer's arms, and hold in position over the front of the bust points.

2. *Waist (Fig. 3.13)*
    Anatomical location point: the true waist level as indicated by tape/cord. Facing the model, the tape wraps around the cord tied around the subject's true waist.

3. *The upper hip (Fig. 3.14)*
    Anatomical location point: the level of the widest part of the stomach in the front and on the hipbones of the pelvis, from the side.
    Facing the model the tape wraps over the pre-prepared twill tape horizontally; it can be helpful to stand slightly to the side of the subject for this measure.

4. *Hip circumference level (lower hip) (Figs. 3.15 and 3.16)*
    Anatomical location point: the trochanter major (the lower pelvic bone connecting the top of the femur bone, at the thigh level). Facing the subject, the measure is taken over the circumference of the lower part of the hips, approximately 8″ below the true waist level. Wrap the tape measure over the twill tape, as previously prepared.

5. *Half back width (Figs. 3.17 and 3.18)*
    Anatomical location point: the scapula (shoulder blades), from the spine of the centre back to the right back armhole.
    The finger in the photograph shows the landmark point, half way between the shoulder ends and underarm landmark point. Facing the back of the subject, place the tape directly on the spine at the centre back and measure across to the point indicated by the finger.

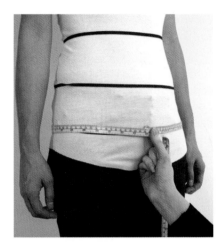

Fig. 3.15 The tape passes over the ties at the lower thigh level

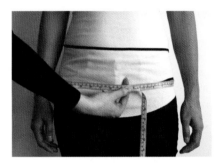

Fig. 3.16 The hip circumference (lower hip level), front view.

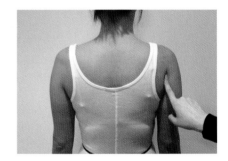

Fig. 3.17 The centre of the right back armhole, located directly between the shoulder bone and underarm point.

Fig. 3.18 Half back measure.

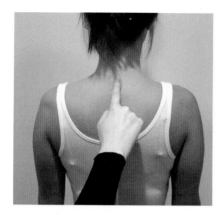

Fig. 3.19 The nape at the back of the neck.

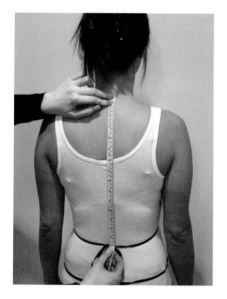

Fig. 3.20 Nape to waist.

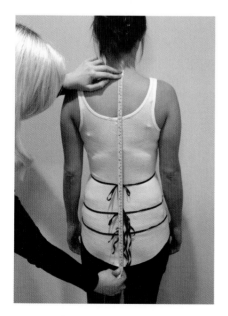

Fig. 3.21 The centre back length to be determined as the jacket length.

6. *Nape to waist*
    (Figs. 3.19 and 3.20)
    Anatomical location point: the nape at the back neck, measured down the spine to the true waist level. Stand behind the model and locate the landmark nape at the centre back neck of the subject. Place the tape and measure down to the true waist level, indicated by the ties.

7. *Centre back length (Fig. 3.21)*
    Anatomical location point: the nape at the centre of the back neck, down the spine, through the waist to the potential jacket length. In the case of the model, the length of jacket will finish at the hip circumference level (lower hip), indicated as the lowest black tape tied around the body.

8. *Shoulder length (Figs. 3.22, 3.23 and 3.24)*
    Anatomical location point: locate the upper region of the humerus bone. Stand to the back of the model, and measure the right back shoulder. Start at zero at the base of the neck, and extend horizontally across the shoulder bone, where the armhole intersects with the shoulder ends. The triangle ruler can be used to obtain a shoulder angle and ask figuration questions; does the model have sloping shoulders? Or square? Down on one side? This will help to analyze if the subject will require custom padding for each shoulder, or reduced thickness at the shoulder pad if the subject is very square in appearance.

9. *Upper arm, bicep (Fig. 3.25)*
    Anatomical location point: upper arm tissue and muscle.
    Turn the model to stand to the side, exposing the right shoulder and upper arm. The tape wraps around the bicep and the value is recorded.

Fig. 3.22 The end of shoulder.

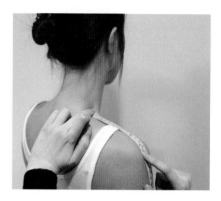

Fig. 3.23 Shoulder length.

Fig. 3.24 The shoulder angle.

Fig. 3.25 Bicep measure.

41

Fig. 3.26 Wrist measure.

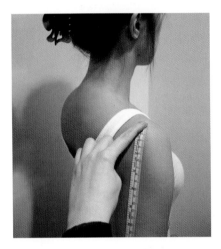

Fig. 3.27 Landmark point, where the armhole intersects the shoulder ends, to the wrist bone.

10. *Wrist (Fig. 3.26)*
    Anatomical location point: the wrist bone (distal end of the ulna) The tape is wrapped around the wrist.

11. *Arm length (Fig. 3.7, 3.28 and 3.29)*
    Anatomical location point: this is where the armhole intersects the shoulder ends (upper humerus bone), measured to the wrist bone (distal end of ulna).
    The model stands to the side, exposing the right side of the shoulder and arm facing outward; arms are placed straight alongside the body. Pass the tape from zero at the shoulder end vertically to the wrist.
    The model bends the arm, and the hand is placed at the hip circumference level (lower hip level indicated with tape). Place the tape at zero at the shoulder ends and over the bend of the elbow, to the wrist.

12. *Neck size (Fig. 3.30)*
    Anatomical location point: base of front neck and nape at centre back neck.
    On the left side of the body, the tape is held in position at the centre

Fig. 3.30 The half neck measure.

front neck and wraps around the base of the neck loosely to the nape at the centre back.

Direct measurements

In addition a set of direct measures are taken, as a cross reference for bespoke patterns when drafting the paper pattern. These will ensure the overall accuracy of the proportion of the finished pattern.

The term 'direct measures' defines the intention to state the quantities of the figure captured in its relative stance and shape. If the measurements are carefully taken, the results are advantageous, constructively enhancing the attention to the finer details of the wearer's attitude, in the pattern.

To take direct measures on the figure the measurements should be made as follows.

1. *The armhole circumference measure (Fig. 3.31)*
   Anatomical landmark: underarm point (as indicated with the triangle ruler) and shoulder ends, where the armhole intersects. Wrap the tape measure around the armhole, in a loose manner.

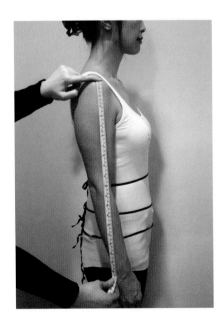

Fig. 3.28 The vertical arm length.

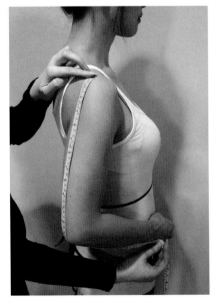

Fig. 3.29 Bending the arm to obtain movement ease for the pattern.

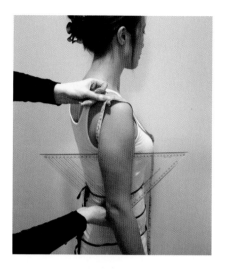

Fig. 3.31 Measuring the armhole circumference.

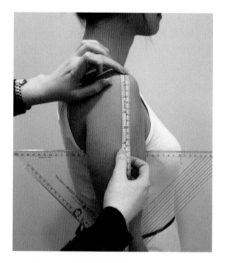

Fig. 3.32 The armhole depth.

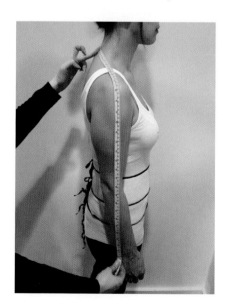

Fig. 3.33 The over shoulder.

2. *The armhole depth (Fig. 3.32)*
   Anatomical location point: the shoulder end where the armhole intersects at the underarm.
   Place the tape at the shoulder end to the underarm point.

3. *The over shoulder (Fig. 3.33)*
   Anatomical location point: The nape at the centre back neck, through the shoulder ends, to the wrist bone.
   Secure the tape at the nape and place the tape horizontally across the shoulder line, past the shoulder ends and vertically through the centre of the arm to the wrist bone.

4. *Half front chest (Fig. 3.34)*
   Anatomical location point: from the centre of the front armhole to the centre front.
   The tape is placed at zero at the centre front to the centre of the left armhole, facing the model.

5. *Width between bust points (Fig. 3.35)*
   Anatomical location point: right bust point to left bust point.
   The tape is placed at zero at the right bust point at the centre of the pins, and is measured horizontally across to the centre of the left bust point.

6. *Front shoulder to waist (Fig. 3.36)*
   Anatomical location point: centre shoulder to true waist level.
   Stand facing the model, placing the tape at zero directly in the middle of the front shoulder guide the tape to the true waist level indicated by the ties.

7. *Front waist length (Fig. 3.37)*
   Anatomical location point: the hollow at the centre of the front neck to the hip circumference level.
   Opposite the subject, the tape is placed at zero at the centre of the front neck, located at the hollow of the throat, and is measured through the centre front line of the model to the lower hip level, indicated with ties.

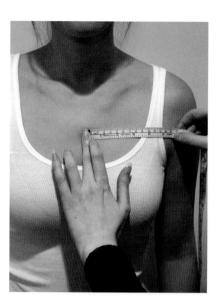

Fig. 3.34 Half front chest.

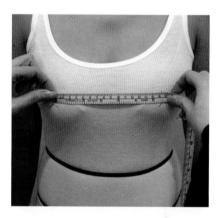

Fig. 3.35 Bust point to bust point.

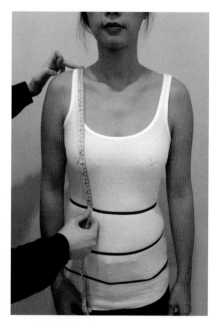

Fig. 3.36 Front shoulder to waist.

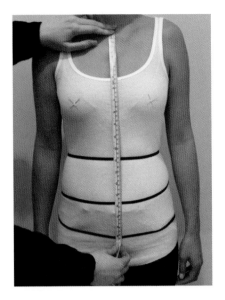

Fig. 3.37 Front waist length.

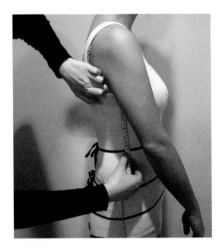

Fig. 3.38 Underarm to waist.

Fig. 3.39 Underarm length.

Fig. 3.40 Elbow circumference.

8. *Underarm to waist (Fig. 3.38)*
    Anatomical location point:
    underarm point to true waist level.
    Measure from zero at the
    underarm point to the true waist
    level. Guide the subject's arm
    slightly forward to obtain this
    measurement.

9. *Underarm length (Fig. 3.39)*
    Anatomical location point:
    underarm point to the wrist bone.
    Stretch the subject's arm outwards
    and place the tape at zero at the
    underarm point and guide to the
    wrist bone.

10. *Elbow (Fig. 3.40)*
    Anatomical location point: elbow
    level.
    Pass the tape around the elbow in
    a loop and record the measure.

Taking measurements from a jacket

It is also a good idea to obtain a set of
measures from the subject wearing a
jacket. It may be something selected for
style purposes, or it could be a personal
choice of the model. These measures
are invaluable to appropriate into the
pattern at drafting stage. The measures
to be considered are as follows:

1. *Coat waist (Fig. 3.42, 3.43 and 3.44)*
    Location: the true waist at the
    centre back to the front edge.
    The coat waist is a half
    measurement, minus the dart and
    seam suppression values, as these
    are already seamed.
    Looking at the coat waist on a
    jacket will help to allocate correct
    suppression at the waist, and
    determine the size of the wrap
    on the front edges, which can be
    interpreted into the flat pattern.
    Place the tape at zero at the centre
    back waist seam of the jacket.
    Measure around the waist level
    where all the darts and seams cinch
    in to the centre front seam using the
    button position as a guide.
    Another way to measure the
    coat waist is to take the full waist

Fig. 3.41 The subject wearing her favourite jacket.

Fig. 3.42 The half coat waist, back view.

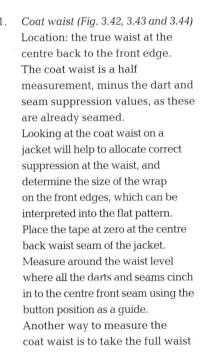

Fig. 3.43 The half coat waist, front view.

measurement by wrapping the
tape around the entire jacket
waist; place the tape at zero on
the left side of the front edge,
wrap around to the right side of
the front edge. Divide the value
by two.

Fig. 3.44 The full coat waist.

Fig. 3.45 The jacket length.

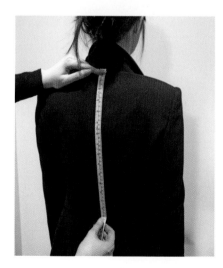

Fig. 3.46 Nape to waist.

2. *Jacket length (Fig. 3.45)*
Location: nape of the back neck to the hem length on the jacket.
Stand at the back of the subject and place the tape at zero at the nape of the back neck, directly on the centre back seam and measure down the seam the to the exact length of the jacket. The jacket is an ideal length for the model's height and postural stance.

3. *Nape to waist (Fig. 3.46)*
Location: nape at the back neck seam to the waist level.
Stand at the back of the subject and repeat instructions for the jacket length, but record the measurement from the nape to the waist level.

4. *Half back (Fig. 3.47)*
Location: locate centrally between the shoulder ends and underarm and square across to the centre back seam.
Stand at the back of the subject and secure the tape at zero exactly in the seam of the centre back and measure horizontally across to the middle section of the back armhole, on the right side of the subject.

5. *Shoulder length (Figs. 3.48 and 3.49)*
Location: base of the neck to the shoulder ends.
The shoulder length can range between 4″ at the slimmest width, for a nipped in shoulder, to a wide 6″, the maximum width for a boxy, wide shoulder line. As the size code grades up, the sizing table indicates that the shoulder should increase by ⅛″. The subject tried on two jackets, both with very different shoulder proportions – one 4″ wide, one 5⅛″ wide, before opting for the slimmer length. Place the tape along the shoulder seam and measure from the base of the neck to the shoulder ends.

6. *Sleeve length (Fig. 3.50)*
Location: centre of sleeve crown to hem of sleeve.

Fig. 3.47 Half back.

Fig. 3.48 Shoulder length slim proportion: 4″

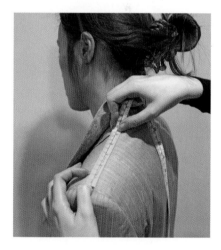

Fig. 3.49 Shoulder length wider proportion: 5⅛″.

The subject stands to the side. Place the tape vertically from the centre of the crown to hem at the cuff of the sleeve.

45

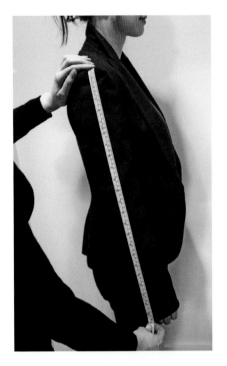

Fig. 3.50 Sleeve length.

Fig. 3.51 Sleeve cuff.

Fig. 3.52 Lapel width.

7.   *Sleeve cuff (Fig. 3.51)*
     Location: hem of sleeve.
     Wrap the tape around the hem
     of the sleeve and record the total
     circumference.

8.   *Lapel width (Fig. 3.52)*
     Location: break line to lapel edge.
     Square horizontally across the left
     side lapel from the break line to
     the edge of the lapel.

9.   *Lapel distance from shoulder
     (Figs. 3.53 and 3.54)*
     Location: point of the lapel to the
     shoulder line.
     Place the tape at zero on the point
     of the lapel. The lapel style in this
     example is a peak, so the tape
     is positioned on the peak and
     measured vertically to the shoulder
     line. Record the distance value. The
     height of the lapel, from the front
     button position to the point, can
     also be measured if desired.

The system to take a set of jacket
measurements can be applied
throughout the fitting process, to record
the dimensions at every fit stage. Once
the pattern is finished, a finished set
of measurements will be given to the
tailor, who will refer to it as a way
to check if the cloth is shrinking or
stretching during the making process.

Size codes and size charts

A standard table of measurements is
studied after careful consideration of the
proportional and direct measurements
taken from the body. A size code can
be allocated, to help the cutter decide
where the subject is uncharacteristic.
The experienced pattern maker
will be able to devise their own
system of working measurement
tables, including as many or as few
quantities as necessary for sizing,
based on their own way of working;
in the fashion industry each design
house has their own set of measures
specific to their intended fit model or
customer that fits the brand aesthetic.
Size charts are extremely helpful in
ready-to-wear, which is where they are

Fig. 3.53 Front view lapel distance from
shoulder.

Fig. 3.54 Side view lapel distance from
shoulder.

Fig. 3.55 Lapel height.

predominantly used; bespoke tailors will use size codes in charts as well, in addition to a working scale, which is an older method of comparison, using chest or bust scales to consider proportions for width and depth. Charts and scales are helpful to reference before commencing a pattern, when using the flat divisional grid system.

The size chart below has been devised specifically for the cutting of a suit jacket. The chart has been calculated for ladies with a medium height ranging between 5ft 5" and 5ft 7" (162.5–172cm), with a proportionate 4"/10.1cm hip increase over the bust size.

The suggested sizes are a means of comparison with the measures recorded from the body. The table can be used as a guide to where the variations in an irregular figure are apparent.

An additional chart for tall or short women follows, with the recommended adjustments.

Proportional measurements size chart for a ladies' tailored jacket.

Ladies' Suit Jacket Sizing								
UK	4	6	8	10	12	14	16	18
US	0	2	4	6	8	10	12	14
France	32	34	36	38	40	42	44	46
Italy	36	38	40	42	44	46	48	50
Germany	30	32	34	36	38	40	42	44
Japan	3	5	7	9	11	13	15	17
Standard Proportional Measurements								
Bust	28" 71.1cm	30" 76.2cm	32" 81.3cm	34" 86.3cm	36" 91.4cm	38" 96.5cm	40" 101.6cm	42" 106.8cm
Waist	24" 61cm	24" 61cm	25" 63.5cm	27" 68.6cm	29" 73.7cm	31" 78.7cm	33" 83.8cm	35" 88.9cm
Hip Circumference (Lower Hip)	30-32" 76.2cm	32-34" 86.3cm	36" 91.4cm	38" 96.5cm	40" 101.6cm	42" 106.7cm	44" 111.8cm	46" 116.8cm
Half Back Width	5¾" 14.6cm	6" 15.2cm	6¼" 15.9cm	6½" 16.4cm	6¾" 17.1cm	7" 17.8cm	7¼" 18.4cm	7½" 19cm
Nape to Waist	15¼" 38.7cm	15⅜" 39cm	15½" 39.3cm	15⅝" 39.6cm	15¾" 39.9cm	15⅞" 40.2cm	16" 40.6cm	16½" 41cm
Full Length	26½" 67.3cm	26¾" 68cm	27" 68.8cm	27" 68.8cm	27" 68.8cm	27¼" 69.2cm	27½" 69.9cm	27¾" 70.5cm
Neck Size	13⅛" 33.2cm	13½" 34.4cm	14" 35.6cm	14½" 36.8cm	15" 38cm	15½" 39.2cm	16" 40.4cm	16½" 41.6cm
Armhole Depth	6¾" 17.1cm	7" 17.8cm	7¼" 18.3cm	7½" 19cm	7¾" 19.7cm	8" 20.3cm	8¼" 21cm	8½" 21.6cm
Sleeve Length	23⅜" 59.3cm	23⅜" 59.3cm	23½" 59.6cm	23½" 59.6cm	23⅝" 59.9cm	23⅝" 59.9cm	23¾" 60.2cm	23¾" 60.2cm
Sleeve Cuff	9⅝" 24.5cm	9¾" 24.8cm	9⅞" 25.1cm	10" 25.4cm	10⅛" 26cm	10¼" 26cm	10⅝" 26.3cm	10¾" 26.6cm
Shoulder Length	4⅜" 11.1cm	4½" 11.4cm	4⅝" 11.7cm	4¾" 12cm	4⅞" 12.3cm	5" 12.7cm	5⅛" 13cm	5¼" 13.3cm

Size chart for petite or tall women, showing the adjustments to the vertical measurements

	Short/petite women: 4ft 11" – 5ft 3" 59" - 63"/149.9cm - 160cm	Tall women: 4ft 7" – 6ft 1" 67" - 73"/170.2cm - 185.4cm
Nape to waist	-¾"/-2cm	+¾"/+2cm
Jacket length	-2½"/-6.3cm	+2½"/+6.3cm
Armhole depth	-⅜"/-0.9cm	+⅜"/+0.9cm
Sleeve length	-1½"/-3.8cm	+1½"/+3.8cm

Fig. 3.56 Size codes.

Chapter 4
The Basic Block

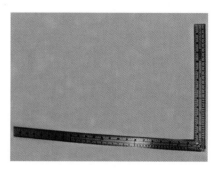

4

Pattern cutting the parts of a tailored jacket begins with the task of drafting a basic block, based on a set of measurements, without the addition of design details.

Construction of a flat pattern for a jacket

The following method is the most commonly used flat pattern making technique in the industry; it is based on a divisional grid devised from a series of hand-drawn pencil lines (or chalk lines as preferred by the cutters on Savile Row). The practice is calculated from given formulae, derived from a size code (see Fig. 3.56) using proportional and direct measurements of the body. The system has evolved over the centuries from scientific study of the human body, passed down from generation to generation. An apprentice will start with this procedure, and modify it to suit their personal cutting experiences gained from observation and fittings. A series of points are plotted as proportional grids to be used as a guideline draft. The master copy is retained and used to trace other patterns from, to incorporate style variations – hence the name 'the basic block'.

NB: All patterns in this book have been drafted by hand and drawn in pencil, at a quarter scale of a full-size pattern. (To obtain a quarter-size pattern, the full-size measures are divided by four.) Should the reader wish to enlarge the patterns to their full size, this can be done using a photocopier to increase the scale or by scanning and re-sizing using Photoshop or similar software.

Opposite page: Fig. 4.1 Preparation to draft the first line of the basic block. Card is laid on the cutting board, alongside shears, pattern rulers, chalk and drawing pencil.

Handling the calculations

The trickiest part about this system is handling the calculations. Most of the sums can be calculated using mental arithmetic counting inches in your mind, or with the aid of tools, if your mental arithmetic is not too good! On Savile Row trainee cutters are taught to 'count', where the trainee will mentally work it out and speak the numbers aloud. A tailor's square can also be used to work out the scale and formulae in inches.

Alternatively, a counting chart (see Fig. 3.1) can be used to add, subtract, multiply and divide inches. The chart

Fig. 4.2 The tailors' square can be used to identify the scale and calculations needed for the formulae.

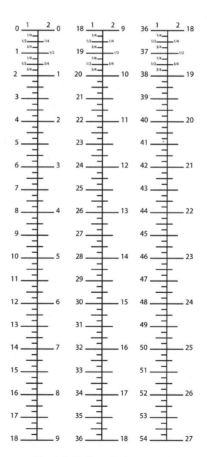

Fig. 4 3 Half-scale fractional counting chart.

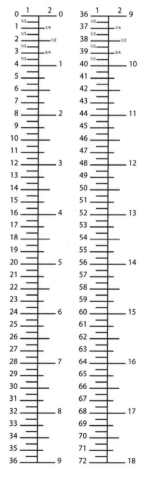

Fig. 4 4 Quarter-scale fractional chart.

allows you to count on the tape measure and convert inches into centimetres, if desired. For the student, print a version of the diagram and work with it alongside the pattern, while drafting.

Alternatively, fractional charts can also be used, as a way to calculate measurements without having to calculate in your head. Half-scale quarter-scale charts are given on Figs. 4.3 and 4.4. To use the charts, locate the number to be divided in the first column, then the answer is found in the second column. For example, to work out half of 10, look at the half-scale chart, find the number 10 in the first column, and look in the column opposite for the answer, which is 5.

USING A CALCULATOR

A calculator can be used instead of the square or charts, in which case all fractions will need to be decimalized.

For example, take the following instruction: 'one fifth of the neck size (The neck size = 14½") plus ⅛'.

This can be expressed using fractions as follows:

$$(\tfrac{1}{5} \times 14\tfrac{1}{2}") + \tfrac{1}{8}"$$

To convert the fractions to decimals, divide the numerator (top number) by the denominator (bottom number).

The decimal version of the equation is therefore:

$$(0.2 \times 14.5) + 0.125$$

Or, alternatively:

$$(14.5 \div 5) + 0.125$$

The result is the same: 3.025", which can be rounded down to 3".

Metric measurements are better suited to the calculator, as it is not necessary to convert fractions to decimals.

As a student or apprentice, try out as many systems as possible and discover the system that works best for you. There is always more than one approach to reach the same conclusion. You may prefer to use mental arithmetic, a tailoring square, counting charts, or to calculate formulae on the calculator. Choose the method you feel most comfortable with.

The working scale

The working scale is a system developed by traditional tailors, and is a well-known method amongst Savile Row cutters for menswear, to apply the depth and width using the chest measurement as the scale. It is a reliable practice for ladies' cutting as well (although it is typically misunderstood due to inadequate explanation of the principles).

In ladies' cutting, it is simply another means of comparison between different sizes, whereby the measurement of the bust size is used to calculate depth and width measurements on the first draft of the divisional grid system. Even though the height and width factors are considered when taking the measurements, when observing the figure on the subject it is advisable to have a working scale as a standard against which these measurements may be compared. It is comparable to a ready-to-wear pattern cutter using size code charts, as in Fig 3.56 from chapter 3, to obtain measurements.

For sizes 36" and under, the working scale is half the bust measure. As all blocks in this book have been drafted with 34" bust size, the working scale is 17". For sizes above 36", another adjustment should be calculated. If we take a subject with a 46" bust for example, there is no proportionate increase to compensate for the irregular figure development of that size, as evidence in patterns of bust size shows that the depth and height remain constant. Therefore, to cope with these statistics, the formula changes to one-third of the bust size, plus 6". So for a 46" bust the scale is 21¼".

To find a cutting scale is a small step towards making a flat paper pattern for a jacket. There are almost as many methods of finding comparative scales as there are flat pattern cutting systems.

Below is a list of proportional depths and widths that can be calculated from the bust scale.

1. Armhole depth: one-third of the bust plus 1¾".

2. Length of the front balance: armhole depth plus one-twelfth of the scale.

3. Position of the front neck point from the centre line: one-sixth of the scale.

4. Front armhole: half the scale minus ¾" for 36" bust and under. Over 36" is one-quarter of the bust measure minus ¾".

5. Position of the nape of the front neck point on the centre line: one-sixth of the scale for 36" bust and under. Over 36" is one-quarter of the bust measure minus ¾".

The basic block (Fig. 4.7)

The following system has been based upon a US size 6, UK 10. Alongside the instructions are the formulae required to plot each point, and the quantity calculated for the suggested size code. The block is drafted as a single half, comprising of a front and back, which is eventually traced off as separate pattern pieces, which are cut on the double when the pattern is ready to toile in fabric. The block is net measurements, with no seam allowances or allocated inlay. These are added once the front and back are traced off as separate pattern pieces. (For seam allowance and inlay allocation, *see* Chapter 8: From block to pattern.) A ½" shoulder pad allowance is incorporated into the draft, and ¾" for waist suppression.

The proportional measures required to draft the pattern are as follows. For bespoke measures insert where applicable. Direct measures can also be incorporated as needed.

1. Height: 5ft 9"

2. Bust: 34"

3. Waist: 27"

4. Hip circumference (lower hip): 38"

5. Nape to waist: 15⅝"

6. Waist to hip circumference: 8"

7. Full jacket length: 27"

8. Half back width: 6½"

9. Armhole depth: 6"

10. Armhole width: 4½"

11. Neck size: 14½"

12. Shoulder length: 4¾"

13. Working scale: 17" (half the bust measurement)

For this particular draft the jacket length is 27", which is a longer length proportion for runway, as the height of the models are tall. The height of the intended wearer is important to record when deciding the jacket length, and this length would be too long for a petite subject. The recorded height for this draft is 5ft 9".

One hip measurement has been applied, that of the hip circumference (the lower hip). For shorter styles the upper hip measurement can be applied if the length goes above the lower hip level.

Begin the pattern by drawing a vertical pencil line, from 0. If using spot and cross, or numbered pattern paper, join the values indicated on the pattern. The line should be long enough for the length of the jacket. This line is labelled the centre back line, and is the centre back (C.B.) of the jacket. It is advisable to draw the line significantly longer than the length of the jacket; this makes it easier to place the pattern master to obtain a 90° line across from it. All triangles and pattern masters have a straight line running through the centre of the ruler, to place directly onto the pattern pencil lines so that the perfect right-angle can be drawn.

For bias grain lines a 45° line is also on the rulers to be used in the same approach; placing the bias line on a straight line of the pattern will give the perfect 45° bias line.

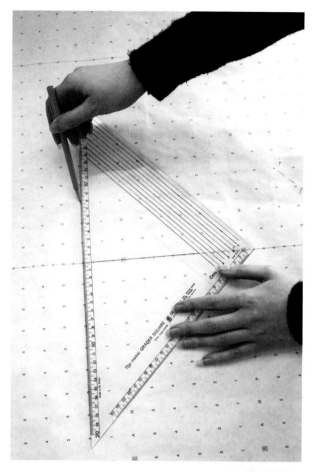

Fig. 4 5 All triangles, squares, or pattern masters have a perfect right angle, enabling 90° lines to be squared on the pattern, from a straight line.

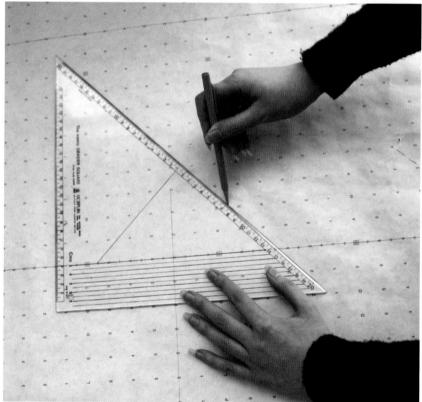

Fig. 4.6 A 45° bias line can also be obtained on the triangle and pattern master.

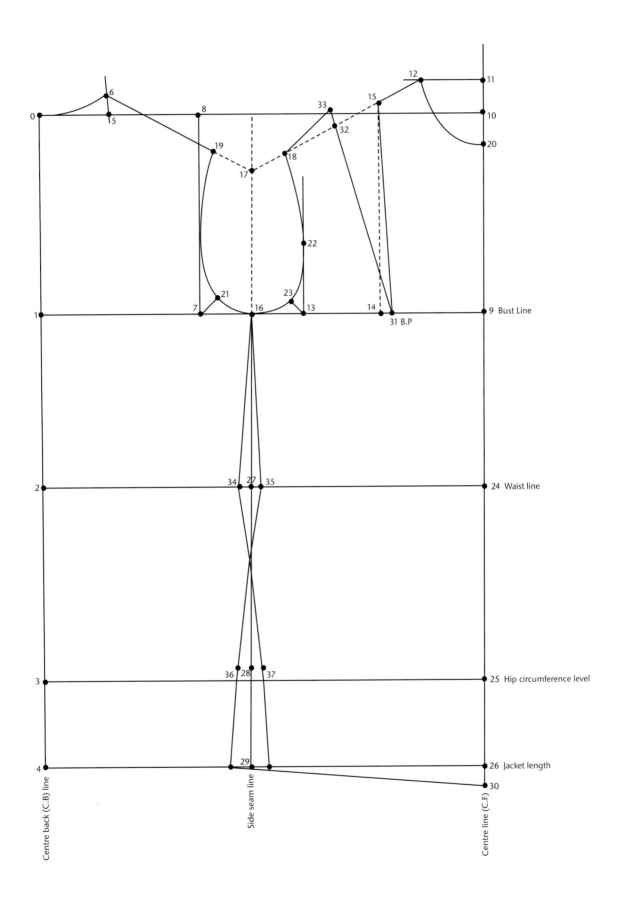

Fig. 4.7 The grid system of the basic block at quarter scale.

1 from 0
Nape to underarm: One-third of the scale (17″) plus 1 ¾″ to include ½″–¾″ for shoulder pad allowance. Do not include this into the draft, if the subject does not require padding in the shoulders.
5¾″ + 1¾″ = 7½″
Mark point 1 with a dot. From point 1 square a 90° line horizontally across the paper, at a right angle to the C.B. line. This balance line is the bust line.

Note: all anatomical balance levels should be labelled on the draft. Students should also number the points as this will make it easier to plot the constructional lines and follow the instructions. It can be confusing without them.

2 from 0
Nape to waist measure: 15⅝″.
Mark point 2 with a dot. Square a 90° line horizontally across the paper, at a right angle to the C.B. line. This balance line is the true waist line.

3 from 2
Waist to hip circumference: 8″.
Mark point 3 with a dot. Square a 90° line horizontally across the paper, at a right angle to the C.B. line. This balance line is the hip circumference level.

4 from 0
Full jacket length: 27″.
Mark point 4 with a dot. Square a 90° line horizontally across the paper, at a right angle to the C.B. line. This line will be the fold line of the hem on the jacket, once the hem inlay has been added. Label line 0 to 4 as the centre back line.

5 from 0
Half back neck: one-fifth of the neck size, plus ⅛″.
(⅛ × 14½″) + ⅛″ = 3″
Mark point 5 with a dot. Square a 90° line horizontally across the paper, at a right angle to the C.B. line.

6 from 5
Rule a line ¾″ upwards, to plot the back neck point at the back shoulder. Mark point 6 with a dot. The back neck point will always be ¾″ higher than point 5, and may alter during the fitting process. This is a standard guideline for now. Join point 6 to 0 with a curve for the half back neck. The curve must measure 2¾″ (the exact measure of 5 from 0). The line 6–5 will curve to fit the measure from 0.

7 from 1
Half back width: 6½″, plus ¼″.
6½″ + ¼″ = 6¾″
Mark point 7 with a dot.

8 from 7
Square a 90° line vertically up to point 8, where the horizontal line squared from zero crosses.

9 from 1
Half bust, plus 2″ ease.
17″ + 2″= 19″
Label line 9 from 1 as the bust line. Square a 90° line vertically up and down, at point 9.

10 from 9
Length of 1 from 0: 8¼″.
Mark point 10 with a dot.

11 from 10
Increase of the front balance to agree with the jacket length: 1⅜″.
The front balance can be derived from dividing the (half bust) scale by one-twelfth.
17 ÷ 12 = 1⅜″
Square a line horizontally across.
Mark point 11.

12 from 11
Location of the front neck point:one-sixth the scale.
(17 ÷ 6) = 2¾″
Mark point 12. (It can also be calculated by taking the measurement of 5 from 0, less a ¼″.)

13 from 9
This point helps to plot the hollow of the front armhole. It can be calculated using the following formula: quarter bust – ¾″.
8½ – ¾″ = 7¾″
Square a 90° vertical line up from 13.

13 from 7
Armhole width direct measurement: 4½″.

14 from 13
Location of the neck point providing the contour shape for the bust prominence point: measure the mid point between points 9 and 13.
Distance between 9 and 13: 7¾″.
Mid point: 3⅞.
Measure ⅜″ back towards the armhole.
Mark point 14 and square up to point 15.

15 from 14
Square up ½″ less than the distance of 9 and 11 on the angle of the shoulder line.

16
Measure the middle of the armhole width, between points 7 and 13 (4½″ ÷ 2 = 2¼″). This is the exact position of the side seam, at the underarm point. Square up and down.

17 from 16
The angle for the shoulder slope, essentially the armhole depth direct measurement plus pad allowance. 5½″ armhole depth + ½″ pad allowance = 6″. This can also be calculated using the bust scale, by dividing the half bust measure by one-third and adding ¼″.
(17″ ÷ 3) + ¼″ = 6″

17 from 15
Rule a straight dotted line to obtain the front shoulder angle, joining points 15 and 17.

18 from 15
Net front shoulder length = 4¾″

19 from 6
Shoulder length plus ½″ ease.
4¾″ + ½″ = 5¼″
Note: this is a standard suggestion for ease; for bigger sizes, or softer cloths add ¾″.

20 from 11
The nape at the centre front neck is measured at the same distance of 11 to 12: 2¾″ (one-sixth of the scale). Draw in the curve of the half front neckline through points 12 and 20.

21 from 7

Rule a line from point 7 at a 45° angle, which measures ¾". Draw in the back armhole, through points 19, 21 and 16.

22 from13

One-sixth of the half bust measurement. 17″ ÷ 6 = 2¾"
This will mark point 22, forming the curve of the front armhole. This anatomical point is also the starting location for the across chest direct measure. The chest measurement can be referenced here if desired, by squaring from the centre line to point 22. Remember to take into consideration the added allowance incorporated into the jacket pattern.

23 from 13

Rule a line from point 13 at a 45° angle, which measures ¾". Draw in the front armhole scye through points 18, 22, 23 and 16.

24, 25, 26

These are squared down from 9. This vertical line is the centre line (C.F.)
Point 24 from 2 is labelled the waist line.
Point 25 from 3 is labelled the hip circumference level.
Point 26 from 4 is labelled the jacket length.

27, 28, 29

These are squared down from 16. Label as the side seam line.

30 from 26

To compensate for the fronts working up, extra length is added on to the bottom hemline, which is joined by a slight curve, smoothed to nothing at the side seam. Recommended value: ¾".

31 from 14

This is the location of the end of the bust dart: ⅜″ from point 14. Label it as the bust point (B.P.).

There are numerous ways to mark the landmark bust point; for standard sizing it can be marked approximately half way between points 9 and 13.

Alternatively, for a bespoke pattern, the measurement between the nipples on the bust of the

subject can be measured, and divided by two, to obtain the half B.P. to B.P. measure, plotted as points 9 to 31. The point itself is indicated with a dot and labelled as B.P. 31. After plotting the bust position, rule a line to point 15 and measure the length, to be used for the other line of the dart.

32 from 15

The width of the dart (measure the distance from points 12 to 15) is 2". Rule a line from point 31 through point 32 and extending past point 32.

33 from 31

33 from 31 should be the same measurement as the length of points 15 to 31, which is why point 33 extends past point 32 where it crosses the shoulder slope. Rule a line from point 33 to the front shoulder end, marked as point 18.

Adding the single side seam to the jacket (Fig. 4.8)

The block can be divided into a series of darts, fitting lines, a single side seam or a side panel between the front and back. The waist suppression is calculated from the number of panels or darts, which will be divided between the half front and back.
The waist suppression of ¾" has been incorporated into the draft at the side seam points 34 and 35.

34 from 27

Measure out to point 34 = ½" from point 27, the very centre of the side seam). Use the vary form curve to join a curved line from point 34 to 16.

35 from 27

Measure ½" from point 27 to point 35. Rule a curved line from 35 to point 16.

The waist suppression calculation

The waist suppression calculation for the remaining seams and darts are derived from the bust.
The draft is calculated from half the bust plus 2″ ease.

(34″ ÷ 2) + 2″ = 19″
The same formula is applied to the waist: half waist, plus 2″ ease
(27÷2) + 2″ = 15 ½"
The difference between the two:
(19″- 15 ½″) = 3 ½"
3 ½″ is the quantity of suppression that needs to be divided into the seams and darts at the true waistline. Proportionally, the back is smaller than the waist by 2″, approximately two-thirds of the surplus (⅔ x 3 ½″) = 2 ¼", which should be added into the back from line 16,34, 37. In the front ⅓ of the surplus (⅓ x 3 ½″) = 1¼"
will be divided into the front from line 16,35,36. How the waist suppression is distributed between darts, panels and seams is a design decision, dependent on the style and the pattern maker.

The hip calculation

Just as the waist suppression can be calculated from the bust scale, so can the flare at the hip circumference.
The draft is calculated from half the bust plus 2″ ease.
(34″ ÷ 2) + 2″ = 19″
The same formula is applied to the hip: half hip, plus 2″.
(38″ ÷ 2) + 2″ = 21″
Difference between the hip and waist:
21″ – 19″ = 2″.

The hip flare is 2″ smaller than the hip circumference measurement, and in order to fit the hip it will need to have the flare added into the pattern. If the half hip is measured on the hip circumference level line on the pattern, the same calculation can be used to identify how much flare needs to be added into the hip.

The half hip on the draft should be 19¾".

Therefore: (21″- 19¾″)= 1¼" of flare to be added between points 36 and 37.

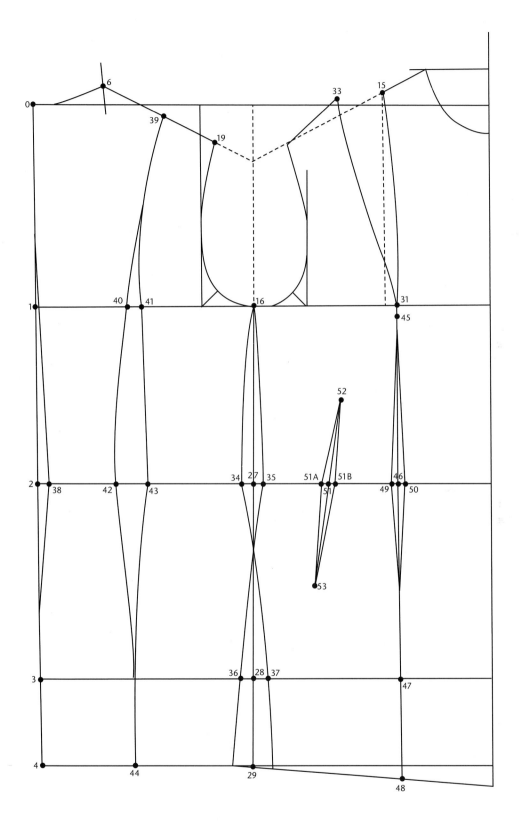

Fig. 4.8 Incorporating the suppression and hip flare for a single side seam draft. (At quarter scale)

36 from 28

For a single side seam, 1¼″ ÷ 2 = ⅝″. Use the vary form curve ruler to draw a shaped line from 36 to 35 at the waist. The line from point 36 continues in the same run to the hemline.

37 from 28

For a single side seam, 1¼″ ÷ 2 = ⅝″. Use the vary form curve ruler to draw a shaped line from 37 to 34 at the waist, continuing down in the same run to the hem. The curve of line 35 and 36 should be the same as line 34 and 37.

Extend the line from points 36 and 37 to the jacket length line, which is the desired flare. A value is not supplied for this measurement, as it should be a continuous line from the hip level, allowing the cutter to fit side flare on the body.

38 from 2

Waist shaping at the centre back waist level = ½″. Shape a line with the vary form curve, from 38 to 0, and from 38 to 4.

39

Mid-way between the front shoulder points 6 and 19.

40 from 1

Style line position, which can be drawn by eye (here it is measured at 3″ from point 1).

40 from 41

½″ shaping under the shoulder blade.

42 from 38

Style line position, which again can be plotted by eye (in this case, 2⅞″).

42 from 43

Shaping allocated into the back, at the waist level.
The total width = 1¼″
Total waist suppression for the back pattern = 2¼″ as previously calculated. (½″ was taken at centre back points 38 from 2, 1¼″ between points 42 and 43 back panel shaping, and ½″ from side seam points 27 to 34 = 2¼″ correct allocation at the back waist level.

44

Join points 44, 42, and 40 to 39, shaping the line with a vary form curve. Label as back panel 1.
Join points 44, 43, and 41 to 39, shaping the line with a vary form curve, label as back panel 2.
These divide the back into two panels.

45 from 31

This is ½″ measured down from the bust point at 31. Square the line vertically through the waist at point 46, to the hip circumference level at point 47, and to the hem at point 48. This forms the front style line.

49 from 46; 50 from 46

¼″ shaping at waist.

49 to 50

Size of the dart = ½″.

51 from 27

Point 51 forms the centre of the second side front dart, exactly half way between points 46 and 27. Rule a slanted line both ways.
The dart width between points 51A and 51B = ¼″
Total waist suppression for the front pattern = 1¼″ as previously calculated. (½″ was taken from first front dart width: points 49 to 50, ¼″ at the second side- front dart width: Points 51A to 51B, and ½″ from side seam between points 35 and 27 = 1¼″ correct allocation at the forepart front waist level.
Therefore: 51A to 51B = ½″ second dart width, with point 51 at the centre.

52 from 51

Mark 3½″: the upper end of the dart.

53 from 51

Mark 4″: the lower end of the dart.
The front separates into two panels.
Points 15, 31, 45, 50, 47, and 48 to the centre line: trace and label as front panel 1.
Points 33, 31, 45, 49, 47 and 48 to the side seam: trace and label as front panel 2.
See Fig. 4.9 to view the separation of the panels.

Shaping

The body is not straight, so all panels, seams and darts should have slight shaping, as opposed to straight lines. A French curve and vary form curve are useful tools to use for shaping. A feeling for the run of the line becomes easier with practice, and an understanding of the shape of the wearer is gained through experience.

The side body jacket draft

The side panel jacket is the preferred distribution of seam panels and suppression, creating a more three-dimensional jacket than the single seam jacket. It will also achieve improved results in fit.

The waist suppression is still calculated as previously calculated, at 3½″, and is divided 2¾″ into the back, and 1¼″ into the front.
The hip flare calculation is also as before: 1¼″.

The basic block with a side body (Fig. 4.10)

Plot points 1 to 33 for the basic block as previously specified.

The amendments to the basic block are as follows:

34 from 2

½″ waist suppression shaped in at the centre back at the waist.

35 from 1

¼″ shaping at the cross back width, on the centre back.

36 from 3

¼″ shaping at the hip line on the centre back.
Draw in the new centre back line using the vary form curve, through points 0, 35, 34 and 36.

37 from 7

Location of the top of the hind seam of the side panel, in the armhole: 2″.

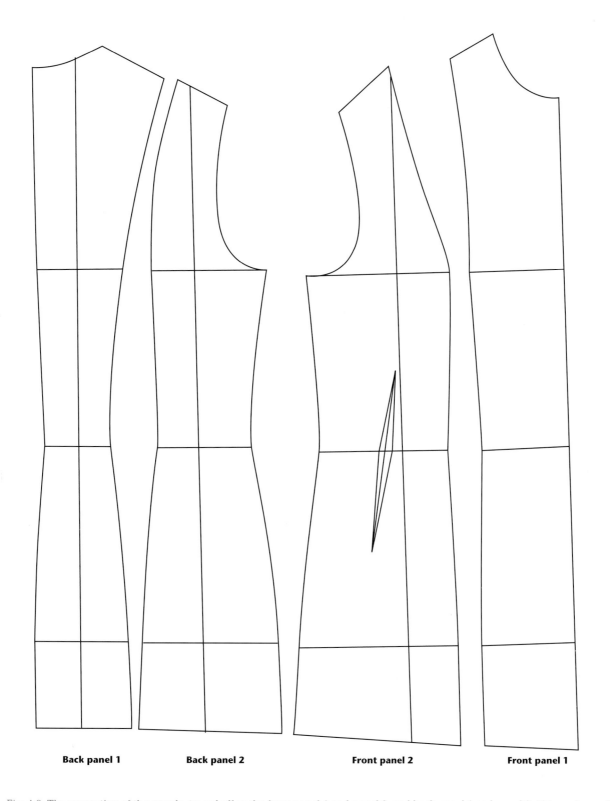

| Back panel 1 | Back panel 2 | Front panel 2 | Front panel 1 |

Fig. 4.9 The separation of the panels, traced off as the front panel 1 and panel 2, and back panel 1 and panel 2. (At quarter scale)

38 from 35
Hind seam of the side panel at the underarm: 6″ from point 35 at the centre back.

39 from 38
Shaping for shoulder blade: ³⁄₈″.

40 from 34
The hind seam of the side panel at the waist level: 5″.

41 from 40
½″ has been allocated at the centre back; 1¼″ of the back suppression should be allocated = 1¼″.

42
Half-way between points 41 and 40. Square a 90° line to point 43, and mark on the hipline.

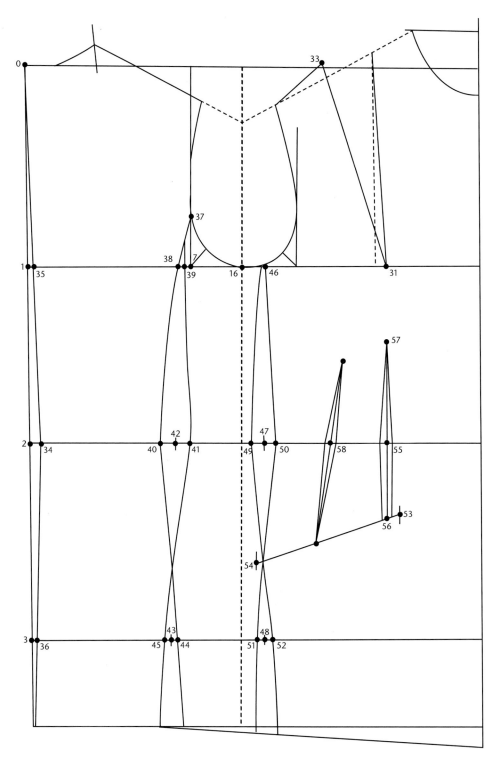

Fig. 4.10 The basic block with a side body. (At quarter scale)

44 from 43

The hip flare calculation value is 1¼".
This has to be distributed between
four lines. 1¼" ÷ 4 = ⅜"
Join points 37, 38, 40 and 44 with a
shaped contoured line, which continues
into the hem. This forms the back pattern.

45 from 43

The hip flare calculation value is 1¼".
This has to be distributed between
four lines. 1¼" ÷ 4 = ⅜"
Join points 37, 39, 41, and 45 with
a shaped contoured line, which
continues into the hem. This forms the
line of the back seam of the side panel.

46 from 16

Point 46 is marked 1" forward of the
dotted line at point 16, representing
the exact side line of the jacket.
Square 90° down to waist and mark
point 47, and point 48 at the hip
circumference level.

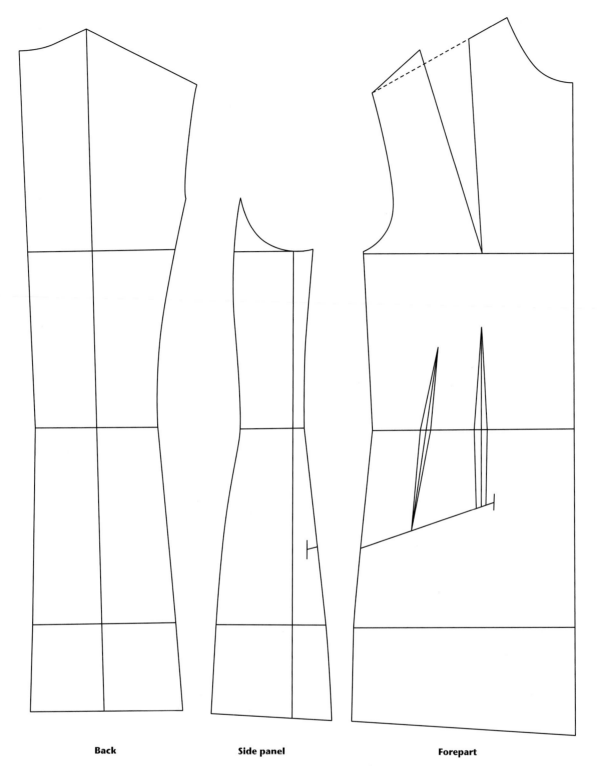

| Back | Side panel | Forepart |

Fig. 4.11 The panels traced off as individual pattern pieces, labelled as the forepart, side panel and back. (At quarter scale)

49 from 47
Shaping at the waist on the forward seam of the side panel: ½".
Point 47 is located centrally between points 49 and 50.

50 from 49
Waist suppression that is already calculated into the draft: 1".

51 from 48; 52 from 48
The hip flare calculation value is 1¼". This has to be distributed between four seam lines.
1¼" ÷ 4 = ⅜"
Total hip flare between points 51 and 52 = ¾"

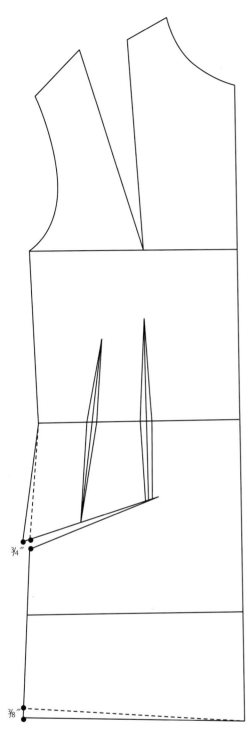

¾"

⅜"

Fig. 4.12 The front bodice traced off as a
separate pattern with a concealed dart in
the pocket position. (Not to scale)

Join points 46, 49, and 52 with
a shaped contoured line, which
continues into the hem. This forms the
line of the front seam of the side panel.
Join points 46, 50, and 51 with
a shaped contoured line, which
continues into the hem. This forms the
side seam of the forepart piece.

Mark the pocket position as desired.
It should not sit too high into the waist
or too low into the hem, and can be
slanted or straight. On the draft it
has been drawn slanted; point 53 is
measured 3" below the waist; point 54
is positioned 5" below the waist.

53 from 54

The pocket length is 6" and marked
slanted. The length should be in
proportion with the size of the jacket
or wearer, between 4½" and 6" is
sufficient. The pocket should start
⅜" in front of the dart and finish at
least ½" into the side panel, for the
standard size.

From point 31 B.P., square a 90° line
to the pocket position. Mark in the
front dart at a ¾" total width of the
dart, ⅜" in both directions from the
dart centre line at the waist (point 55)
and pocket line (point 56).

Point 55

Centre of the first front dart. The total
dart width = ½".

57 from 56

The desired length of dart is 7".

58

Located mid-way between points 55
and 50, and is the centre of the second
front dart. The total dart width = ¼".

Trace off the pieces from the
separate patterns (see Fig. 4.11). It
is helpful to label with the correct
title information: the 'forepart' is the
traditional name of the front pattern
piece, indicated by the points of the
centre line, hemline and 51, 50, and
46. The 'side panel' is the given name
for the side body, identified by points
46, 49, 52, 45, 41, 39 and 37. The back
is obviously the 'back', indicated from
the centre back seam and points 44,
40, 38 and 37, see Fig. 4.11.

A dart to the value of ⅜" is added in
the pocket position, to prevent drags
on the upper hipbone. Be sure to add
the value (⅜") at the hem, so it fits
when seamed to the side panel. A step
at the top line of the dart is also added
to account for the value of the front
dart; which adds up to ¾", the size of
thr front dart.

The basic block should remain
the master copy and be used as the
foundation to devise new patterns of
jacket styles. A lapel and button wrap
are not included to the basic block
at this stage. The style variations
documented in later chapters all use
the side body draft (instructions 0–33
from Fig 4.7, the basic block, and
34–58 from Fig 4.10, the side body
draft). A single seam body is rarely
used, as it is more practical to divide
waist and hip suppression between
two seams.

Bust suppression can be divided
through darts and can be displaced
to various locations through the bust
point with a practice known as dart
manipulation.

Dart manipulation

Dart manipulation is a technique used to design the position of the darts on the front bodice. More frequently used on dresses, it is a useful tool to interpret into patterns for ladies' jackets. The position of the dart can be moved around the body to any position, in accordance with the design, as long as the point of the dart remains at the point of the bust. There are two methods:

1. The pivotal transfer technique. Using a bodkin at the B.P., pivot the pattern to close the dart and move to the desired position on the bodice. Fig 4.14 demonstrates how to move the shoulder dart into the underarm position using this method; by marking point 1, the right hand side

of the dart, then point 2, the new dart position onto pattern paper. Trace around the blocks from points 1-2, and use a bodkin to pierce the bust point of the pattern and pivot point 3 to pint 1, closing the dart and displacing the suppression at point 2. The remaining section from point 3 to 2 is then drawn in completing the process.

2. The slash and spread technique – my preferred system, and the system used in the examples to follow. Draw a new line from the bust point in the desired area on the front; cutting through the new line and existing dart, then closing to open in the new position. Thus, slash and spread with scissors, to close and re-open in a new position on the bodice.

To 'slash' a line means to cut with scissors through a line to a certain point, but not through that point. To 'spread' is to open the slash lines to add the required volume. It is commonly used throughout pattern making, and is especially effective to open and close darts on the forepart.

Trace the net forepart pattern from the bodice block previously drafted, and experiment moving the darts, which provide the shape. The bust dart is currently positioned in the centre of the front shoulder.

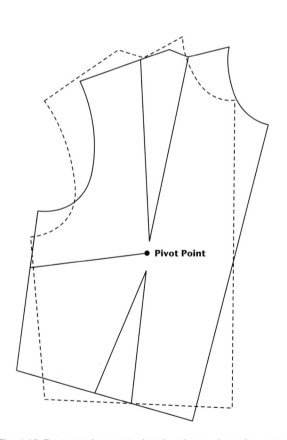

Fig. 4.13 Darts can be manipulated and moved to other parts of the basic block by using the bust point as a pivot point, by swinging the block to open and close desired darts. (Not to scale)

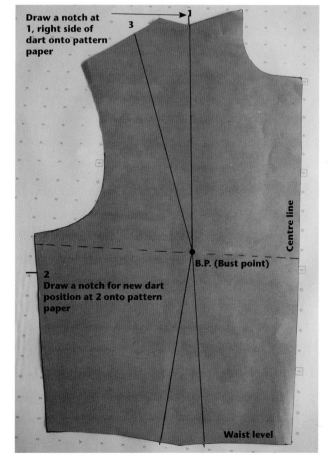

Fig 4.14: The pivot technique is used to close the shoulder dart and move into the underarm.

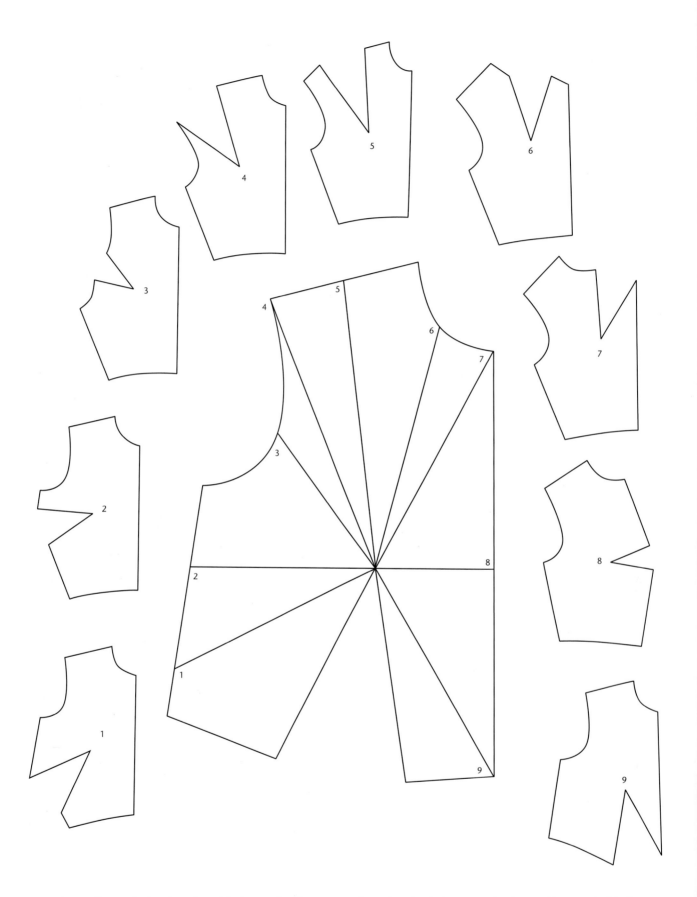

FIG 4.15: The single dart front basic block is used to demonstrate the multitude of placements for dart positions on the block. (Not to scale)

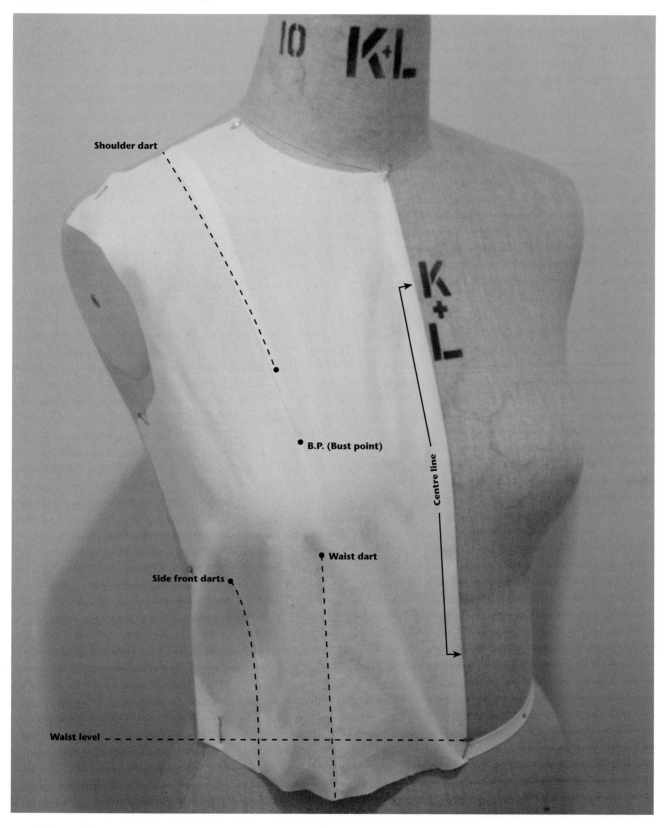

FIG 4.16: The basic block as a half toile cut off at the waist level, showing the current dart position placements on the pattern, which is in the shoulder seam and waist.

The Under Arm Dart

To move the suppression from the shoulder to the underarm position, mark the exact location of the new dart (Fig. 4.19i). Point A is the underarm, and point B is the end of the new dart, measured 2¼″ from A. Rule the angle of the dart from point B to the exact bust point (B.P.). Cut around the net edges of the pattern, slashing through the shoulder dart at points C and D, to the bust point and through the new dart line. Close the suppression at points C and D, taping the net lines together exactly, and open the dart at point B.

Trace the new forepart pattern onto a clean sheet of pattern paper with the new dart position. The dart should not be sewn exactly to the bust point, as it can cause imperfections in the silhouette; it has been marked ½″ back from the bust point, labelled as point E (Fig. 4.19ii).

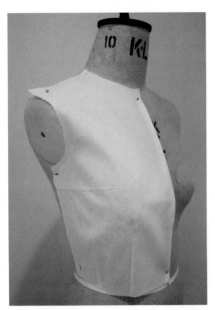

Fig. 4.17 Half toile of front bodice with under arm dart, showing the top- side pinned to the dress form. For the purpose of the exercise the length has been chopped off at the waist.

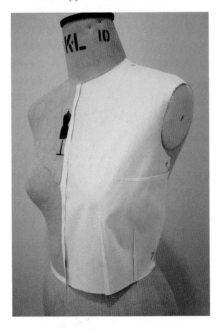

Fig. 4.18 Under side of front bodice toile with underarm dart, showing the direction the darts fold towards on the inside of the bodice, pinned to the dress form.

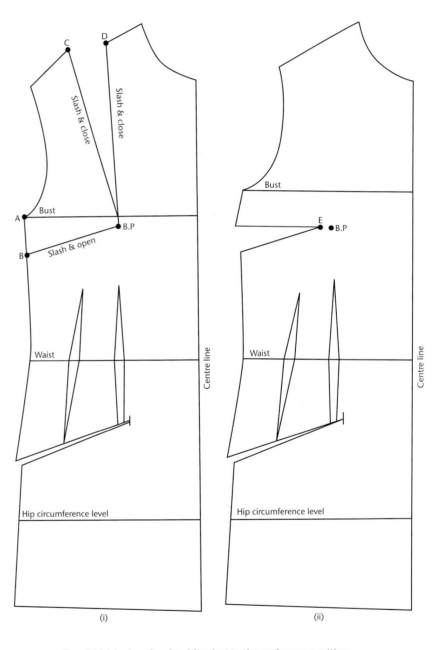

Fig. 4.19 Moving the shoulder dart to the underarm position.
The shoulder dart is slashed, closed and re-opened in the under arm position.
(Not to scale)

The Neck Dart

To move the suppression into a neck dart, indicate points A and B at the shoulder dart, and mark the new dart position in the neck at point C, to the desired length from the centre line. Rule a line to the bust point (Fig. 4.22 i), and decide the exact length of dart, indicated by point D, about 1″ back from B.P. Cut around the net edges of the pattern, slashing through the shoulder dart to the bust point and through the new neck dart. Close the suppression at points A and B and open the dart at point C.

Trace the new forepart pattern onto a clean sheet of paper with the new dart position (Fig. 4.22ii) .

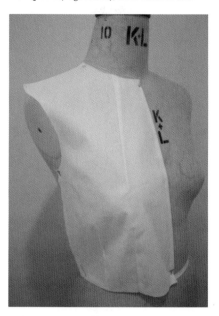

Fig. 4.20 Half toile of front bodice with neck dart, showing the top- side pinned to the dress form.

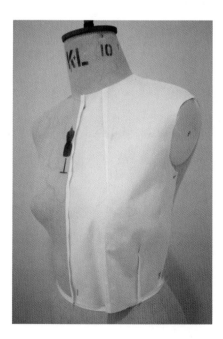

Fig. 4.21 Under side of front bodice toile with neck dart, showing the direction the darts fold towards on the inside of the bodice, and pinned to the dress form.

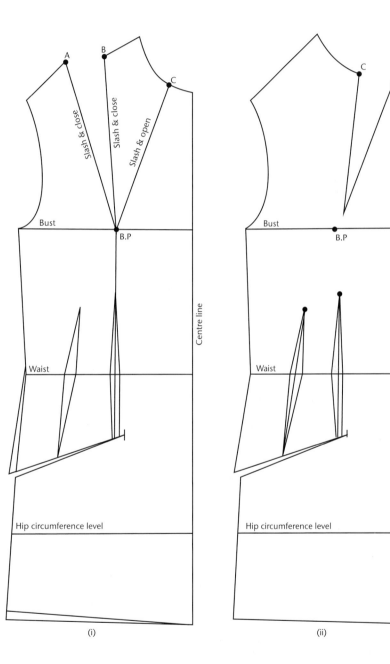

Fig. 4.22 The neck dart.
The shoulder dart is closed and then moved to the front neck position.
(Not to scale)

65

The Waist Dart

In Fig. 4.25, diagram (i), the shoulder dart value has been placed into the front waist dart. It is not necessary to mark a new dart in this example because the dart already exists. It is simply a case of displacing the suppression into the existing front dart.

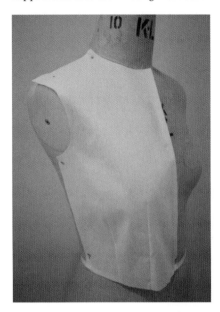

Fig. 4.23 Half toile of front bodice with all the suppression concentrated in the waist dart, showing the top- side pinned to the dress form.

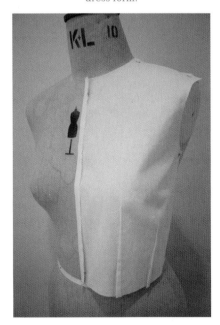

Fig. 4.24 Under side of the front bodice toile with shoulder suppression concentrated in the waist dart, showing the direction the darts fold on the inside of the bodice, and pinned to the dress form.

To do this square down from the bust point and label point A at the top end of the dart, Point B at the centre line in the middle of the dart at the waist, and point C at the bottom of the dart where the pocket position crosses. Label points D and E at the hip pocket, and F and G at the shoulder dart. Cut around the net edges of the forepart pattern, slashing through the shoulder dart (points F and G), through the B.P. to point A, continuing through the centre of the dart (points B and C), and through the hip pocket (points D and E). Close the suppression at F and G, taping the net lines together, and open

the waist dart and hip pocket.

Trace the new forepart pattern onto a clean sheet of pattern paper with the new front dart width (ii).

When the bust suppression is fully displaced into the front waist dart, it can sometimes be tricky to tailor. If the area surrounding the bust point is not shrunk away correctly with an iron, the bust can appear too pointy; and if the cloth does not shrink very well, like so many lightweight cloths do not, then it will appear to be constructed badly. A wool suiting is the preferred choice for this style of dart manipulation, as the bust can be shaped and pressed with ease.

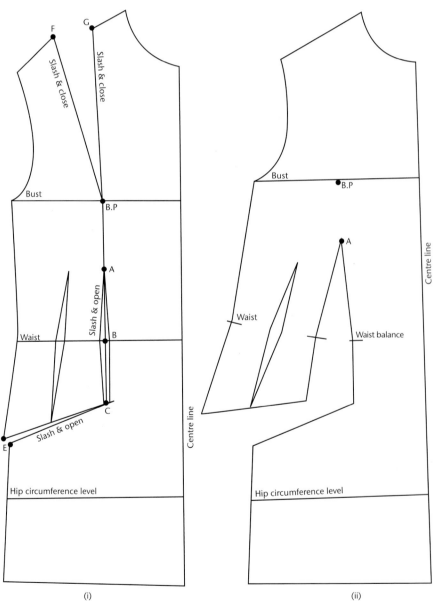

(i)   (ii)

Fig. 4.25 The value of the shoulder dart is placed in its entirety into the waist dart. (Not to scale)

The Combined Neck and Waist Dart

To balance the suppression the amount can be divided into the front waist dart and a neck dart, so that it is not fully concentrated in one place; hence the combined neck and waist dart. In

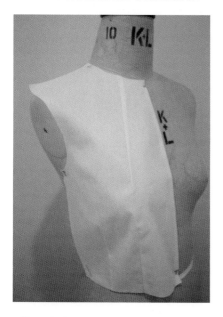

Fig. 4.26 Half toile of front bodice with the suppression spread equally between the neck and waist dart, showing the top-side pinned to the dress form.

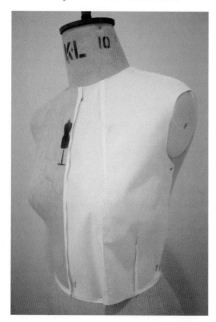

Fig. 4.27 Under side of the front bodice toile with shoulder suppression spread equally between the neck and waist dart, showing the direction the darts fold on the inside of the bodice, and pinned to the dress form.

this example, repeat the same points at A, B, C, D, E, F and G (Fig. 4.28i). Mark the new neck dart position at point H, 2″ from the centre line, and rule the new dart line to the bust point. Mark point I the desired length of the dart. Cut around the net edges of the forepart pattern, slashing through the neck dart line (H and B.P.), the shoulder dart (points F and G), point A continuing through the centre of

the dart (points B and C), and the hip pocket (points D and E). Close the suppression at F and G, taping the net lines together, and open the neck dart, waist dart, and hip pocket, balancing the suppression equally between the neck and waist.

Trace the new forepart pattern onto a clean sheet of pattern paper with the new front dart width (ii).

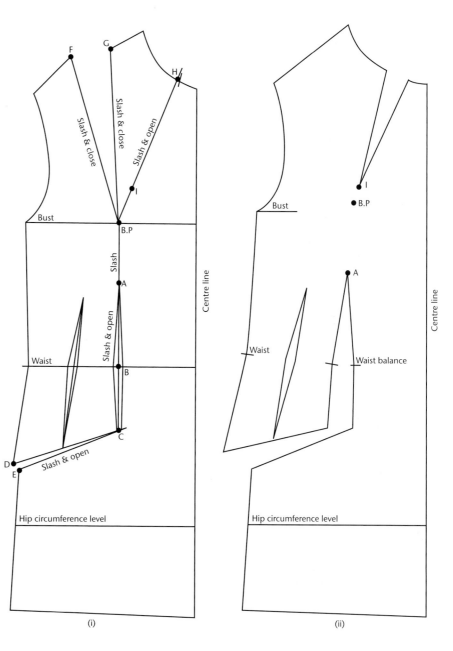

Fig. 4.28 The combined neck and waist dart.
The value is spread equally between the first waist dart and neck dart, to balance the suppression. (Not to scale)

67

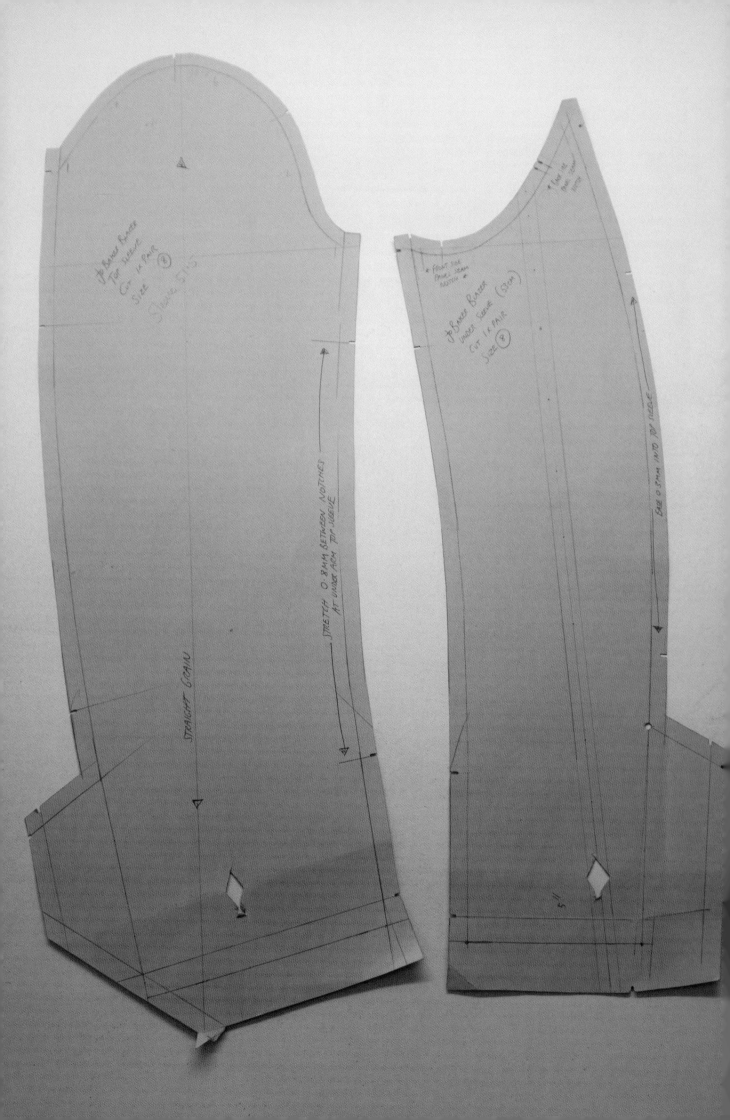

Chapter 5
The Sleeve Block

Pattern cutting tailored sleeves is the challenging part of a jacket pattern. This is because there are so many considerations that affect the construction of a well-balanced sleeve. This chapter reveals the secrets to obtaining beautiful sleeves by incorporating various elements into the pattern: the fabric choice, fullness/ease at the crown of the sleeve, and precise pitching in the armhole to hang vertically without unsightly drag lines and distortions.

There are two types of sleeve construction: a one-piece sleeve or a two-piece sleeve. The one-piece sleeve will typically have an elbow dart and will be used for more sporty styles, dresses and blouses. It will have one underarm seam to run in conjuction with the side seam of the jacket. A traditional tailored jacket will have a two-piece sleeve, as it is considered to be more refined. This style of sleeve will have the underarm seam and a hind arm seam to create ergonomic run of seams, which is more in keeping with the slimline silhouette of a tailored jacket.

The sleeve pitch and balance

The sleeve when basted into an armhole must be so balanced that a good 'sleeve pitch' is obtained when the arm is in its natural position at the side. Correct pitching gives essential movement, and removes unsightly dragging lines, which disorder the hang of the sleeve. Therefore a point in the front armhole is identified, and

Opposite page: Fig. 5.1 A traditional tailored jacket will require a two-piece sleeve, consisting of a top sleeve and an under sleeve, with a cuff vent at the hem. Its seams are ergonomic to follow the curve of the arm.

called the 'front pitch'. A second point in the back called the 'back pitch' is marked; both pitches decide the balance of the sleeve in the armhole. The entire sleeve hinges from the front pitch point: lowering this point will result in a backward hanging sleeve; raising this point will result in a forward hanging sleeve. The back pitch position is decided by the hind seam position to the armhole, and the distribution of fullness, also known as ease, allocated in the crown height, to be in balance with the front pitch. Fullness/ease is extra width added into the pattern, which allows movement of the bicep and the top of the sleeve to roll at the seam.

It is necessary to add inlays to a first pattern sleeve block and hand baste the sleeve into the armhole of the jacket to check the sleeve pitch; either on the mannequin or by holding the jacket and placing in your hand, to see the hang of the sleeve.

A useful trick is to observe the position of the cuff in relation to the hip pocket flap (Fig. 5.2); for a standard size, with normal posture, the sleeve should sit in the middle of the flap. This can be marked with a faint chalk line or a hand basted mark stitch, to assist in observing the correct pitch. A lot of runway models stand very upright, so jackets to be shown on the runway are cut with a lower pitch, so the sleeve will sit further back from the mark at the centre of the pocket flap. In contrast, for the wearer who stands more forward the sleeve will sit forward of the centre of the pocket.

Adjustments to the pitch on the pattern can be re-marked in the forepart and back armhole of the basic block, and on the two-piece sleeve draft. If there are several alterations from the fitting, which include changes to the armhole, the sleeve

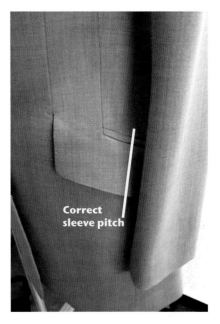

Fig. 5.2 The cuff in line with the centre point of the hip pocket. In the fitting a mark will be made in chalk on the flap to record the hang of the sleeve.

must be re-basted, and the pitch re-checked, as it will hang differently with the new amendments. The new sleeve pitch will then need to be recorded on the new pattern.

The sleeve block

This section is focused entirely on drafting a tailored two-piece sleeve for the basic block with a side body. A one-piece sleeve is hand draped on the mannequin later in the book. Two versions of two-piece jacket sleeves are explored here: the 'three-quarter sleeve' and the 'fifty/fifty', as it is known in tailoring terminology. The names are a reference to the position of the underarm seam.

To produce the two-piece sleeve draft, an additional copy of the front and back basic block armhole should be traced off and used for taking

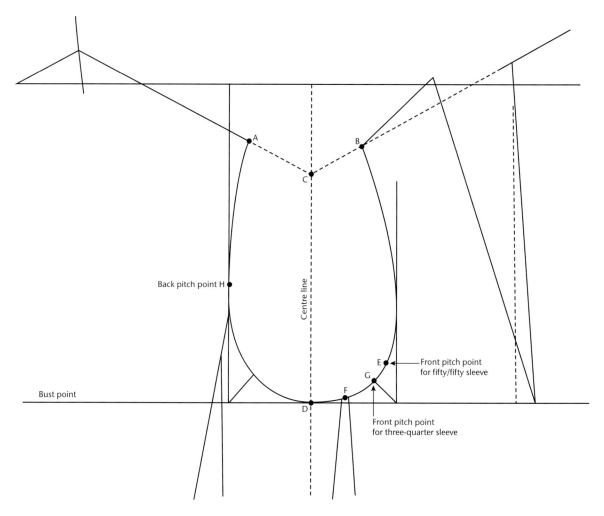

Back pitch point H

Centre line

E — Front pitch point for fifty/fifty sleeve

G

F

Bust point

D

Front pitch point for three-quarter sleeve

Fig. 5.3 A copy of the front and back armhole should be traced to reference the run of the lines and measurements needed to transfer into the sleeve draft. (Not to quarter scale)

measurements, and transferring the run of the lines into the shape of the sleeve circumference (Fig. 5.3).

The measures required to draft the pattern are as follows.

1. Total armhole circumference, measured from points A to B, on the basic block draft: 16½". This measurement will be applied to the size of the sleeve head, which has to be checked and measured to be the same as the armhole, with an additional fullness/ease allowance at the crown.

2. The total armhole depth from points C to D, including the pad allowance of ½": 6". It is essential to check that the crown height of the sleeve is the exact measure of the armhole depth on the basic block.

3. The front pitch point for the fifty/fifty sleeve is measured at 1" from point F (the forepart side seam) to point E, labeled as the front pitch point for fifty/fifty sleeve on the armhole. Point G is the front pitch point for the three-quarter sleeve, and is measured at ¾ " from point F.
Point E on the armhole is where the underarm seam of the sleeve will be placed, when basting the sleeves into the armhole. The pitch may change during the fitting process in accordance with the wearer.

4. The back pitch point from the bust line: 3¾", located at point H on the basic block draft.

5. Width of the top sleeve for a regular sleeve with a lot of crown fullness: 8½". Width of the top sleeve for a slimmer sleeve with reduced crown fullness: 8". The width of the top sleeve is determined by the desired fit of the sleeve and how much fullness is to be added at the crown of the sleeve.

6. Sleeve length: 23½".

7. Sleeve cuff, regular sleeve: 10¾". Sleeve cuff, slimmer sleeve: 10".

Adjusting the sleeve fullness according to the weight of the cloth

All sleeve patterns should be adjusted for the weight of cloth. The regular sleeve (Fig. 5.5) has 2½" of fullness at the sleeve head (point 17). At point 20 the under sleeve has been pivoted to decrease the width of the under sleeve to 2″ of fullness, so that the tailor has the option to use less ease if necessary.

This seems an excessive amount of fullness to control when putting sleeves into the armhole. However, if the sleeves are hand basted very carefully, fixing the majority of the fullness at the crown, it shrinks beautifully under a tailoring iron if the cloth is a soft wool with a weight of around 12–13oz (340–370g) and above; then with the addition of sleeve head roll, it creates a beautiful high roll at the sleeve head.

This sleeve draft is calculated for softer weights of cloth: if a lighter weight wool cloth is desired, amend the instructions to add the adjustments for the slimmer sleeve with reduced fullness/ease. The fullness/ease amount for this pattern is significantly reduced to 1½″. The key message here is that the fabric needs to be selected before drafting the pattern, so that that the necessary points can be considered and adjusted, in accordance with the type of cloth.

A 10–11oz (280–312g) wool should have the fullness reduced to 1¾″, which is demonstrated at point 20 (Fig. 5.5) where the under sleeve hind arm has been pivoted to lessen the width, therefore decreasing the extra fullness.

A cloth with a weight below 10oz (280gms) should be adjusted again. The width of the top sleeve at point 2, in the slimmer fifty/fifty (Fig. 5.11) sleeve, should be reduced by ¼″, and at the under sleeve, point 17. An 8–9oz cloth (227–255g) should have around 1½″ fullness. The cuff width is also reduced to balance the line of the width at the sleeve crown.

For a lightweight suiting at 7oz (198g) or below, if there is too much fullness, pleats will be created when pressed, so the pattern has to be adapted again. It is advisable not too add too much fullness for this weight, a maximum of 1⅜″. The pattern will need to be adjusted further, following the previous steps described for the slimmer sleeve.

Fig. 5.4 The extra fullness at the sleeve crown creates a roll at the top sleeve.

For fabrics which will not take the fullness or press well, like leather, gabardine, or sport fabrics, ¾″ fullness should be enough, and in some cases none at all. It is always advisable to carry out a trial with the intended cloth, before cutting the pattern in the actual fabric, to see how it performs.

There are two versions of each block: the regular sleeve, which has 2½″ fullness (with the option to pivot to 1¾″, depending on the cloth), and the slimmer sleeve, which has 1½″ fullness.

The fifty/fifty two-piece regular sleeve (Fig. 5.5)

The 'fifty/fifty' sleeve is a reference to the position of the underarm seam: the proportion of the under sleeve to the top sleeve is exactly one half, a fifty/fifty distribution between the two.

It is not uncommon for traditional tailors to mark two points for the hind arm seam. This is so that there is flexibility to adjust the sleeve in accordance with the armhole when the jacket has been made up in the actual cloth, as it is not always easy to predict the characteristics of all fabrics and capture this in a flat pattern. It will also allow the tailor to adjust ease and alter the sleeve to correspond with the fitting. One set of points is wider, and the other slimmer; then seam allowance and 1″ inlays can also be included. This is common practice on Savile Row, London, and can be observed in both the fifty/fifty and three-quarter drafts.

To draft the points for a regular sleeve width, rule a straight 90° line, which is longer than the measurement of the sleeve length. Indicate point 0 on this line.

1 from 0

The height of the back pitch from the bust line on the back armhole (Fig.5.3 point H), minus ½″.
3¾″ − ½″ = 3¼″

2 from 1

The top sleeve width is measured diagonally between points 1 and 2: 8¼″. The measurement is applied along the diagonal line from point 1 on the draft. Point 2 can be adjusted to increase the width of the top sleeve (or decrease for the slimmer sleeve).

3 from 2

Calculate one-third of the distance between points 1 and 2, plus ¼″.
(8½ ÷ 3) + ¼″ = 3⅛″
Square a 90° line up and down.

4 from 3

Mark point 4 exactly in the middle of line 0 to 3, and measure back towards the hind arm by ¾″.

5 from 1

Measure ½″ below point 1.

6 from 5

The crown height corresponds with the total armhole depth of the basic block: 6″. Square across to point 7, which also squares up from point 3.

7

The mid-point of the top sleeve, which matches to the shoulder seam of the basic block back and forepart pieces. Rule a dotted line from point 7 to points 1 and 2.
Draw in the shape of the top sleeve

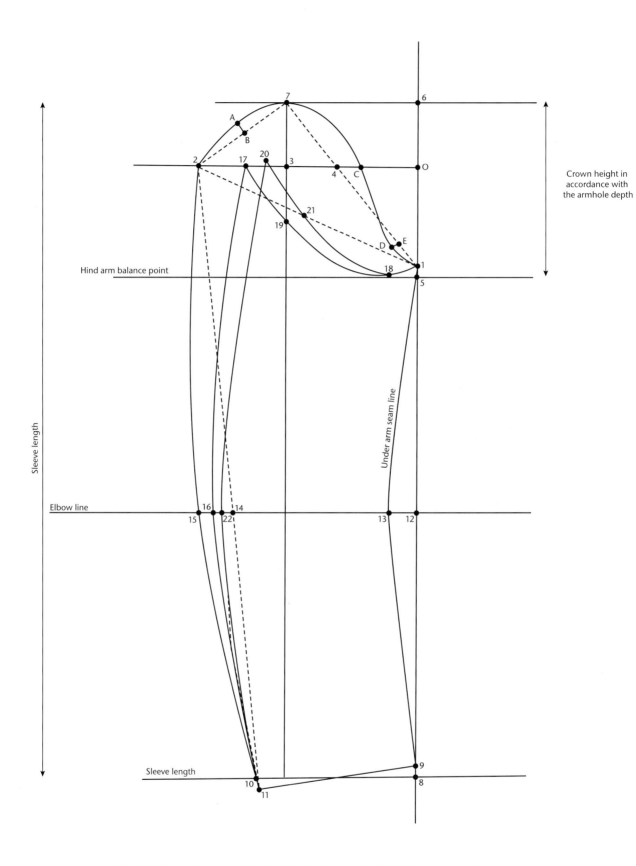

Fig. 5.5 The main constructional points for the regular fifty/fifty two-piece sleeve
with pivoted under sleeve points to adjust fullness distribution for the cloth. (At quarter scale)

Chapter 5 / The Sleeve Block

between points 1, 2 and 7. Firstly indicate point B, located centrally between points 2 and 7, and square out to point A.

A from B
Hollow the shape outwards roughly ³/₈". Draw in the shape of the back top sleeve, through points 2, A, and 7.

C from 4
Hollow the shape outwards by ⁵/₈". Point C is marked on horizontal line from 0. Mark point E approximately 1" from point 1.

D from E
Hollow the shape inwards by ¼". It can be difficult to draw a smooth curve with a pattern master, or French curve. Experienced pattern makers will use a template of a sleeve shape cut on heavy card to draw around with ease between the points (see template 10); this will speed up the process.

8 from 6
Total sleeve length: 23½". Square a 90° line across.

9 from 8
At the hem of the underarm seam, measure ³/₈" above point 8 for the angle of the cuff.

10 from 8
Half the total cuff width.
10¾" ÷ 2 = 5³/₈"

11 from 10
The hind arm seam hem. Square down from point 10 by ³/₈". Join points 9 and 11 with a straight line, the hem of the sleeve. Rule a dotted line from point 11 to point 2.

12
The elbow line, located half way between between points 1 and 9.

13 from 12
Measure 1" along the elbow line. Join point 13 to points 9 and 1 using the vary form curve stick. This is the underarm seam.

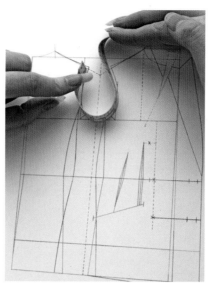

Fig. 5.6 Measuring the circumference of the armhole.

14
Located on the elbow line, where it crosses through the dotted line between points 2 and 10.

15 from 14
The elbow point at the hind arm seam of the top sleeve: 1¼".
Join point 15 to points 11 and 2 using the vary form curve stick.

16 from 15
The elbow point for the hind arm seam of the under sleeve: ¼".

17 from 2
The upper point of the hind arm seam of the under sleeve: 1⁵/₈".
Join points 17, 16 and 11 using the vary form curve. Point 17 is an important point, which can be pivoted to adjust the size of the sleeve to be slimmer or wider. Check that the distance between points 2 and 11 is the same as between points 17 and 11, as these two seams sew together.

18 from 1
The front pitch point: 1".
Join points 1, 18 and 17 with a hollow curve in keeping with the armhole on the basic block.

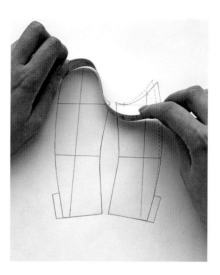

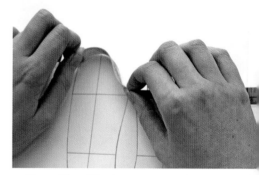

Above: Figs. 5.7 & 5.8 Measuring the circumference of the top sleeve.

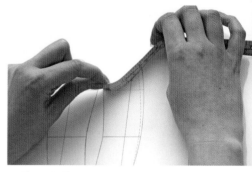

Fig. 5.9 The tape measure is placed carefully around the curve to obtain an accurate measurement.

19
The net armhole measurement of the basic block, to include the back bodice and the forepart, is 16½" (Fig. 5.6). This measurement is obtained from placing the tape measure around the net seam lines of the armhole, adding the back to the front.
Measure the circumference of the top sleeve with a tape measure between points 2 and 1 (Figs. 5.7 and 5.8) and

continue around the under sleeve (Fig. 5.9) from point 1 through point 18, marking point 19 the exact armhole measurement of the basic block. The distance measured between 19 and 17 indicates the amount of fullness/ease incorporated into the pattern.

19 from 17

The fullness/ease amount included in the regular fifty/fifty pattern is 2½". It is at this part in the process where point 17 is pivoted to point 20 on the draft, by the desired amount to reduce the fullness/ease in the pattern. For a first sleeve pattern, it is safer to have two hind arm points on the pattern of the under sleeve. Further seam allowances and inlays are then added

to the wider hind arm after it has been traced as a pattern piece. This is so that when it is chopped in cloth, the tailor has the freedom to adjust the sleeve, dependent on the cloth and how well the fullness/ease shrinks under the iron. If it starts to pleat, and it will not press away, the tailor can reduce the size of the sleeve. This is represented at point 20.

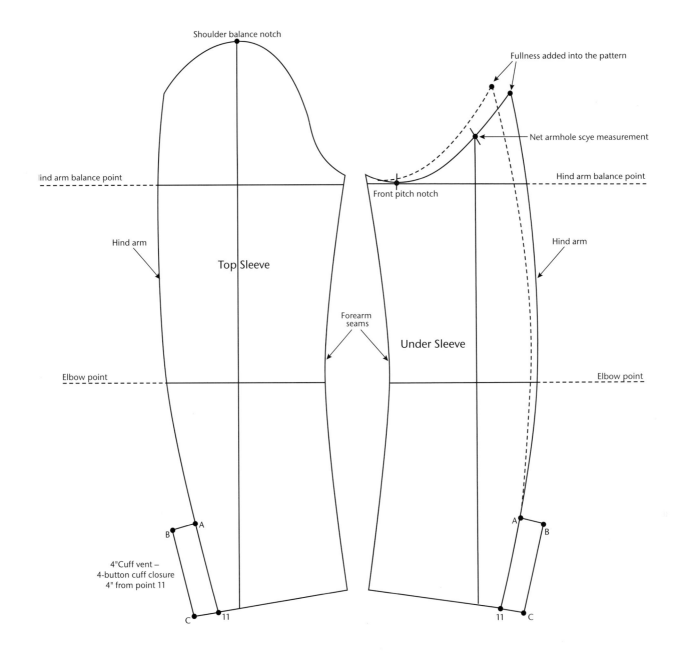

Fig. 5.10 The regular fifty fifty top and under sleeves are traced from Fig 5.5 as separate pattern pieces, with no seam allowance.
(At quarter scale)

20 from 17

The reduced ease upper hind arm.
By narrowing this point, the ease will
be reduced to 2". Hollow a curve
between points 1, 18 and 20.

21

The net armhole is 16½".
Re-measure the circumference of
the top sleeve and under sleeve from
points 2 to 1, and through points 1, and
18. Mark point 21. Points 21 to 20 are
the new fullness/ease value, which
has now been reduced to 1¾".

22 from 16

Narrower hind arm elbow point: ½".
Join points 20, 21 and 11 with a vary
form curve.
Trace off the top sleeve as a separate
pattern through points 1, 9, 11, 2 and
7. Trace off the under sleeve through
points 1, 9, 11, 16 and 17 and 11, 22,
and 20 (Fig 5.10).
The addition of the cuff vent at point A
has been added for a four-button cuff
closure, on the top sleeve and under
sleeve. Measure 4" up from point 11
at the hind arm hem for a 4-button
functioning cuff vent.
Square out from point A to B: 1⅜";
square out from point 11 to C: 1⅜".
Draw in the vent. Draw onto both the
under sleeve and top sleeve.

The fifty/fifty two-piece slimmer sleeve (Fig. 5.11)

A cautious pattern cutter will draft a
wider sleeve for the first pattern, with
added inlays, as it is easier to pinch
in during the fitting, and fit closer to
the arm while it is worn. It is more
difficult to fix the sleeve width if the
proportion is too slim to start with,
as it is impractical to resolve the fit
issues. If a slim sleeve is required, it is
a sounder choice to reduce the pattern
gradually, through two stages of fitting.
The previous sleeve draft allowed
the cutter to pivot the under sleeve to
adjust the fullness/ease from 2½" to 2".
For slimmer style sleeves and lighter
weight cloths, the ease amount may
still be too much to baste into the sleeve
head. The pattern can be adjusted

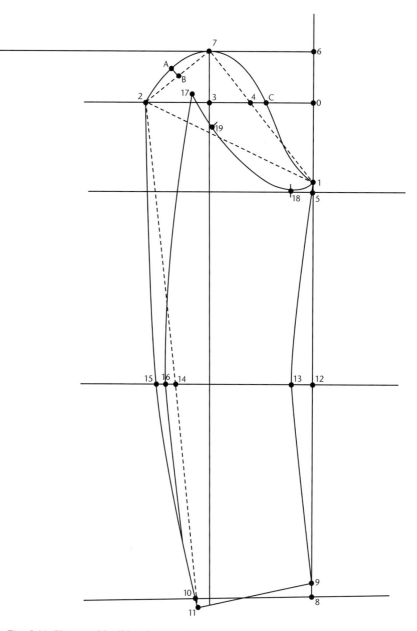

Fig. 5.11 Slimmer fifty/fifty sleeve width, with reduced fullness. (At quarter scale)

further to be slimmer and have reduced
fullness/ease, if it is needed.

To draft the slimmer fifty/fifty sleeve,
cross-reference the regular fifty/fifty
sleeve, and repeat directions from
points 0 to 19, including A, B and C,
with the exception of the following
points. The sleeve ease/fullness is 1½".

2 from 1

Width of the top sleeve: 8".
The value has been reduced by ¼",
when compared to the regular width.

10 from 8

Slimmer cuff: 10". Half the total cuff
width: 5".
The cuff is reduced to fit closer to the
wrist, in this example approximately
⅜", to be in proportion to the new top
sleeve width at point 2.

14

Still located on the elbow line where
it crosses through the dotted diagonal
line between points 2 and 10. It simply
moves in more narrowly towards the
underarm, as the values at points 2
and 10 are reduced.

15 from 14

The elbow point at the hind arm seam of the top sleeve is 1″.
Draw in the new hind arm seam of the top sleeve between points 2, 15, and 11.

16 from 15

The elbow point of the hind arm of the under sleeve is ¼″.

17 from 2

The upper point of the hind arm on the under sleeve is 2″.
Draw in the new hind arm seam of the under sleeve by joining points 17, 16, and 11. Check that points 2 and 11 are the same length as points 17 to 11, as these two seams are sewn together.
A wider hind arm point has not been included on this draft; if it is desired a second hind arm point can be added by repeating instructions from the regular sleeve, or by pivoting point 17 according to the cloth being used.

18 from 1

The front pitch point: 1″.

19

The net armhole measurement on the basic block, measured with the tape measure around the circumference of the sleeve from points 2, 7, 1, on the top sleeve and through points 1, 18, to 19 is 16½″.
Once the pattern dimensions have been checked and you are satisfied with the outcome, separate the two sleeves by tracing the top sleeve and under sleeve. Add the cuff vent closure, and required seam allowances and inlays. This is explored further in Chapter 9.
Cut a first toile of the regular and slimmer fifty/fifty sleeve and fit on a mannequin or model, checking both proportions to see what is preferred. Record the observations and alterations on the pattern. Continue the process until the balance of the sleeve is correct.

The three-quarter regular sleeve (Fig. 5.13)

On the 'three-quarter sleeve' (also known as the 'false forearm sleeve' by Savile Row tailors), the forearm seam is displaced under the arm. The ratio of the top sleeve to the under sleeve is three to one, hence the name. It is the most commonly used sleeve for ladies' jackets as it is aesthetically more appealing: the underarm seam is hidden, whereas on the fifty/fifty sleeve it is visible.

It should be noted that the front pitch will sit ¼″ lower into the armhole for this style of sleeve: ¾″ from points G to F on Fig. 5.3, resulting in the back pitch point being raised by ¼″ to 3½″. This is to compensate for the adjusted seams.

The width of the top sleeve can be adjusted to sit lower into the back, according to the style. It should be noted that the elbow point (point 15) is narrower and the hind arm is straighter on this draft; therefore, 15 from 14 is 1″.

To draft the three-quarter sleeve, trace the fifty/fifty regular two-piece sleeve draft, or apply directions from 0 to 22; both will need the following modifications.

To displace the forearm:

23 from 5

Reduce the forearm of the under sleeve at the underarm: ¾″.

24 from 13

Reduce the forearm of the under sleeve at the elbow: ¾″.

25 from 9

Reduce the forearm of the under sleeve at the hem: ¾″.
Draw in the new forearm seam of the under sleeve, joining points 23, 24, and 25.

26 from 5

Increase the width of the forearm of the top sleeve at the underarm: ¾″.

27 from 13

Increase the width of the forearm of the top sleeve at the elbow: ¾″

28 from 9

Increase the width of the forearm of the top sleeve at the hem: ¾″.

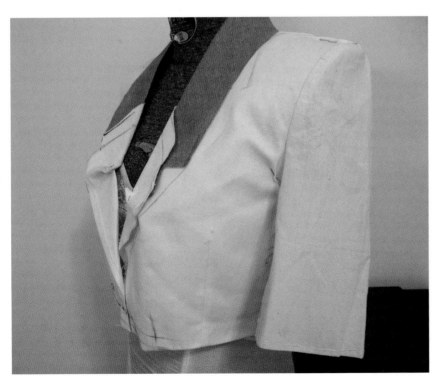

Fig. 5.12 The sleeve has been cut in calico and hand basted into the body of a jacket toile to check ease/fullness distribution and pitch points.

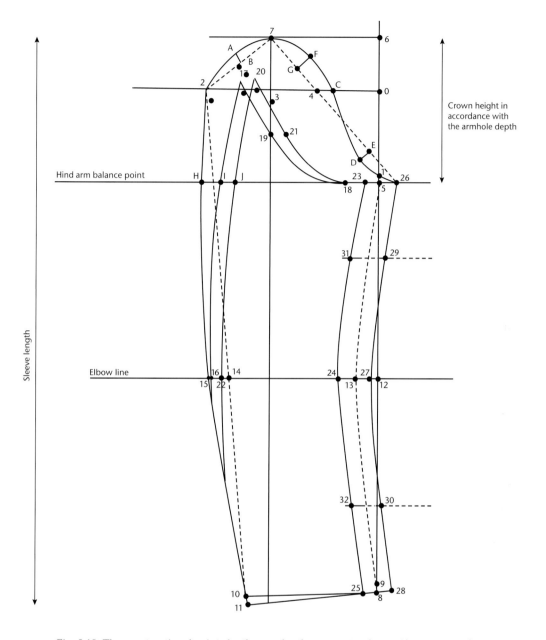

Fig. 5.13 The constructional points for the regular three-quarter sleeve. (At quarter scale)

Draw in the new forearm seam of the top sleeve, joining points 26, 27, and 28.

29 and 30

The forearm balance notches of the top sleeve are placed 4″ from points 26 and 28. On the top sleeve between balance notches 29 and 30 the forearm seam must be stretched with an iron and eased in when machining to the under sleeve. This is essential to allow the displaced seam to drape around the arm, without causing any unsightly drags. Points 31 and 32 on the under sleeve are squared across from 29 and 30.

Draw in the top sleeve shape as described for the fifty/fifty sleeve going through points 2, 7, 1 and 26.

A to B: square out ½″.
C to 4: square out ⅝″.
D to E: square in ½″.

Point G is marked in the middle of the dotted line between 4 and 7.
F to G: square out ¾″.

The universal template (template 10) for the sleeve head can be used here to draw in the shape of the top sleeve, joining points 2, A, 7, F, C, D, 1, and 26.

18 from 23

Draw in the run of the under sleeve circumference. The front pitch is lowered by ¼" on the front armhole to compensate for the extra width added to the top sleeve. Therefore point 18 from 23 is ¾".

21

Re-measure the total armhole circumference of the basic block and re-mark points 20 and 21.
It should be observed that the under sleeve at point 11 is raised by ¼" to

point 10 at the cuff. Point 10 to 25 is the hemline for the under sleeve; point 11 to 25 is the hem line for the top sleeve. If this adjustment is not applied, drag lines will be created at the hind arm balance level (points H, I, and J on the sleeve draft), and will also hinder movement of the arm.
Points 17 and 20 of the under sleeve have been lengthened by ¼" above the horizontal line from 0, to

compensate for this. When the blocks are traced off as separate pattern pieces, make sure the hind arm balance points are transferred onto each piece and match correctly. Points H, I, and J should be used as back balance notches for the top and under sleeve (See Fig. 5.14).

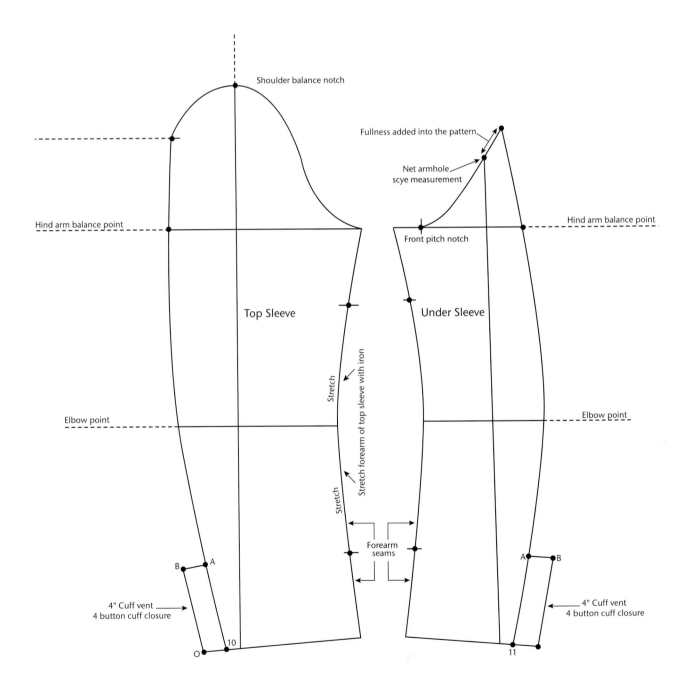

Fig. 5.14 The three-quarter sleeve traced off as separate pieces with no inlay or seam allowance. (At quarter scale)

The three-quarter slimmer sleeve (Fig. 5.15)

To draft the slimmer version of the three-quarter sleeve, repeat directions from points 0 to 32, including points A to J. On Fig. 5.15 the wider hind seam has been excluded from the draft at points 16, 17, 19 and I. If it is preferred two hind seam points can be plotted to be cautious, but for the purpose of this exercise, only the slimmer hind seam at points 20, 21, and 22 have been marked. Sleeve ease/fullness: 1½".

2 from 1

Width of the top sleeve: 8".

10 from 9

Slimmer cuff: 10". Half the total cuff width: 5".

14

This is still located on the elbow line where it crosses through the dotted diagonal line between points 2 and 10. It simply moves in more narrowly towards the underarm, as the values at points 2 and 10 are reduced.

15 from 14

Elbow point at the hind arm seam of the top sleeve: 1".
Draw in the new hind arm seam of the top sleeve between points 2, 15, and 11.

18 from 23

The front pitch point is re-measured from the new underarm point at 23. As it is a three-quarter sleeve, it will sit lower in the armhole to compensate for the extra width in the top sleeve: ¾".

21

The net armhole measurement on the basic block measured with the tape measure around the circumference of the sleeve from points 2, 7, 1, and 26 on the top sleeve and through points 23 and 18 to point 21 on the under sleeve is 16½". Trace off the top sleeve and under sleeve. Use points 20, 22 and 10 for the hind arm of the under sleeve. Use points 2, 15, and 11 for the hind arm points of the top sleeve. The hind arm balance level should be marked as notches on each piece, indicated by points H and J.

As soon as the basic blocks for the bodice and sleeve have been drafted and corrected through various stages of the fit process, the finished pattern can be interpreted into countless jacket style variations.

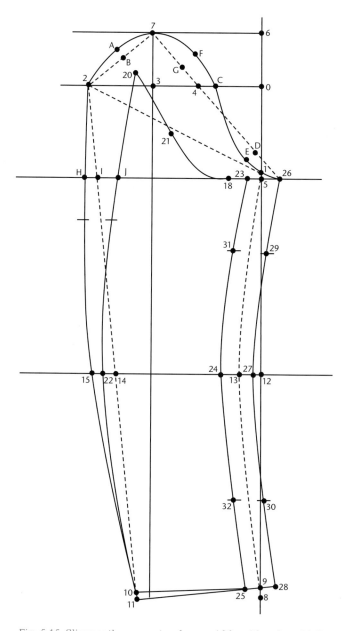

Fig. 5.15 Slimmer three-quarter sleeve width, with reduced fullness.
(At quarter scale)

Chapter 6
Style Variations

The basic block can be adapted into any style of blazer: single-breasted, double-breasted, overcoats, tuxedos, crop jackets and sports jackets. It is the foundation of developing paper patterns for all manner of beautiful tailored jackets. This chapter touches on a small selection of the endless style variations that can be adapted from the divisional grid system.

1. The single-breasted blazer

The chapter explains how to make the necessary adjustments to a new pattern traced from the basic block, to accommodate the style variations for classic suit jackets. The design modifications, which vary between styles, can be applied to the pattern to create a new style, which will need to be checked and finalized through several stages of the fitting process.

History of the single-breasted blazer

The term 'single-breasted', annotated to 'S.B.' refers to a narrow wrap with a single column of buttons. Classic S.B. jackets will always be a one button, a two-button, or a three-button. Sometimes a four-button jacket will appear on a ladies' jacket, but it is rare. The number of buttons is the decision of the designer or wearer, but it is important when starting a flat pattern to know the number of buttons before plotting the break line position and lapel, which is plotted to roll ½"/1.2cms above the top button.

Historically, S.B. jackets replaced draped garments during the Middle-

Ages, in the Renaissance period. Pins on coats were replaced by buttons and buttonhole fastenings. Frock coats were created for gentlemen; they were shortened at the end of the nineteenth century and crossed over into women's clothing, with more and more women's tailors emerging in London and Paris. In 1916, Chanel unveiled the first flannel S.B. blazer, and it became an essential part of a woman's wardrobe.

Single-breasted blazers are the most commonly worn jacket, by both men and women; it transcends fashion, as the ultimate style essential.

The following draft is a pattern for the body of a 'semi-fitted' jacket (meaning it is not closely fitted to the body), resulting in a boyish fit/boyfriend blazer. It has two buttons at the centre front closure, a notch lapel, side panel and centre back vent. The sleeve to accompany the draft is taken from the traditional two-piece copy of the three-quarter sleeve; it has a four button functioning vent at the cuff closure.

The measures required to draft the pattern for this style of blazer are as follows:

Fig. 6.2 Richard Nicoll single-breasted blazer on the form.

1. Height: 5ft 9"

2. Bust: 34"

3. Waist: 27"

4. Hip circumference (lower hip): 38"

5. Nape to waist: 15⅝"

Fig. 6.3 Two-dimensional flat working drawing of S.B. blazer, hand drawn; to assist plotting style lines on the basic block draft.

6. Waist to hip circumference: 8″

7. Full jacket length: 27″

8. Half back width: 6½″

9. Armhole depth: 6″

10. Armhole width: 4½″

11. Neck size: 14½″

12. Shoulder length: 4¾″

13. Working scale: 17″ (half the bust measurement)

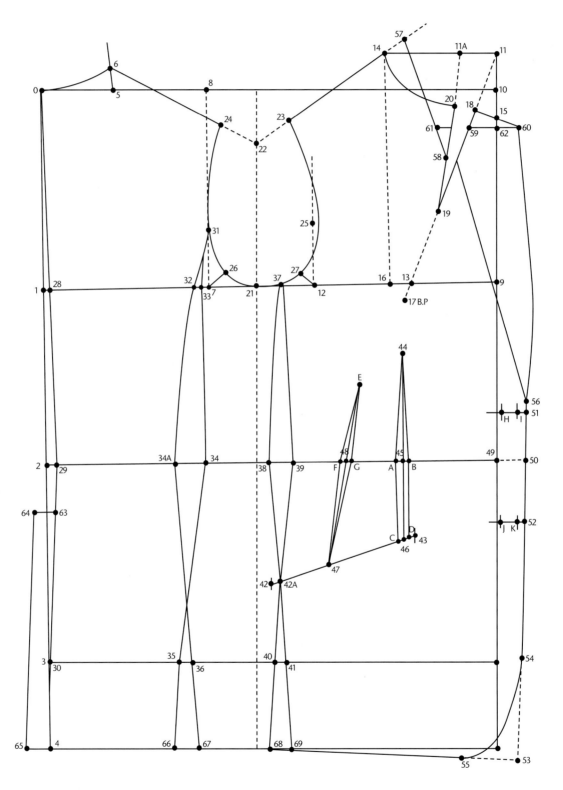

Fig. 6.4 The divisional grid system is used to plot the points for the two-button single-breasted blazer. (At quarter scale)

The measures are for a standard US size 6 (UK size 10). To achieve an oversize, relaxed proportion, use larger measurements from the chart, which are two sizes too big for your size.

Begin the pattern by adapting the basic block with side body jacket draft, and repeating the previous instructions for points 0 to 11, and marking them on the new draft. The points differ from point 12 onwards, due to the addition of the neck dart, which completely removes the shoulder dart. There are also additional darts and shaping through the seams, to counteract the removal of the shoulder dart.

⁎11A from 11
The size of the required bust suppression should be equal to the original suppression in the shoulder dart; this can be calculated by working out one-twelfth of the half bust.
$17'' \div 12 = 1\frac{1}{2}''$

12 from 9
The front of the armhole. Calculate a quarter of the half bust, minus ¾".
$(17 \div 4) - \frac{3}{4}'' = 7\frac{3}{4}''$
Square a 90° line up.

13
Located mid-way between 9 and 12.

16 from 13
Approximately ½" back from mid point 13. Square up to point 14 with a dotted line.

14
The line squared horizontally from point 11, line 16 to 14 is the same measurement as point 9 to 11.

15 from 11
The centre front neck point is measured at the same distance as 0 to 5: 3".

17 from 13
Square down ⅜". Mark this landmark as the bust point. Draw a dotted line between point 17 and point 11, and also point 17 and point ⁎11A.

19 from 18
Length of the neck dart at points 18 and 19: 4¼".

20 from 19
Length of the dart: 4¼". Draw in the dart. Draw in the curve of the front neck joining point 14 to point 20 and point 15 to 18.

21
Mid-way between point 7 and point 12. Square up and down with a dotted line.

22 from 21
The angle for the shoulder slope, essentially the armhole depth direct measurement plus pad allowance. 5½" armhole depth + ½" pad allowance = 6".
Join with a dotted line from point 22 to point 6 and a dotted line from point 22 to point 14.

23 from 14
Net front shoulder length: 4¾".

24 from 6
The net back shoulder length plus ½" ease.
$4\frac{3}{4}'' + \frac{1}{2}'' = 5\frac{1}{4}''$.
This is a standard suggestion for ease; for bigger sizes, or softer cloths add ¾". Draw in the back armhole, through points 24, 26 and 21.

25 from 12
One-sixth of the half bust measurement scale:
$17'' \div 6 = 2\frac{3}{4}''$

26 from 7
Draw a 45° line from point 7: ¾".

27 from 12
Draw a 45° line from point 12: ¾". Draw in the front armhole through points 23, 25, 27 and 21. At point 25 shape the front armhole in by ¼".

28 from 1
Shaping at the cross back width, on the centre back: ¼".

29 from 2
Waist suppression shaped in at the centre back at the waist: ½".

30 from 3
Shaping at the hip line on the centre back: ⅛".
Draw in the new centre back line using a vary form curve, through points 0, 28, 29, 30, and 4.

31 from 7
Square up 2" from point 7 to 31, for the location of the upper part of the side seam, in the back armhole.

32 from 7
Square across horizontally ⅜" to point 32.

33 from 32
Shaping for shoulder blade: ⅜".

34 from 34A
Shaping at the side panel back seam, at the waist level: 1¼".

36 from 35
The hip flare value is 1¼" to be divided into the forepart, side panel and back (points 35 & 36, and 40 & 41), which has to be distributed between the two points. Therefore 36 from 35: $1\frac{1}{4}'' \div 2 = \frac{3}{4}''$.
Join the points 31, 32, 34A, and 36, with a shaped contoured line, which continues into the hem at point 67. This forms the Back Panel.
Join the points 31, 33, 34, and 35, with a shaped contoured line, which continues into the hem at point 66. This forms the line of the back seam of the side panel.

37 from 21
Marked 1" forward of the position of the side seam.

39 from 38
Waist shaping total: 1".

41 from 40
The hip flare value is 1¼".
The required hip flare at the hip circumference line (lower hip) has to

be distributed between the two points.
Therefore 41 from 40: $1\frac{1}{4}" \div 2 = \frac{3}{4}"$.
Join points 37, 38, and 41 with
a shaped contoured line, which
continues into the hem at point 69.
This forms the line of the front seam of
the side panel.
Join points 37, 39, and 40 with
a shaped contoured line, which
continues into the hem at point 68.
This forms the sideline of the front
forepart piece.

The Pocket Position
Mark the pocket position as desired,
but it is dependent on the length of the
jacket. It should not sit too high into
the waist or too low in to the hem, and
the angle can be slanted or straight.
On the draft it has been drawn
slanted; point 42 is measured 5"
below the waist, point 42A is indicated
exactly where the pocket angel
crosses the side. Point 43 sits 3" below
waist. Rule a line through points 42
and 43, the length = $5\frac{3}{4}"$.
The centreline of the first dart (point
46) should sit $\frac{3}{4}"$ back from point
43. Square a line up to point 44, the
desired length of the dart. On the
draft the length = $7\frac{1}{2}"$ from the pocket
position. Square down to Point 45,
located at the centre of the dart at the
waistline, and down to point 46 on the
pocket line.

B from A
Total width of the dart at the waist: $\frac{1}{2}"$.

D from C
Total width of the dart at the pocket
position: $\frac{1}{2}"$.

47 from 42
Measure $2\frac{1}{2}"$ along the pocket line.
Draw in the angle of the second dart in
the desired diagonal direction. Point E
indicates the length of the dart: $7\frac{1}{4}"$.

48
Mid-way between points 39 and 45.

G from F
Total width of the dart at the waist
level: $\frac{1}{4}"$.

49
Located on the centre line, at the true
waist level, squared down from point 9.

50 from 49
Single-breasted button wrap
extension: $1\frac{1}{2}"$. Square up and down
to the hem point 53, with a dotted line.

51 from 50
Measure 2" above waist line, for the
position of the top button.

52 from 50
Measure $2\frac{3}{8}"$ below the waist line for
the second button position.
The total distance between the top
button and the bottom button: $4\frac{3}{8}"$.

54 from 53
Mark 4" up from point 53 to point 54,
and shape the front edge and hem in
a curve to point 55. A template can be
used to draw a classic rounded front
edge, as Fig. 6.4.

56 from 51
Mark a point above the top button
position to allow the lapel to roll: $\frac{1}{2}"$.

57 from 14
Measure $1\frac{1}{8}"$ from point 14. This is
the collar stand depth from the neck
point. To draw in the break line: rule
a straight line from point 57 to point
56; as the line is interrupted with the
neck dart the line is staggered and stops
at point 58. Measure between points
19 and 58 on the dart; point 59 from 19
should measure the same distance on
the opposite side of the dart. Continue
to rule the break line from point 59 to 56.

61 from 60
Square a 90° line from the centre line,
across the lapel. The line is identified
as the desired lapel width. Point 61 is
plotted on the break line. Point 60 is
the width of the lapel. On the draft this
is 3". Shape the edge of the lapel with
a curve stick to the desired style line;
or draw around a lapel template to

obtain a classic notch revere. Template
1 will suffice.

62
Measure $1\frac{3}{8}"$ back from point 61 and
square up to point 15.

63 from 4
Length of the centre back vent: $10\frac{1}{2}"$.

64 from 63
Width of the centre back vent: $1\frac{1}{2}"$.

65 from 4
Width of the centre back vent: $1\frac{1}{2}"$.

Identify points 66, 67, 68 and 69 along
the hemline, as a continuation of the
flare from the hip circumference level.
Trace off and separate the panels
(Fig. 6.5) into a back panel (i), side
panel (ii) and forepart panel (iii), as
a net pattern to prepare to add seam
allowances and extra inlays, for
chopping in cloth. Be sure to add the
value of the dart (C and D) to the side
of the forepart where it finishes at the
pocket position

A from 42A
Value of the dart at the pocket
position: $\frac{3}{4}"$. Re-draw the front
sideline and taper in to the waist level.
A dart in the pocket, also known as
the belly cut, can be incorporated
into the forepart if it is desired.

B from 42A
The belly cut width if desired: $\frac{3}{8}"$.
Rule a line from point B to 43.

C from 68
The belly cut width added to the hem,
so the length is still the same: $\frac{3}{8}"$.

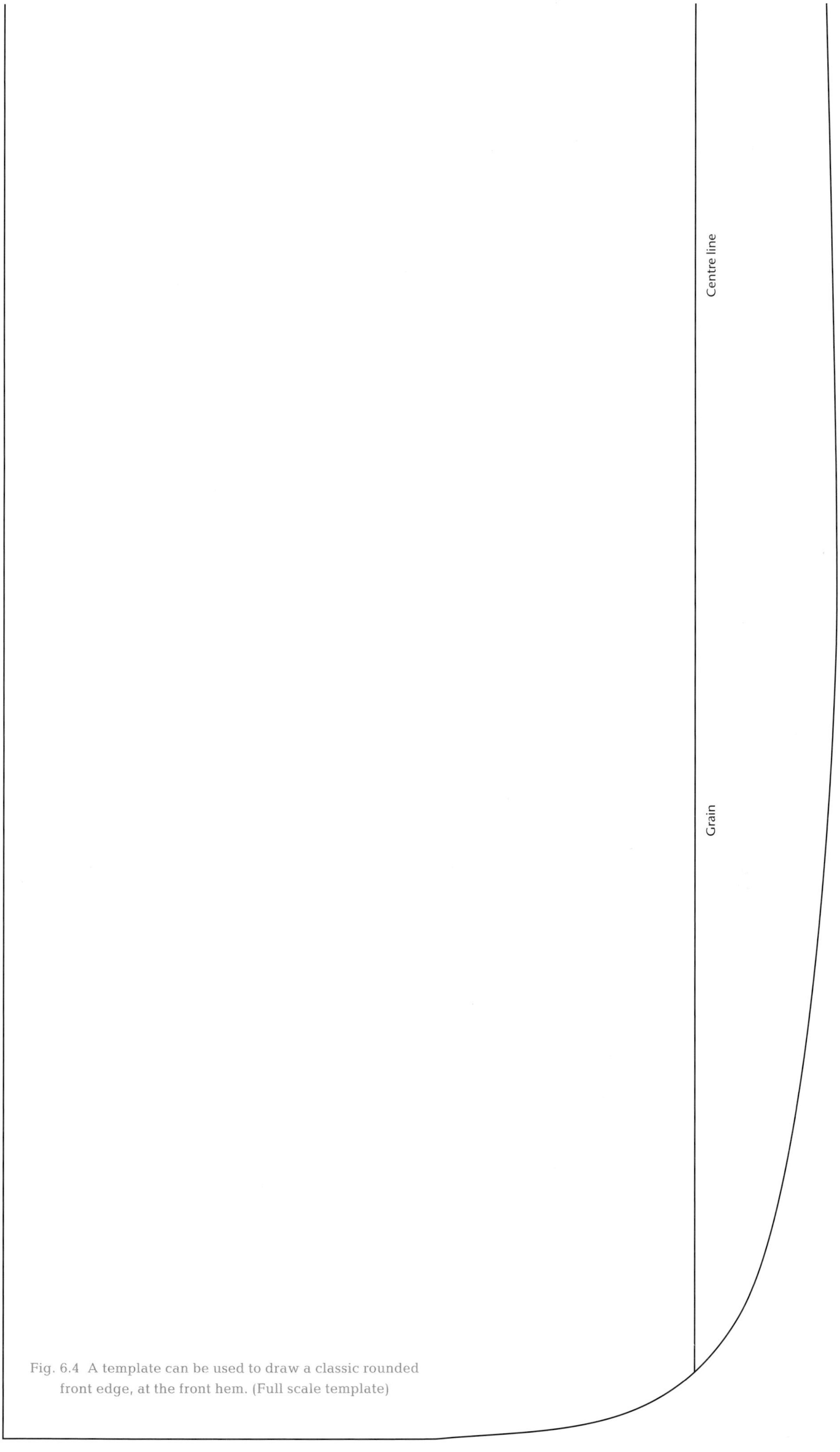

Centre line

Grain

Fig. 6.4 A template can be used to draw a classic rounded
front edge, at the front hem. (Full scale template)

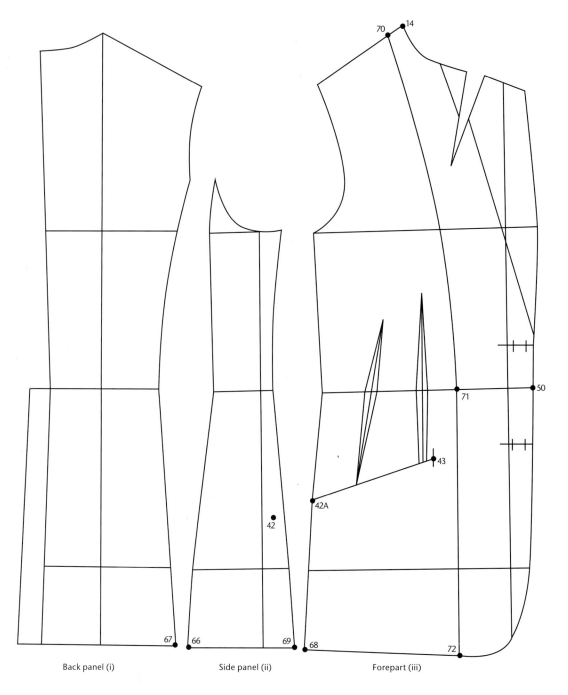

Back panel (i) Side panel (ii) Forepart (iii)

Fig. 6.6 The single-breasted blazer, traced off as separate net pattern pieces with no inlays and seam allowance. (At quarter scale)

Plotting the points for a facing pattern on the traced forepart

Facings are sewn to the front edge of a ladies' jacket, are bagged out and folded back on the inside of the front edge. Facings are the only way to finish the front edge of a jacket, to neaten the edge and prevent the fronts from stretching out of shape.

70 from 14

Referring to forepart (iii) on Fig. 6.6, measure along the shoulder line: ¾″.

71 from 50

At the waist line of the front edge mark 3¼″. Join points 70 and 71 with a curved line. Square a 90° line down from point 71 to point 72 on the hemline. This line is sewn to the internal lining.

Linings, facings and interlinings are explored further in Chapter 8, 'From Block to Pattern'.

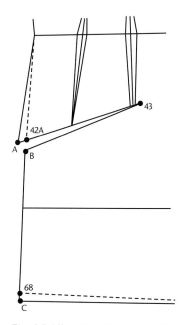

Fig. 6.7 Allocating the value of the first front dart, and a belly cut into the pocket position on the traced off forepart.

Fig. 6.8 The two-button closure.

Button variations – indicating buttonhole positions

TWO-BUTTON PLACEMENT (FIG. 6.9i)

I from 51
The first buttonhole position is marked ½″ from the front edge.

All buttonhole positions are marked ½″ from the front edge, for one-, two-, and three-button variants. Unless an unusually large button is being used, a standard button for a tailored jacket is a 30-ligne, normally in horn. Fig 6.10 indicates a chart showing button ligne measurements used within the industry. For a 30-ligne button, the length of the buttonhole should be 1″.

H from I
The length of the buttonhole determined by the size of the button, known as the 'ligne'. It is marked at 1″ on the draft for 30 ligne button sizes.

K from 52
The second buttonhole position, ½″ from the front edge.

J from K
The length of the buttonhole: 1″ on the draft.

THREE-BUTTON PLACEMENT (FIG. 6.9ii)

To convert the draft into a three-button S.B. closure, the angle of the centre line must firstly be adjusted (points A and B). If this amendment is not applied to the draft, the front balance will be long and will flare open; extra width at the hipline is required to compensate for this. This same adjustment is applied to double-breasted fronts and long overcoats.

A
The location where the hem crosses the centre line.

B from A
Measure ½″ and mark point B.
Re-draw the new angle of the centre line from point B to nothing at point 11.

50
Size of the button wrap from the new centre line at the waist line: 1½″.

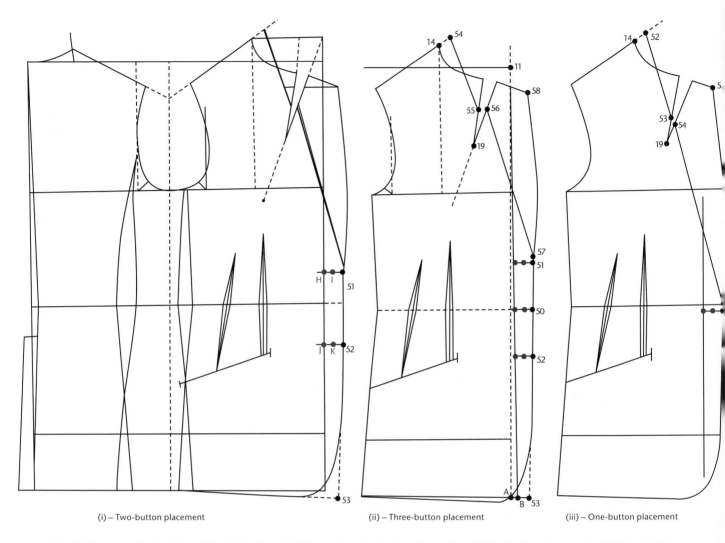

(i) – Two-button placement   (ii) – Three-button placement   (iii) – One-button placement

Fig. 6.9 Button style adaptions of the single-breasted blazer, showing button alternatives (i) Two-button placement, (ii) Three-button placement, and (iii) One-button-placement. (Not to quarter scale)

51 from 50

Top button position: 3″ from the waist. This measurement will depend on the height of the wearer. For a shorter length the distance between buttons should be reduced to be in proportion with the length of the blazer.

52 from 50

Lower button position: 3″ from the waist. The total distance between each button on this draft is 3″. The number increases for the two-button width (4⅜″) between points. The value is smaller for the three-button, to accommodate the extra button. Square down to point 53, where it crosses the hemline. Re-draw the front hem curve.

54 from 14

The break line. Measure 1⅛″ from point 14; this is the collar stand depth from the neck point, and remains the same value as recommended for the two-button and one-button draft. Rule a line from point 54 to point 57. Point 57 is ½″ above the top button position (point 51). The break line stops at the dart, point 55. Measure from point 19 on the dart to point 56 the same value as the measurement of 55 from 19, on the opposite side of the dart. Continue to rule the break line from point 56 to 57.

The buttonhole positions have been indicated, and are marked ½″ from the front edge. Length of the buttonhole: 1″.

Point 58: Re-measure and mark the lapel width so that it is still 3″ from break position.

ONE-BUTTON PLACEMENT
(FIG. 6.9III)

The one button position is marked exactly at the true waist (point 50). However, it is personal preference to position the button to be lower than the waist as it is more flattering for the female form, as it elongates the body. A direct consequence of marking the button lower than the waist, is that it is trickier to fit, as drag lines will sometimes appear at the side waist point; this is easy to rectify by amending the balance notches of the waist. Time for extra fittings is helpful

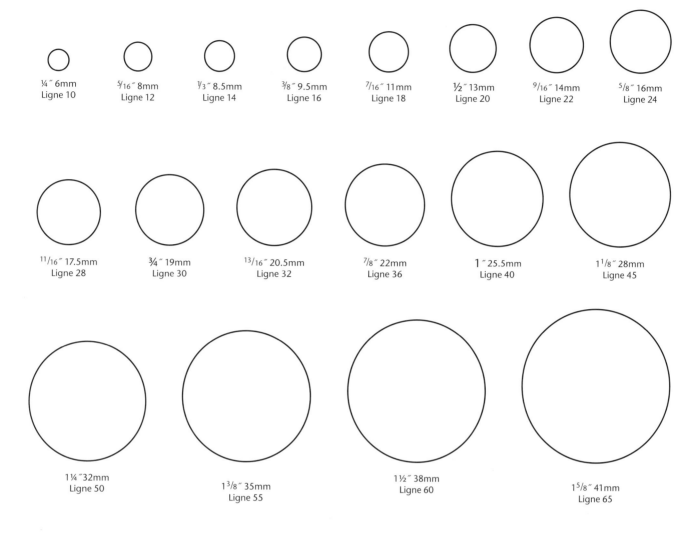

| ¼″ 6mm
Ligne 10 | ⁵/₁₆″ 8mm
Ligne 12 | ⅓″ 8.5mm
Ligne 14 | ⅜″ 9.5mm
Ligne 16 | ⁷/₁₆″ 11mm
Ligne 18 | ½″ 13mm
Ligne 20 | ⁹/₁₆″ 14mm
Ligne 22 | ⅝″ 16mm
Ligne 24 |

¹¹/₁₆″ 17.5mm Ligne 28 ¾″ 19mm Ligne 30 ¹³/₁₆″ 20.5mm Ligne 32 ⅞″ 22mm Ligne 36 1″ 25.5mm Ligne 40 1⅛″ 28mm Ligne 45

1¼″32mm Ligne 50 1³/₈″ 35mm Ligne 55 1½″ 38mm Ligne 60 1⅝″ 41mm Ligne 65

Fig. 6.10 The button ligne size chart for tailored jackets. The length of buttonholes is determined by the size of the buttons.
(Full size scale)

to make sure the jacket is clean and free from the unsightly lines of an ill-fitting garment.

Point 51 from 50

Mark ½″ below the waist position and square a horizontal line across to the centre line, to indicate the button position. Buttonhole length on the draft: 1″.

Point 52 from 14

The break line. Measure 1⅛″ from point 14; this is the collar stand depth from the neck point, and remains the same value as recommended for the two-button draft. Rule a line from point 52 to point 50, which stops at the dart, point 53. Measure from point 19 on

Fig. 6.11 Buttons at sleeve cuff: 20 ligne.

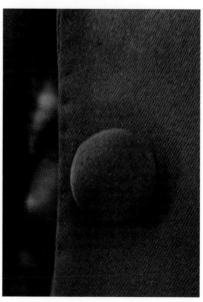

Fig. 6.12 Centre front button: 30 ligne.

the dart to point 54 (the same value as the measurement of 53 from 19) on the opposite side of the dart. Continue to rule the break line from point 54 to 50.
Point 55
Re-measure the lapel width so that it is still 3″ from the break position.

2. The double-breasted blazer

**History of the
double-breasted blazer**

The term 'double-breasted' or 'D.B.' refers to the wide overlap extension, and two parallel columns of buttons. One column of buttons is purely decorative, known as the 'show' buttons, while the other row

of buttons along the edge of the front are functional, to fasten. To strengthen the fastening an internal button, called the 'jigger', is always added to fasten the overlapped layers together from the inside.

The fastening method is indicated using number terminology: the first number is the number of functional buttons below the lapel; the second is the total number of show buttons. The possibilities for columns of buttons are endless, just some of which are noted below.

- One-button, show three: One functioning button and three show.

- One-button, show two: One functioning button and two show.

- One-button, show one: One row of functional buttons, with one show button.

- Two-button show three: two rows of functional buttons and three show.

- Two-button show two: two rows of functioning buttons and two show.

- Three-button, Three show: Three rows of functioning buttons, with three additional show buttons.

- Four-button, Four show: Four rows of functioning buttons, with four show buttons.

- The five-button, Five show: Five rows of functioning buttons, with five show buttons.

The five-button double-breasted style is more common on coats, like the men's peacoat in Fig. 6.13, or traditionally naval uniforms, rather than jackets these days, but is another example of varied fastenings on double-breasted pattern adaptions.

The style of lapel on a double-breasted blazer is always a peak lapel, or pointed in appearance and fastens right over left, for a ladies' jacket.

Double-breasted styles were originally gentlemen's garments, reserved officially for military and naval uniforms in the form of pea coats and reefer jackets. They became a standard in men's apparel from the 1920s, and became popular in women's dress when they were worn by the likes of Katherine Hepburn and Marlene Dietrich. Their popularity continued through the 1940s and '50s with exaggerated proportions and shoulder widths.

Their popularity waned a little in the 1960s and '70s, with a brief revival in

Fig. 6.13 The term double-breasted refers to the wide overlap extension and two parallel columns of buttons.

Fig. 6.14 Power dressing exploded in the 1980s with the ladies double-breasted suit jacket; as worn by Joan Collins. (Photo: ABC Photo Archives/Disney ABC Televsion Group/Getty Images)

1967 of naval reefers due to The Beatles wearing them for the *Sergeant Pepper's Lonely Hearts Club Band* album cover, with skinny drainpipe pants. The D.B. became an eccentric style choice for musicians and artists of the time.

With the explosion of power dressing in the 1980s, the double-breasted blazer in women's fashion was all the rage once again. It is less common now, and reserved exclusively for bespoke tailors or luxury brands in men's and women's wear.

The cropped length double-breasted blazer (Fig. 6.22) (one button, show two)

The following draft is a pattern for the body of a fitted double-breasted blazer, with a princess seam running from the pocket to the neckline, which is a one-button closure with two show buttons. This is for a shorter length

Fig. 6.15 The 'one-button, show two' double-breasted blazer. The original inspiration image: David Bowie from the *David Live* album. (Photo: GAB Archives/Redferns/Getty Images)

blazer; the length finishes at the hip circumference level. It has a peak lapel, side panel and no vents. The sleeve has a five-button cuff closure. It was inspired by a jacket worn by David Bowie, on the *David Live* album. The double-breasted button wrap has been considered for 36 ligne silver gilt buttons, which are plugged through the fronts after hand basting canvases into the forepart. The measures required to draft the pattern are as follows.

1. Height: 5ft 9″

2. Bust: 34″

3. Waist: 27″

4. Hip circumference (lower hip): 38″

5. Nape to waist: 15⅝″

6. Waist to hip circumference: 8″

Fig. 6.16 Side front view of blazer.

Fig. 6.17 Side back view of blazer.

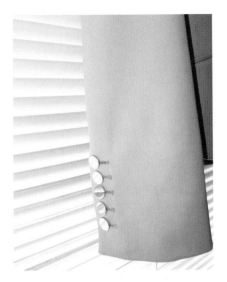

Fig. 6.18 The five-button cuff closure.

7.   Full jacket length: 27⅝"

8.   Half back width: 6½"

9.   Armhole depth: 6"

10. Armhole width: 4½"

11. Neck size: 14½"

12. Shoulder length: 4¾"

13. Working scale: 17" (half the bust measurement)

To draft, trace off the single-breasted blazer with side panel, marking all points, and repeating instructions for points 0 to 41 on the S.B. draft (Fig. 6.4), with the exception of point 4, which will not exist, as the jacket length on this draft finishes at the hip circumference level, and point 19 as the dart is converted into a princess seam over the contours of the bust.

3 from 0
The new jacket length to finish on the hip circumference level, as the style is a shorter length, is 23⅝". Square a 90° line horizontally across the draft.

19
The end of the neck dart from the S.B. draft. Points 18 to 19 are the length of the neck dart: 4¼". Square across to

Fig. 6.19 Working drawing to aid the pattern cutter to apply proportions to the draft.

points 19A and 19B, which is shaping in the princess seam.

19A to 19B
Total on the draft: ¾".

42, 43, 44, and 45
The new angle of the pocket in proportion to the jacket length. It is 1½" higher than the position on the single-breasted blazer draft (Fig. 6.4), where

Fig. 6.20 Illustration of the
double-breasted blazer.

Fig. 6.21 The cropped length double-breasted blazer, with one functioning button and
two show buttons. It is the author's sample on the dress form.

the position of the line is lower due to
the longer length of the S.B. The length
of the pocket is 5 ¼", which is narrower
than the length on the S.B. draft, due to
its new position on the upper hip level.

43 from 45

The pocket extends past the dart by
½". 43 to 45 is ¾".

46

Marked at the waist in the centre of
the dart. Point A from B is the size of

the dart, measured at ½" total. Rule
lines from A and B to the pocket line,
and label points C and D.

47

Plotted centrally between points 39 and
A. E to F is the size of the dart: ¼" total.
Rule a diagonal line through the centre
of the dart and mark points G and H.
Length of the dart: 5¼". Rule the lines
of the dart from E and F, to G and H.

The princess seam over the bust

Having a princess seam over the bust
will achieve a closer fit to the form and
when fitted correctly will accentuate
the contours of the female form. In the
double-breasted example, it is cut to
follow the bust and finish at the front
neckline. Traditionally, pattern makers
will cut the line to finish at the shoulder
or at the armhole, but it is a personal
preference to end it at the neckline,
as it is hidden under the lapel, giving
a modern, cleaner finish. The value of

the neck dart, which is used in the S.B. blazer, is incorporated into the seam.

48

Marked at the centre line, where the waist crosses horizontally. Square down to point 50 on the hemline.

49 from 48

The centre line requires some flare at the hem from nothing at point 15.

At point 48 it extends ⅜″ to point 49. Rule a line to point 51, continuing the angle of the flare. This is so that the fronts can fasten over the stomach without flaring open from the top button position, which is a common problem in double-breasted pattern cutting. Cutters will sometimes need to add more flare to their front edges, during the fitting stages to rectify the fronts with this

recurring issue. Sometimes if the fronts are too long, they will create the same appearance, which is a slightly different adjustment. If the fronts of a double-breasted blazer are too long in the fitting, the excess can be pinched out of the lapel, until the forepart is level as it should be, and perfectly vertical on the wearer. The pinched out amount is then 'straightened' at the neck

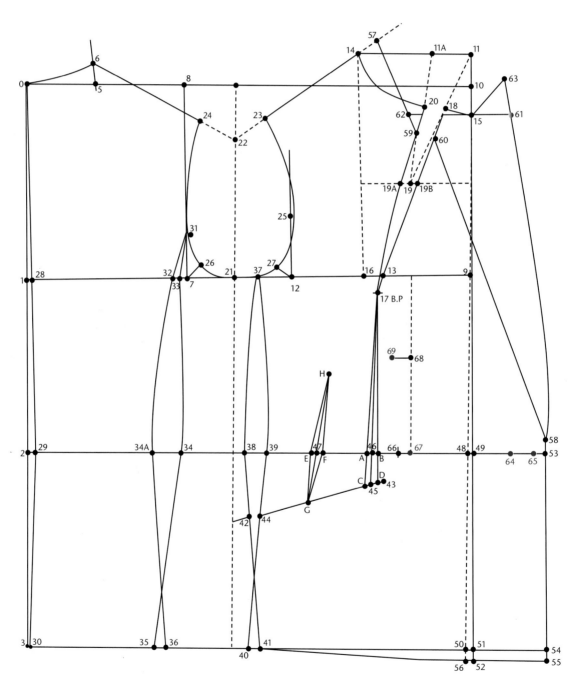

Fig. 6.22 Cropped double-breasted ladies' jacket – divisional grid system. (At quarter scale)

point. This can be observed in the fitting process (Chapter 11).

51 from 50
Flare added at the hem level on the new jacket length: ⅝".

52 from 51
Length added to the hem: ¾".
Rule a new centre line through points 52, 51, 49 and 11. This adds extra swing and length onto the centre line, which is essential for a double-breasted front-wrap extension. The same amendment is also used for converting jackets into overcoats, or can be used on a three-button blazer.

53 from 49
Double-breasted extension: 3¼".
The extension width depends on the size of buttons used, and style preference. As silver gilt buttons require a wider button wrap overall, the extension should be at least 3¼", this is due to the method of construction to plug them into the fronts. For horn buttons of the same size, an extension of 3" is required.
Square down to points 54 and 55.
Point 55 is marked ¾" below point 54, to add extra length in the front balance. The front edge on a double-breasted is never curved like on the S.B., it is always cut straight and square. There is, however, a slight curve along the line of the hem, through points 55, 56, and 52, to nothing at the side point 40. Use a vary form curve to draw the curve.

57 from 14
Collar stand: 1¼".
The collar stand is ⅛" wider than the stand on the S.B. draft; on this particular style the stand sits higher into the back neck.

58 from 53
Added spring above the button position: ½". It also looks nicer if the roll of the break line finishes higher than the first top button.

59
Draw in the break line. Place the ruler from point 57 to point 58. Rule a line (as it is interrupted by the princess seam it should stop at point 59).

60
The measurement of point 59 from B.P. 17. Rule a line from point 60 to 58. Points 57, 59, 60 and 58 form the break line.

61 from 62
Square a line from point 15 to points 61 and 62. The desired peak lapel width is 3½".

63 from 15
The angle of the peak specific to the style: 2½".
   On the draft, when the lapel folds back, the line of the peak should point in the direction of the shoulder end where the sleeve heads joined. (*See also* Chapter 7 on collars and lapels, which provides further tips for drafting the peak lapel and collar.)

Marking button and buttonhole positions

CALCULATING BUTTON WRAPS FOR DOUBLE-BREASTED BLAZERS
Before marking buttonholes and show button positions, the button wrap must firstly be plotted. This will depend greatly on the desired width between the buttons and final coat waist measurement after fitting on the wearer. All the D.B. drafts included in this chapter have used an extension width = 3¼" from the new centre line.

65 from 53
Exactly ¾" from the front edge, due to the size of the gilt buttons.

64 from 65
This is the size of the buttonhole, dependent on the size of the button. On the draft it is 1 ⅛".
   The buttons are traditional silver gilt, with a tall neck, which are plugged through the top layer of the jacket and internal canvas, and secured by inserting a twill tape through the

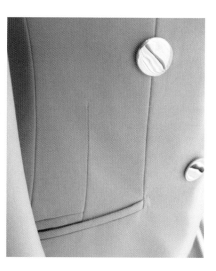

Fig. 6.23 Traditional gilt blazer buttons, 36 ligne size.

hole and hand stitching in place. Therefore, it is always safer to measure the ligne width and judge the length accordingly. As the gilt buttons selected on the blazer are a 36 ligne, it is bigger than the 25 ligne horn buttons used on the S.B. blazer, the button hole length should be marked at 1⅛".

66 from 49
A mark for the button wrap, where the front edge will overlap. The wrap is equal to the D.B. extension from the centre line (points 49 and 53): 3¼". The total button wrap is 6½" approximately, between 53 and 66, which is the extension from the centre line of points 49 to 53 multiplied twice. Square a line up to the bust line.

67 from 66
Position of the functioning button from the button wrap (point 66): ¾". Square a dotted line up to the bust line.

68 from 67
The position of the show button. It is approximately 4". Some tailors mark the show button at a 90° vertical angle directly above point 67, directly above the lower button. It can also be positioned ¾" wider towards the side panel (depending on the size of the jacket and the seaming position). This is a style choice determined by the cutter or wearer.

69 from 68

Square across from point 68: ¾".
An internal jigger button is also sewn
to this button, to secure the button
wraps. It is hand sewn to the neck of
the top button (point 69) on the inside
of the facing.

Trace and separate the panels (Fig.
6.24) into: back panel (i), side panel (ii)
and forepart panels 1 and 2 (iii) as a
net pattern, in preparation for adding
seam allowances and extra inlays,

for chopping in cloth. Be sure to add
the value of the dart to the side of the
forepart (point A1), where it finishes at
the pocket position, and the belly cut
(point B1).

A1 from 44

Size of the dart at C, and D at the
pocket position added to the side: ½".
Re-draw the side, and smooth back
into the waist.

B1 from 44

Size of the dart/belly cut in the pocket:
³/₈".

C1 from 40

Extra length to accommodate the
addition of the dart: ¾".

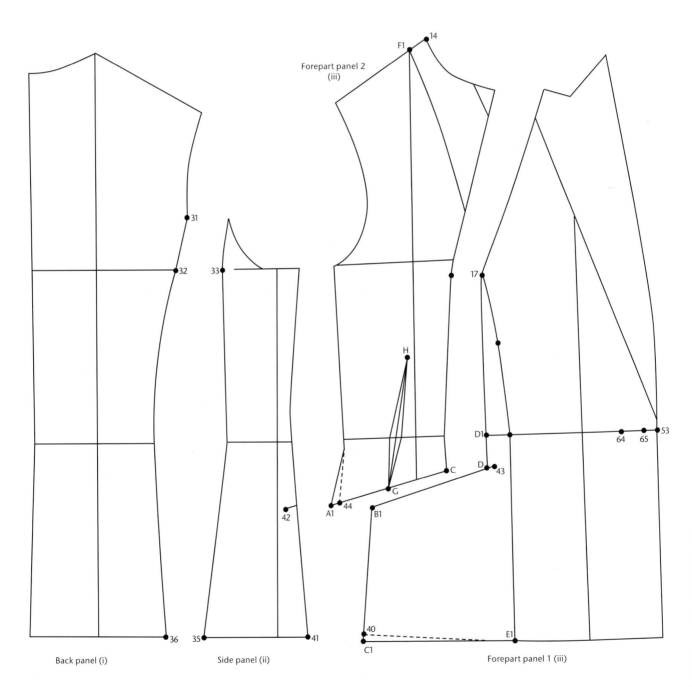

Fig. 6.24 The separate panels with no inlays or seam allowances, or added vents. (Quarter scale)

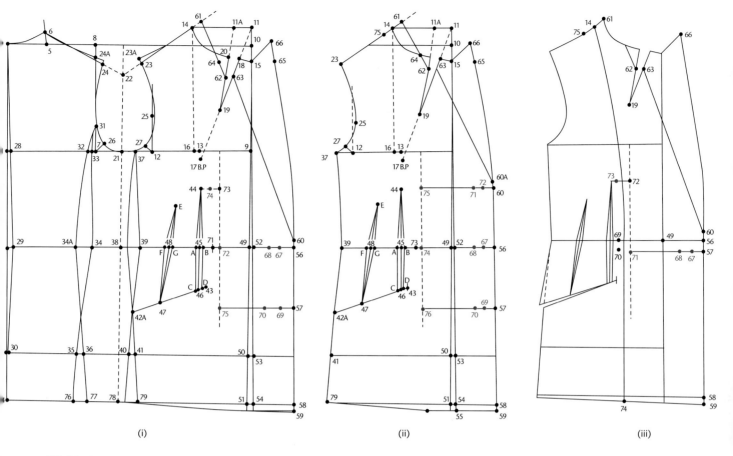

FIG 6.25 Examples of button variations in double-breasted blazer styles; which vary according to the number of functional and show buttons. (i) The Two-Button, Show Three D.B (ii) The Three-Button, Three Show Buttons (iii) The one-Button, Two Show Buttons. (Not to quarter scale)

The facing points

Close the seam from bust point 17 running through the neckline; or tape forepart panel 1 and 2 together from point 17.

D1 from 53

Width of the facing from the front edge = 6″.
Square down to E1 on the new jacket length line.
F1 from 14: The width of the facing at the shoulder and neck point = ¾″.
Join F1 and D1 with a vary form curve.

Double-breasted button variations

The styles in Fig. 6.25 are three very different button adaptions applied to the draft of the S.B. blazer. Each button variation has been applied to Fig. 6.24 block. The extension for the button wrap has been considered for 36 ligne horn buttons.
Two-button, show three D.B. (Fig. 6.25i)
Three-button, no show D.B. (Fig. 6.25ii)

One-button, show two D.B. (Fig. 6.25iii)
The measures required to draft these styles are as follows.

1. Height: 5ft 9″
2. Bust: 34″
3. Waist: 27″
4. Hip circumference (lower hip): 38″
5. Nape to waist: 15⅝″
6. Waist to hip circumference: 8″
7. Full jacket length: 27″
8. Half back width: 6½″
9. Armhole depth: 6″
10. Armhole width: 4½″
11. Neck size: 14½″

12. Shoulder length: 4¾″
13. Working scale: 17″ (half the bust measurement)

THE TWO-BUTTON D.B., WITH THREE SHOW BUTTONS (Fig. 6.26)
To draft the pattern, 'two-Button, with three show buttons', trace off the single-breasted jacket, repeating the instructions and marking points 0 to 49 as indicated on the S.B. draft (Fig. 6.4). The shoulder has a slight pagoda shape, and kicks up at the ends, to be re-shaped back into point 14 at the neck point.

23A from 23

The value by which the shoulder is raised for the pagoda silhouette: ⅜″.

24A from 24

The value by which the shoulder is raised by for the pagoda silhouette: ⅜″.

97

49

Square down to the hipline point 50, and the hemline point 51.

52 from 49

Flare added to the centre line at the waist level: ³⁄₈".

53 from 50

Flare added to the centre line at the hip circumference level (lower hip): ³⁄₈".

54 from 51

Flare added to the centre line on the hem at the full jacket length level: ½".

55 from 54

Add extra length into the front balance: ¾".

Rule a new centre line through points 11, 52, 53, 54 and 55. This adds extra swing and length onto the centre line, which is essential for a double-breasted front-wrap extension.

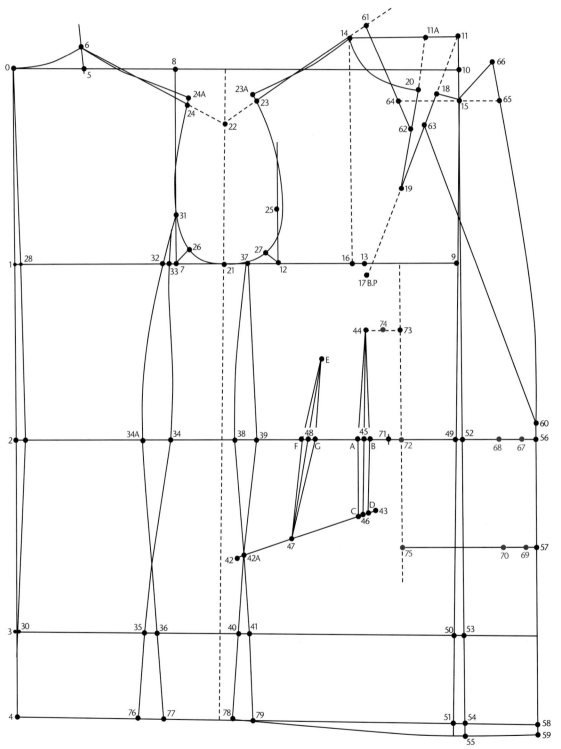

FIG 6.26 Quarter-Scale two-button, show three D.B Style.

56 from 52

Double-breasted extension in the draft example: 3″. In this example the extension is narrower than the previous D.B. draft, due to the style. The extension depends on the desired distance between buttons horizontally. Some styles require a wider horizontal width, others slimmer; the button size will affect the choice as well: either way it is the choice of the pattern maker/designer. Square down to point 57. The vertical distance between the rows of buttons is 4¼″. Square down to point 58 on the hem at the lower hip level. Point 59 is marked ¾″ below point 58, to add extra length in the front balance. Draw in the new front edge through points 56, 57, 58, and 59.

60 from 56

Roll above the button position: ½″.

61 from 14

Collar stand: 1¼″.
Draw in the break line, which is interrupted by the dart. Place the ruler between points 61 and 60. Point 62 is where the ruler hits the first line of the dart. Point 63 is plotted at the exact measurement of line 62 and 19. Rule a line from point 63 to point 60.
Points 61, 62, 63 and 60 form the break line.

64 from 65

The desired lapel width, minus the neck dart width. In the draft it is 3½″.

66 from 15

The angle of the peak specific to the style: 2½″.
On the draft, when the lapel folds back the line of the peak points in the direction of the shoulder end at the sleeve head.

67 from 56

Button row one. Mark the buttonhole position ½″ from the front edge.

68 from 67

The buttonhole size depending on the size of buttons used. In the draft: 1⅛″.

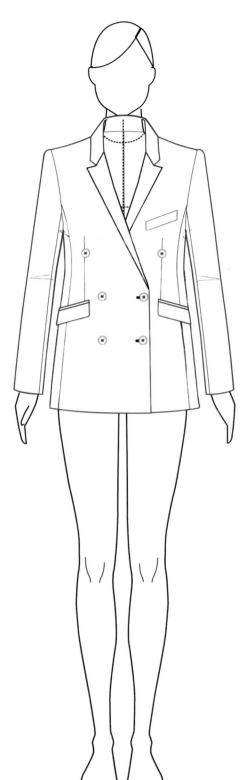

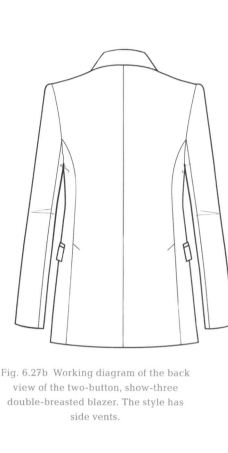

Fig. 6.27b Working diagram of the back view of the two-button, show-three double-breasted blazer. The style has side vents.

Fig. 6.27a Working diagram of the front view of the two-button, show-three, double-breasted blazer. The style has peak lapel, chest outer breast pocket and jet and flap pockets.

69 from 57

Button row two. Mark the buttonhole position ½" from the front edge.

70 from 69

The buttonhole size depending on size of buttons used. In the draft: 1⅛".

71 from 56

Total button wrap: 6". The extension width from 52 to 56 multiplied by two (3" × 2).

72 from 71

Button row one, functioning button is marked ½" from point 71.

73 from 72

The desired length between show buttons: 4¼". As mentioned previously, the show button can be marked at point 73 directly above point 72. It is a personal style preference to have the show button (point 74) on this style of D.B. to angle ½" towards the top end of the first dart.

74 from 73

Top show button: ½" from point 73.

75 from 72

The desired length between buttons: 4¼".

Points 76, 77, 78, and 79 are the flare lines continued to the jacket length line. Trace and separate the panels (Fig. 6.29) into: a back panel (i), side panel (ii) and forepart panel (iii), as a net pattern, in preparation for adding seam allowances and extra inlays, for chopping in cloth. Be sure to add the value of the dart to the side of the forepart (point A1), where it finishes at the pocket position, and the belly cut (point B1).

A1 from 42A

The size of the dart at C and D at the pocket position added to the side: ½". Re-draw the side, and smooth back into the waist level.

B1 from 42A

The size of the dart/belly cut in the pocket: ⅜".

C1 from 78

Extra length to accommodate the addition of the dart: ⅜".

The Facing Points

18, 19, and 20

Close the neck dart.

71 from 56

The width of the facing from the front edge: 6".
Square down to 80 on the new jacket length line.

FIG 6.28 The one-button, show two, D.B. blazer on the dress form. It is at finishing stage, ready for a fitting to determine the final wrap width and mark button positions based on this value.

81 from 14

Width of the facing at the shoulder and neck point: ¾".

Join 81 and 71 with a vary form curve.

ADDING SIDE VENTS

For side vents, inlay is added to the back and side panel. To mark:

82 from 77, and 82 from 76

Vent length: 9½" on the back and side panel.

For the remainder of the points on the back panel (i):

83 from 82

Folded over allowance, which is the top side of the vent: 1".

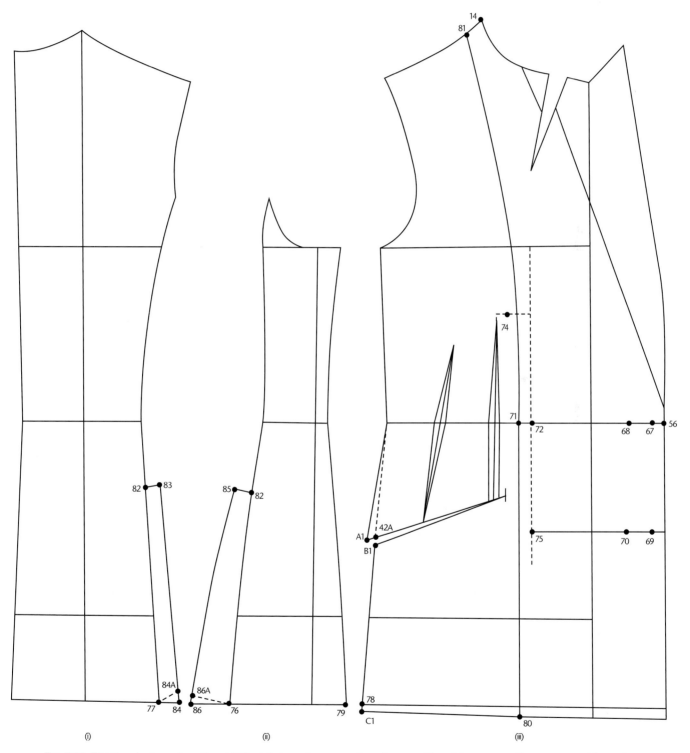

Fig. 6.29 The 'two-button, show three' D.B. style traced as separate patterns, with no inlays, seam allowances, or side vents.
(At quarter scale)

84 from 77
Folded over allowance: 1″.

84A from 77
The corner of the back vent is cut away when the vent is bagged out during the construction process, and this has been identified with a dotted line.
Join 83 to 84A with a slight curve.
For the remainder of the points on the side panel (ii):

85 from 82
The under part of the vent: 1½″.

86 from 76
Extra width for the under side of the vent: 2½″.

86A from 76
The under part should sit ¼″ higher than the topside of the vent, indicated with a dotted line.
Join 85 to 86A with a curve.

THE THREE-BUTTON D.B.,
WITH THREE SHOW BUTTONS
Refer to Fig. 6.25 (ii), 'three-button, three show D.B.'.
To draft the pattern the previous draft can be traced and adapted accordingly to add a new row of buttons, by using "The Two-button D.B, show three" (quarter scale Fig. 6.26). The jacket length and lapel style remains the same. It is only the layout of the button position that is slightly different. Mark all points, repeating instructions 0 to 56 from Fig. 6.26, with the following modifications.

57 from 56
Distance between each button: 4¼″.

58
Located on the centre line of the jacket length level.

59 from 58
Extra length in the front balance: ¾″.

60 from 56
The top column of buttons. Distance between each button: 4¼″.

60A from 60
The break springs ½″ higher than the top button position.

61 from 14
Collar stand: 1¼″.
Draw in the centre line through points 56, 57, 58, and 59.
Draw in the break line, which is interrupted by the dart. Place the ruler between points 61 and 60A. Point 62 is where the ruler hits the first line of the dart. Point 63 is plotted at the exact measurement of point 62 from the end of the dart (point 19). Rule a line from point 63 to point 60A.
Points 61, 62, 63 and 60A are the break line.

64 to 65
The desired lapel width, minus the dart width. In the draft it is 3½″. Do not include the value of the dart.

66 from 15
The angle of the peak specific to the style: 2½″.

67 from 56
The middle column of buttons. Mark the buttonhole position ½″ from front edge.

68 from 67
The buttonhole size depending on the size of buttons used. In the draft: 1⅛″.

69 from 57
Bottom column of buttons. Mark the buttonhole position ½″ from front edge.

70 from 69
The buttonhole size depending on the size of buttons used. In the draft it is 1⅛″.

72 from 60
The top column button position: ½″ from the front edge.

71 from 72
The buttonhole length: 1⅛″.

73 from 56
Total width of the button wrap: 6″, which is the extension width of 56 and 52 multiplied by two (3″ × 2).

74 from 73
The middle button position is ½″ from the button wrap.
Square up to point 75 the top button and down to point 76 the bottom button. Line 74, 75 and 76 is represented with a dotted line ½″ away from point 73, the button wrap extension.

THE ONE-BUTTON,
SHOW TWO-BUTTON D.B.
Refer to Fig. 6.25 (iii): the 'one-button, show two' variation.
To draft this example trace the D.B. block from Fig. 6.26, marking all points and repeating instructions 0 to 56. Fig. 6.25 (iii) documents the modifications from points 56 to 73.

57 from 56
The button line is altered and placed ½″ below the waist to elongate the peak lapel, as it has only one set of buttons.

67
The buttonhole position is ½″ from the front edge.

68 from 67
The buttonhole size depending on size of buttons used; in this draft it is 1⅛″.

69 from 56
Button wrap at the waist: 6″.

70 from 69
The button wrap at point 70, to be in line with the new button line: ½″ below point 69.

71
Position of first functioning button: ½″ from button wrap position, point 70. The desired length between show buttons is 4″ in the example. Square up to point 72.

History of the tuxedo jacket

The tuxedo is also traditionally a menswear jacket, dressed as part of a dinner suit, strictly for formal occasions. Yves Saint Laurent was credited with designing the first ever dinner suit for women, called 'Le Smoking' – a black tuxedo for women. Its first version was introduced in his Paris haute couture collection in 1966 – it had mixed reviews at the time, being described as old-fashioned when compared to the collections being shown in 'swinging London'. It was called 'Le Smoking', to reference its heritage of being worn for black tie/tuxedo. That changed in 1967, when Helmut Newton photographed the suit for *Vogue* and it was the first of its kind to earn consideration from the fashion press. 'Le Smoking' still continues to be featured in Saint Laurent collections to this date.

It was actually nearly half a century earlier, when 'Weimar' art culture was flourishing in underground Berlin, that female cabaret performers wore men's tuxedo suit jackets. During this frivolous time the performers donned men's clothes to perform their raucous shows. Margo Lion famously performed overtly androgynous and bisexual routines wearing a tuxedo. Lion also inspired Marlene Dietrich, and they both became icons of the German Berlin cabaret scene.

Dietrich was the most famous pioneer of this androgyny. She teamed up with film-maker Josef von Sternberg, who frequented the Berlin clubs, to capture the movement in films like *Der Blau Engel*. Their partnership provided a spring-board for Dietrich's career, and finance from Hollywood enabled them to produce other films, where Dietrich famously wore bespoke men's suits, handmade by men's tailors, memorably performing in *Blonde Venus* wearing white top hat and evening tails, and in the film *Morocco* wearing a black tuxedo suit.

Since its origins in the early 1900s, the tuxedo jacket has seen endless incarnations over the years and

Fig. 6.30 Marlene Dietrich wearing evening tuxedo and top hat in the film *Morocco*, 1930, her first Hollywood film with Josef von Sternberg.
(Eugene Robert Richee/MoviePix/Getty Images)

continues to be a timeless iconic jacket for both men and women.

Characteristically the jacket is black, but midnight navy and white are also highly favoured colours. The lapel of the jacket is cut as a peak, padded with a soft felt, and covered with shiny silk or matt corded silk. The felt prevents the silk from being marked from the internal hand pad stitching, which can show through from inside when the jacket is steamed. The buttons are covered in the matching silk to complement the cloth. The fit, length and proportion are a style

decision of the wearer or designer, and tuxedos can be either single-breasted or double-breasted.

Modern tuxedos

SOFT GREY TUXEDO DINNER JACKET

The following example is a modern tuxedo, a longer length proportion, in soft grey 10oz (280g) wool, with matching grey silk on the outer edge of the lapel. The colour was deliberately chosen to diverge from the traditional colours to update the blazer to a cool, modern style. It was originally cut and hand made as a

Fig. 6.31 Author's own tuxedo jacket on the dress form; side view.

Fig. 6.32 Author's own tuxedo jacket on the dress form; back view.

mannequin show sample, to be a modern update to the tuxedo jacket; the traditional characteristics are still the same, however.

The pattern draft is closely fitted at the waist and over the bust. It is a single-breasted jacket, with a princess seam running from the pocket to the neckline. It has a one-button centre front invisible closure, where the button is hidden inside the placket, for a minimal look. It has a peak lapel, with what is known as an inset lapel, which is fabricated in wool. This is where the peak lapel has not been entirely covered with silk; the front facing encloses an edge of silk or cloth; this can be reversed so that the inset can be silk instead. The draft has a centre vent, and there is

a four-button invisible placket on the cuff closure.

Both of the double-breasted drafts described previously can be interpreted into a tuxedo style as well, as they have a peak lapel; be sure to cut the facing in silk, which will then become quintessentially 'Le Smoking'.

The measures required to draft the pattern (Fig. 6.37) are as follows.

1. Height: 5ft 9″

2. Bust: 34″

3. Waist: 27″

4. Hip circumference (lower hip): 38″

5. Nape to waist: 15⅝″

6. Waist to hip circumference: 8″

7. Full jacket length: 29″

8. Half back width: 6½″

9. Armhole depth: 6″

10. Armhole width: 4½″

11. Neck size: 14½″

12 Shoulder length: 4¾″

13. Working scale: 17″ (half the bust measurement)

Fig. 6.33 This type of peak lapel is called an inset; the inset is traditionally covered with silk. In this soft grey tuxedo the outer edge is framed with silk and the inset is wool.

Fig. 6.34 The pocket flaps at the hip are grown-on to the side body of the jacket, eliminating a section of the seam between the jet and flap.

To draft the pattern, trace off the existing draft for the single-breasted jacket with side panel, marking all points and repeating instructions for points 0 to 43 on the S.B. draft (Fig. 6.4), with the exception of Point 4. Point 4 is a longer length jacket proportion. Therefore:

4 from 0
Jacket length: 29".

19
The original end point of the neck dart. Square out to 19A and 19B, which is the new shaping of the princess seam.

42, 42A, and 43
The new angle of the pocket in proportion to the length. Point 43 is 3¼" below the waist. Point 42 is 5" below the waist. The length of the pocket is 5½".

Mark in point 42A on the forepart side seam. On this draft point 43 does not extend ½" wider than the dart, as the pocket flap has been grown-on to the body, it replaces point D on the dart. Therefore the flap needs to finish at the end of the dart.

44
Continue point 44 at the end of the dart to point 17, converting it into a princess seam running into the neck.

45
Marked at the waist in the centre of the dart. Point A from B is the size

of the dart, measured at ½". Square down vertical lines to the pocket line and label points C and D.

46
Marked at the centre of the dart, at the pocket angle.

48
Plotted centrally between points 39 and A, the total of F to G is ¼". Rule a 45° line through the centre of the dart (point 48) and mark points E and 47, the ends of the dart. Rule dart lines through points F and G.

7
For now the buttonhole position is still indicated on the draft, even though eventually it will be concealed within

Fig. 6.35 Original hand illustration of the tuxedo suit.

Fig. 6.36 Front and back view of soft grey tuxedo: working drawing.

the hidden placket at the opening of the centre front.

The hidden placket is drafted as two rectangular pattern pieces with the following dimensions: (without seam allowance)

Length = 4 ¾".

Width = 2".

A seam allowance of 3/8" is added to the edges after plotting the rectangular pattern piece.

J from I

The side back of the flap is angled, as it is more flattering on the hip area, ¾". Rule a line between point 42 and J.

49

Located on the centre line, where it crosses the waist line.

50 from 49

The single-breasted button wrap extension: 1½".

51 from 50

The buttonhole position marked ½" below the waist line and ½" away from the front edge. This is to balance the length of the jacket with the position of the button.

52 from 51

The size of the buttonhole depending on the size of the button. In the draft it is 1". Square down from point 50 to point 53 the line of the jacket length. For now the buttonhole position is still indicated on the draft, even though eventually it will be concealed within the hidden placket at the opening of the centre front.

The hidden placket is drafted as two rectangular pattern pieces with the following dimensions: (without seam allowance)

Length = 4 ¾".

Width = 2".

A seam allowance of 3/8" is added to the edges after plotting the rectangular pattern piece.

54 from 53

The front balance of the draft is lengthened by ³/₈".

55 from 53

The curved front hem. Measure 3" from point 53.

56 from 54

The curved front hem. Measure 3" from point 53. Draw in the shape of the front curve at the hem.

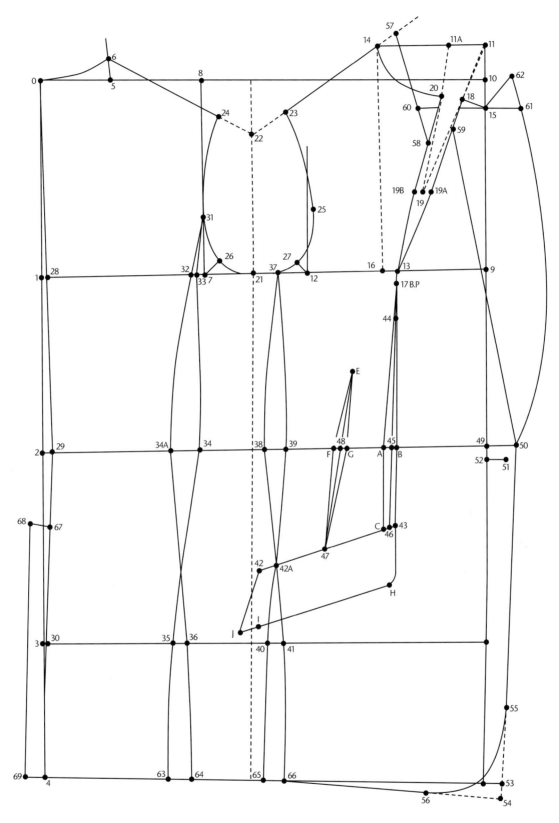

Fig. 6.37 Constructional points for the longer length tuxedo jacket style. (At quarter scale)

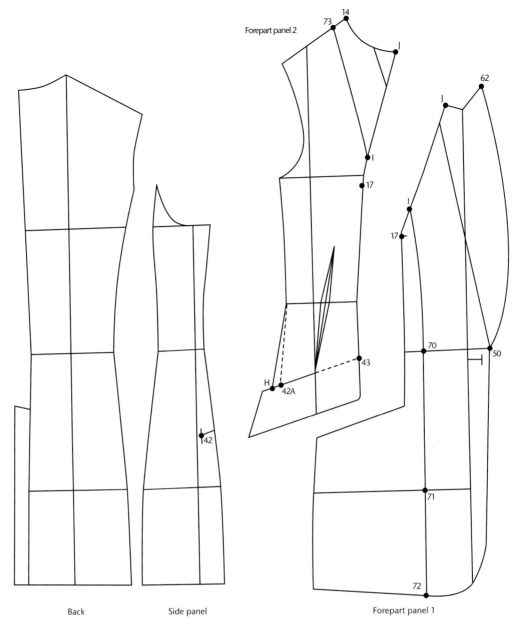

Forepart panel 2

14
73

17

17

62

70
50

71

72

H
42A
43

42

Back   Side panel   Forepart panel 1

Fig. 6.38a The block traced off as individual net pattern pieces. Forepart panel 2 shows the pocket flap grown-on. (Not to quarter scale)

57 from 14

The collar stand: 1¹⁄₈″ from point 14, this is the stand depth from the neck point. Rule in the break line from point 57 to point 50; it stops at the dart, point 58. Measure from point 17 on the dart to point 58 and mark point 59 on the opposite side of the dart to the exact measurement, as this will seam together when the jacket is constructed.

61 from 60

Squared from the centre line through point 15 to the exact width of the peak lapel at point 61. This particular lapel is wide in style: 4″.
Be careful not to incorporate the value of the princess seam dart value into the measure.

62 from 61

The desired height of the point in the peak lapel. In the draft it is 1⁵⁄₈″. Draw in the outer line of the lapel between points 62, 61 and 50, with a French curve stick, which has a more prominent curve shape than the vary form curve. The style line of this lapel is excessively curved in comparison to all other jackets documented in the chapter so far.
    Points 63, 64, 65, and 66 are indicated at the jacket length level; the lines of the seams from the hip circumference level continued to the hem. These lines are known as the flare; they can be pinched in during a fitting if they are too wide.

To mark the centre vent:

67 from 4

Length of the vent: 11½″.

68 from 67

Width of the vent: 1¼″.

69 from 4

Width of the vent: 1¼″.
Join points 68 and 69 with a straight line. Trace off and separate the panels as net pattern pieces, Figs. 6.38a & b, in preparation to add seam allowances and inlays for cutting into cloth. Due to the princess seam the forepart is divided into two separate patterns; as the seam does not continue all the way to the hem and finishes at the dart, be

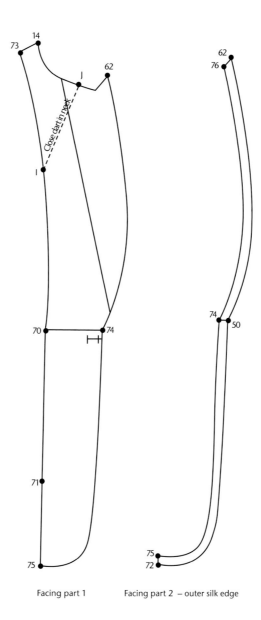

Facing part 1   Facing part 2 – outer silk edge

Fig. 6.38b Tracing off the points of the facing and separating into part 1 and 2, due to the inset. (Not to quarter scale)

sure to add the value to the side (½″ total dart size on the draft).

H from 42A
Total width of the dart at the pocket position, taken from the width of points 43 and C: ½″.
A dart/belly cut is not added onto the pocket in this particular style, due to the grown-on pocket flap.
A facing should be indicated on the forepart panel 1 and traced off as a separate piece, with the inset marked onto the pattern.
To draft the facing points: Close the dart running from the bust point through the neckline indicated with the points I and J – this can be completed by cutting out the net forepart panels 1

and 2 and taping each side of the dart together for the purpose of drawing on the facing. It is always advisable to remove any neck dart or seam from a facing pattern (Fig. 6.38b).

70 from 50
Measure from the front edge along the waist line: 3¼″.
Square down to point 71 and 72.

73 from 14
Measure across from the front neck and shoulder point at 14: ¾″. Join points 73, I, and 70, with a vary form curve.
For the inset mark a parallel line 1″ from the front edge. Therefore:

74 from 50
Silk outer edge at waist: 1″.

75 from 72
Silk outer edge at hem: 1″.

76 from 62
Silk outer edge at shoulder and neck point: 1″.
Trace around the net pattern of the facing and its outer edge; label as 'facing part 1' and 'facing part 2'.

THE SHORTER LENGTH TUXEDO (FIG. 6.39)

The second style of tuxedo is a lower hip length fitted jacket. The style has no vents, a one-button centre front closure, with a four-button cuff vent.

Originally a wedding tuxedo, it is constructed in ivory wool cloth, 9oz (255g), with ivory shiny silk covering the entire lapel.

The measures required to draft the pattern are as the previous draft, with the exception of the jacket length.

1.   Height: 5ft 9″

2.   Bust: 34″

3.   Waist: 27″

4.   Hip circumference (lower hip): 38″

5.   Nape to waist: 15⅝″

6.   Waist to hip circumference: 8″

7.   Full jacket length: 23⅝″

8.   Half back width: 6½″

9.   Armhole depth: 6″

10. Armhole width: 4½″

11. Neck size: 14½″

12. Shoulder length: 4¾″

13. Working scale: 17″ (half the bust measurement)

To draft the pattern trace off the single-breasted jacket (Fig. 6.4), marking all points, and repeating instructions 0 to 50, with the following modifications

4
Point 4 will not exist as the jacket length on this draft finishes at the hip circumference level.

3 from 0
The new jacket length to finish on the hip circumference level: 23⅝″. Square a 90° line horizontally across the draft. The hip flare at points 35, 36, 40, and 41 can be adjusted as desired. For this style of blazer adding ⅛″ extra width at each point will help accentuate the hourglass silhouette, giving the appearance the waist is cinched in.

42, 42A, 43 and 46
The pocket position is re-marked to be closer to the waist level line.

43
1¼″ below waist.

42
2½″ below waist.

42A
On the side of the forepart line.

43
The pocket extends past the seam by ½″. Indicate point D, which is ¾″ from point C.

51 from 50
The buttonhole position is marked ½″ from the front edge on the waist line.

52
Where the centre line crosses the hem.

51 from 49
The size of the buttonhole depending on the size of the button. In the draft it is 1″.

53
The front balance of the draft is lengthened, marked ⅜″ lower than the hip circumference level.

54 from 53
The curved front hem. Measure 3″ from point 53.

55 from 53
Measure 3″ from point 53.
Draw in the shape of the front curve at the hem. When compared with the other front edges on previous drafts, this is more curved, achieved with the French curve stick.

56 from 50
The spring and roll on this style of blazer is cut higher above the buttonhole, marked 1″ along the round of the lapel edge.

57 from 14
The collar stand. Measure 1⅛″ from point 14; this is the collar stand depth from the neck point. Rule a line from point 57 to point 56; it is interrupted at the dart, points 58 and 59. Stop at point 58. Measure points 17 to 58, and mark point 59 on the opposite side of the dart, based on this measure.

15
Square a 90° line across both ways, mark point 60.

61 from 60
Lapel width: 4″.

62 from 61
The desired height of the point in the peak lapel. In the draft it is 1⅝″. Through points 62, 61, 56 and 50 draw in the line of the lapel using a French curve to draw the exaggerated curve of the edge.
Trace off and separate the panels as net pattern pieces, ready to add seam allowances and inlays for cutting into cloth (Fig. 6.42). Due to the princess seam the forepart is divided into two separate patterns. As the seam does not continue all the way to the hem and finishes at the dart, be sure to add the value to the side (½″ total dart size on the draft).

A from 42A
Total width of the dart at the pocket position: ½″.

A dart is added onto the pocket, to aid the fit over the stomach area.

B

Point B is lowered ³⁄₈″ to accommodate the dart, which means extra length should be added at the hem.

C from 40

Lower the side hem point by ³⁄₈″.

To plot facing points D, E, and F, close the neck seam suppression.

D from 50

Width of the facing at the waist level: 3¼″.
Square down to point E.

F from 14

Width of the facing at the neck and shoulder point: ¾″.
Join the line D to F with a vary form curve.

That completes two very different lengths of tuxedo styles. Try drafting double-breasted versions, or varying the lapel proportions and number of buttons at the front edge. This is what updates a traditional tuxedo jacket.

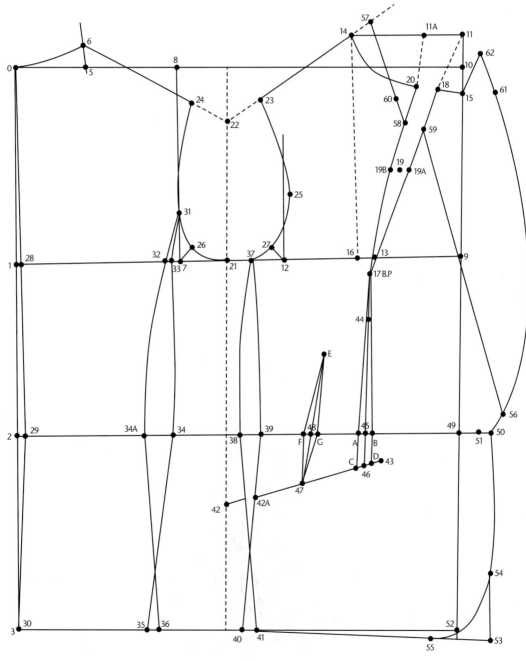

Fig. 6.39 The constructional points for the ivory silk tuxedo jacket. (At quarter scale)

Fig. 6.40 Ivory silk tuxedo jacket.

Fig. 6.41 The brown paper pattern pieces for the ivory silk tuxedo jacket.

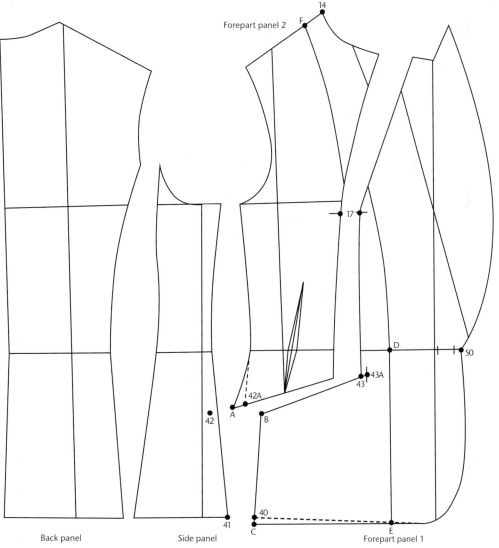

Forepart panel 2

14

F

17

D 50

43A
43

42A
A
B

42

40
41
C E

Back panel   Side panel   Forepart panel 1

Fig. 6.42 The ivory silk tuxedo traced off as individual net pattern pieces.

4. Shoulder lines, shoulder pads and sleeve heads

Classic, soft shoulder lines: soft, sloping, straight

The shoulder is defined with a felt-covered internal shoulder pad, intended to give the wearer the illusion of having a more balanced shoulder line. The shoulder line of a tailored jacket can be drawn straight, sloping, or shaped with a curve to follow the contours of the shoulder bone. The front shoulder may be drawn with a curve (as shown in Fig. 6.44), which appears softer in appearance, whilst the back shoulder

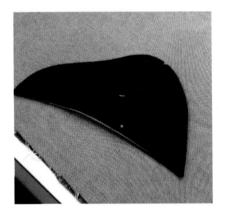

Fig. 6.43 The shoulder pad is intended to give the wearer a more balanced shoulder line.

retains its original angle and is eased onto the curve of the front shoulder.

The shoulder ends, points 23 and 24 on the S.B. jacket (Fig. 6.4), are currently cut as a sloping shoulder angle, which tilts the shoulder end to be lower than the neck. This type of shoulder line is very common in menswear, but is not advisable to suggest for a subject with disproportionate shoulders, as in the fitting it will be harder to achieve a good balance. The angle can be adjusted by raising points 23 and 24, which gives the appearance of a straight shoulder line, but sometimes it is necessary to reduce at the neck points to achieve a straighter silhouette.

The differences of shoulder angle can be compared in (FIG 6.45), the straight shoulder is indicated in red and appears square, when compared to the existing sloping angle of the shoulder, represented by points 6 and 24 in the back, and 14 and 23 in the forepart. Points 24A, 23A, 6A, and 14A are straightened by ¼″, at the ends and neck. The amount to straighten is defined by the natural shoulder line of the wearer, but if the model has very sloping shoulders, the straight shoulder will have to be built up with layers of wadding to support the extra height. The same applies to a subject with

broad shoulders: a sloping shoulder line will be difficult to fit a pronounced physique. The shoulder pad can be custom sewn to compensate for the different shoulder proportions of the wearer, by adding extra padding to the shoulder or reducing the thickness. They can create the illusion of having broader or less sloping shoulder lines.

Shoulder disproportions: down right or down left

In bespoke tailoring, the pads are used to correct shoulder disproportions. A wearer may have one shoulder significantly lower and dropped, only on one side – commonly phrased as a 'down right shoulder' or a 'down left shoulder'. This can be judged when seeing a client for the first time to take their measurements; training the eye to observe these imperfections will help when cutting the pattern, and especially judging the amount the shoulder is lower than the other side.

Most women tend to be down right from the consistent wearing of handbags on their right shoulder and 'down right' and 'down left' can be identified on the pattern pieces using the following system (Fig. 6.46).

A from 24, and D from 23
½″ below the original front and back shoulder ends.

B from 6, and E from 14
¼″ below the neck point.

H from 27A
The under-armhole point is also dropped ½″, to retain the same armhole depth. Re-draw a new armhole, so that the curve is a smooth line through points A, C, G, H, F and D. At points 31, 31A, 27 and 27A, the line will be lowered by ³⁄₈″ to help draw a new run.

A from B
Be sure to re-measure the shoulder length to be the same shoulder length as points 24 from 6.

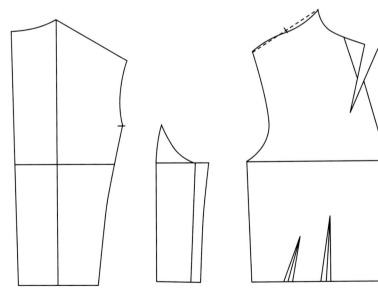

Fig. 6.44 A classic soft shoulder: the front shoulder is shaped with a slight curve, while the back remains straight, and is eased onto the front curve of the shoulder. (Not to quarter scale)

D from E

Re-measure the shoulder length to be the same shoulder length as points 23 from 14.

This adjustment will improve the overall fit of the jacket for the wearer with a down shoulder. It can be helpful to make a right side pattern and a left side pattern, for all jacket body pieces, to be sure to cut the correct side of the pattern in cloth. The more experienced bespoke cutter will be able to cut straight into cloth, and will mark stitch the right and left shoulder line, as an indication to the tailor who will make it. For a down left shoulder, use the same method, but reverse the markings. Having one down shoulder will also affect the front pitch point of the sleeve; this will need to be lowered, otherwise the sleeve balance will hang more forward on the dropped side.

Adjusting shoulder pad allowance

All drafts have ½" shoulder pad allowance incorporated into the pattern. A cutter should measure the thickness of the pad, to cross-reference before starting the pattern, and adjust accordingly. The shoulder pad thickness can be measured using a tape measure or ruler placed at the centre of the pad to obtain the necessary pad allowance (Fig. 6.47).

To add extra pad thickness into the pattern, *see* Fig. 6.48. Points 24 and 23 are indicated as the original shoulder ends from the S.B. draft; points 6 and 14 the original neck points. Points 23A and 24A are the increase in pad thickness; remember that an allowance of ½" has already been included, so if the pad width is ¾", it should be increased by ¼", to nothing at the neck points. The same applies to the crown of the top sleeve, at point 7: the increase at point 7A is the same value applied to the front and back shoulder (¼"), and the line is re-drawn back into nothing on the sleeve circumference. To decrease the width, repeat the instructions, by lowering the shoulder ends.

For a jacket with no shoulder pads, the pad allowance should be removed

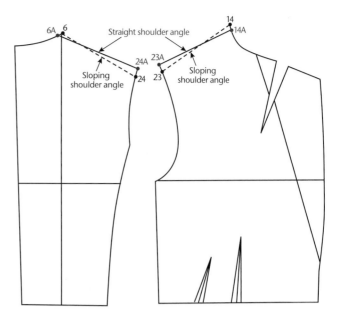

Fig. 6.45 Comparative shoulder angles: the sloping shoulder, and the straight shoulder represented on the same draft. (Not to quarter scale)

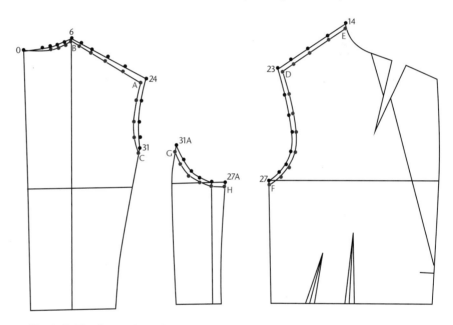

Fig. 6.46 The dropped shoulder adjustment. A down right shoulder line has been identified with red dots and the regular shoulder line with black dots. A person will have one down right or down left shoulder. (Not to quarter scale)

entirely from the pattern (Fig. 6.49), by re-marking the shoulder slope to remove the allowance. The shoulder ends at points 23 and 24 should be lowered ½", from nothing at the neck, points 14 and 6. At the sleeve crown point 71, on the top sleeve reduce the sleeve height by ½".

Fig. 6.47 The shoulder pad thickness can be measured to obtain the pad allowance.

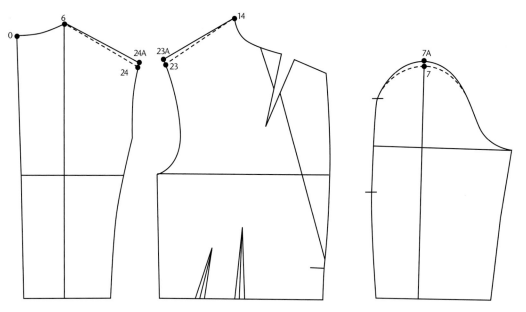

Fig. 6.48 Increasing the shoulder line and sleeve head to add extra shoulder pad allowance.

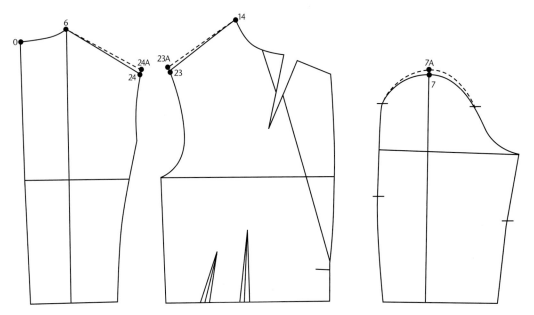

Fig. 6.49 Decreasing the shoulder line and sleeve head to eliminate shoulder pad allowance.

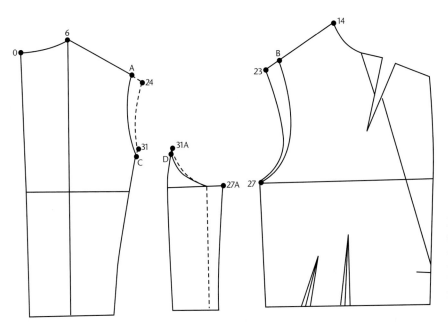

Fig. 6.50 A narrow shoulder proportion – adjustments to the draft on the single-breasted blazer. The shoulder length is 4¼".

Adjusting the shoulder length to create new widths in proportion

THE SLIM SHOULDER LINE (Fig. 6.50)
In fashion, the differentiation of shoulder lines, and inclusion of pads depends greatly on the vision of fashion designers and the current trends of the day.

Slim shoulders were popular on men's Teddy boy suits in the 1950s, introduced into British subculture after the war by Savile Row tailors. Inspired by Edwardian fashions, skinny lapel widths and nipped in shoulders filtered into women's tailored jackets as well, and became associated with rock and roll music during the 1950s and '60s. The proportion became briefly popular again during the 2000s. Shoulder length of the basic block: 4¾".

Shoulder length of the narrow shoulder proportion: 4¼".

To judge the exact narrow shoulder can be tricky on a model with particularly broad shoulders. The length may have to be adjusted by ⅛"to ¼" in stages, so that the sleeve does not drag across the shoulder bone. If this happens the shoulder length is too narrow, and it is wise to keep widening by ⅛" until the drags disappear. To draft narrow shoulder points:

24 from 6, and 23 from 14
The original shoulder lengths on the single-breasted jacket.

A from 6
The new back shoulder length plus ¼" fullness/ease: 4½".

B from 14
The new front shoulder length: 4¼" The armhole should also be adjusted in accordance with this measure, through points A, C, D, 27A, 27, and B. For the sake of having a smooth line, point 31 has dropped to point C, and D from point 31A.

THE WIDE SHOULDER LINE
(Figs. 6.51 and 6.52)
Wide shoulder lines were popular during the 1940s, with the start of the Second World War. The decade was defined by militarized women's

GRACE JONES/NIGHTCLUBBING
NOUVEL ALBUM

"I´ VE SEEN THAT FACE BEFORE" (LIBERTANGO)

c'est une publication phonogram

Fig. 6.51 Grace Jones on the album cover "Nightclubbing" – Another advocate for androgynous dressing during the eighties, making a statement with wide, masculine shoulder lines.
(Photo: John D. Kisch/Separate Cinema Archive/Archive Photos/Getty Images)

fashion, influenced by masculine styles and heavily padded shoulder lines to depict a solid shoulder proportion. This was revived again in the 1980s with power dressing. A wide shoulder line really depends on the wearer, and it should be significantly wider, when compared to the size of

the model, to the point where it is soft and drops past the shoulder bone, or is built-up with extra padding to support the extra weight.

The shoulder length of the basic block: 4¾".

Begin with a 6" shoulder for this draft, by adding the 1¼" to points 23 and 24, and re-draw the armhole to be smooth with the new proportion. (When the front and back shoulder seams are placed together it should look like an egg shape, with a smooth curve.) If a 6" shoulder is not enough, try adding an ⅛" until the proportion is right, and fit the shoulder on a model or on the mannequin. The same applies if it is too wide: remove an ⅛" until it is in keeping with the proposed design. Remember the back shoulder has ½" ease for movement, so the value of point A from 6 is 6½"; point B from 14 on the front shoulder is 6". Points C, D and E show the new run of the armhole, in proportion to the newly adjusted wide shoulder line.

For extremely wide shoulders, sometimes the armhole will have to be lowered, as the further the point falls into the arm, the smaller the armhole depth becomes. Calculate exactly on the toile the amount the shoulder ends drop into the upper arm, and drop the underarm by the same amount, to retain the armhole depth. The new armhole will need to be re-measured and checked with the existing sleeve patterns, and adjustments made to the crown height and sleeve circumference in accordance with the new proportion.

There are several pattern making tricks that can be used to create a wide or built up shoulder line: the box shoulder line, pagoda and darted sleeve are just some of the variations that can be applied to the shoulder line of the basic block and sleeve, to alter the shoulder proportion. The front pitch point will also need to be adjusted in the fitting, as the sleeve balance will hang differently now.

THE BOX SHOULDER LINE
In the following example, the silhouette resembles a box shoulder line, a new proportion I developed while working on Savile Row. It is where a section of the shoulder has been grown-on to the top sleeve.

This variation of shoulder was used for bias silk blouses in the 1930s, construed as epaulettes and referred to as narrow strips transferred onto sleeve heads, but in the 1940s it was translated into dresses, as a military influence. The blazer shown here has incorporated the same cutting technique: cut wider in length, this blazer has a shoulder length of 6⅛", and has been exaggerated in proportion. The epaulette section has been bonded to a hat canvas – an interlining used for moulding the base of a hat. It is perfect for sustaining the wide, box-like silhouette, hence the name I gave it, and the silk epaulette section is combined with a 10oz (280g) worsted wool suiting. It is almost a new tuxedo minus the peak lapel, as it has a classic notch instead.

The sleeve head itself does not require any fullness in the crown, as it does not require a sleeve head roll. A shoulder pad has been added into the jacket, which was built up with layers of wadding to build structure to support the style.

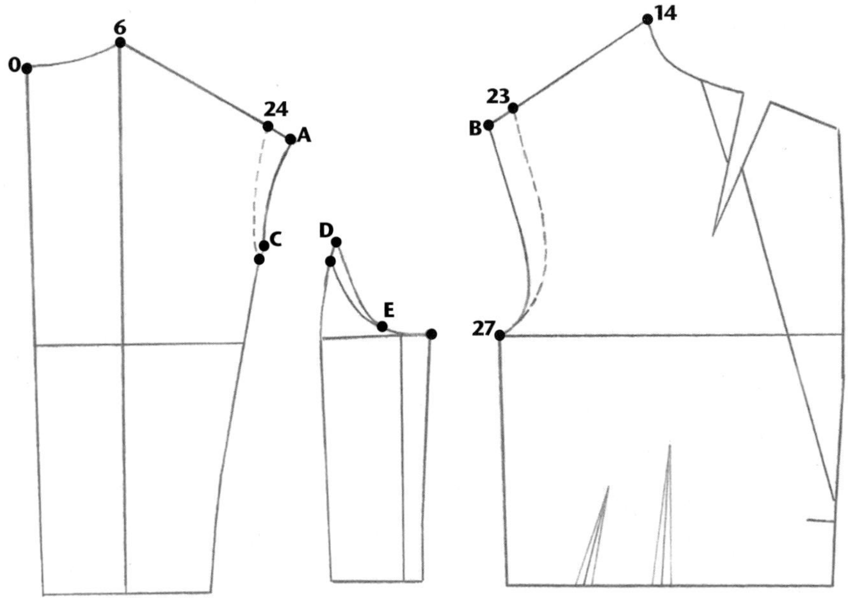

A to B
(Fig. 6.58) Position A is the neck point side of the shoulder seam and position B is the armhole end of the shoulder seam.

Use the single-breasted blazer (Fig. 6.4), two-button, and slimmer three-quarter sleeve as blocks (Fig. 5.15), and trace a new net copy. Fold the ease out of the back shoulder and place the net shoulder seams of the front and back together exactly, and lay onto drafting paper. Rule an extended 90° line through A and B, continuing from the shoulder seam through the edge of the paper.

At point B place the centre grain line of the net top sleeve on the line drawn previously. The highest point of the centre of the sleeve should touch point B, the end of the shoulder. The dotted line shows extra width (⅜") added into the front of the cap circumference; the amendment helps prevent front draglines and helps to eliminate the ease/fullness, as this style of sleeve does not require any. In sleeves with a lot of fullness, the cap can be placed ⅜" inside point B, reducing the crown height to remove more ease.

Draw in the strap design to the desired width; in this example the strap is narrower at the neck end (1½") and wider at the armscye end (2").

1 from A, and 2 from A
¾"

Fig. 6.52 Adjusting the single-breasted blazer to have a wider shoulder line: 6".

3 from B and 4 from B

1″

Rule a straight line between points 1, 3 and 2, 4. Rule a second curved line, shown with a dotted line.

5

This is the front balance notch marked centrally onto line 2 to 4 and onto the curved dotted line.

6

The back balance notches, two marks located centrally on line 1 to 3 and on the curved dotted line.

Make sure you transfer these notches onto the strap and onto the front and back bodice when tracing off the pieces. The curved line should curve outward ⅛″ from the balance notches.

7

The underarm seam on the top sleeve. Trace off all pieces separately (Fig. 6.59). Be sure to check the measurement of the sleeve circumference, including the under sleeve in relation to the front pitch point. There should be no fullness between points 7 and 4 and the front pitch point on the under sleeve. The same applies in the back of the sleeve: there should be no fullness. If there is still fullness the sleeve can be taken in at point 7 and at the hind arm seam.

The shoulder will need to be built up, by hand sewing layers of wadding and sponge on a custom pad to prevent the shoulder ends of the jacket from collapsing.

THE PAGODA

The pagoda shoulder line is when the ends of the shoulder kick up higher than the point at the neckline. The extra height is then filled with a custom shoulder pad built up with layers of sponge and wadding. Made popular in the 1970s by celebrity bespoke tailor Tommy Nutter, who cut suits for Mick Jagger and Paul McCartney, and Fred Burretti, the clothes designer for David Bowie during the Ziggy Stardust era, in 1973.

Fig. 6.53 The box shoulder line – Author's own jacket on the dress form.

Fig. 6.54 The box shoulder line – aerial view.

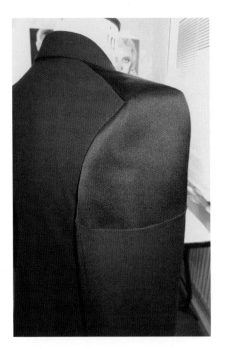

Fig. 6.55 : The box shoulder line – Side back view.

RAISING THE SHOULDER LINE AND CROWN HEIGHT OF THE SLEEVE
(Fig. 6.61)

To draft a pagoda shoulder line, take the single-breasted blazer (Fig. 6.4) and the top and under sleeve patterns previously drafted (Fig. 5.15).

First decide the desired height of the shoulders. The following has been drafted based on the Tommy Nutter blazer worn by Bianca Jagger in the image.

24 from 6
The net shoulder length minus the back shoulder fullness: 4¾".

A from 24
The desired height at the back shoulder ends; in this case, ½".

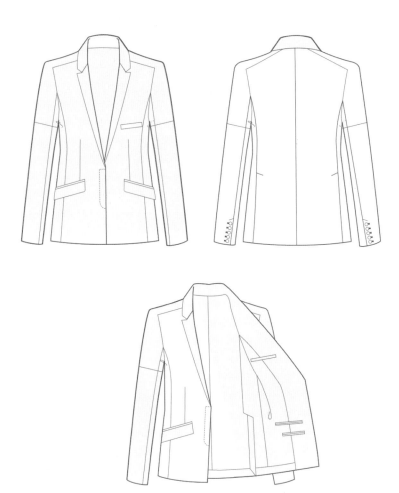

Fig. 6.56 The technical working drawings of the jacket with box shoulder proportion.

Fig. 6.57 Original fashion illustration depicting the silhouette of the box shoulder.

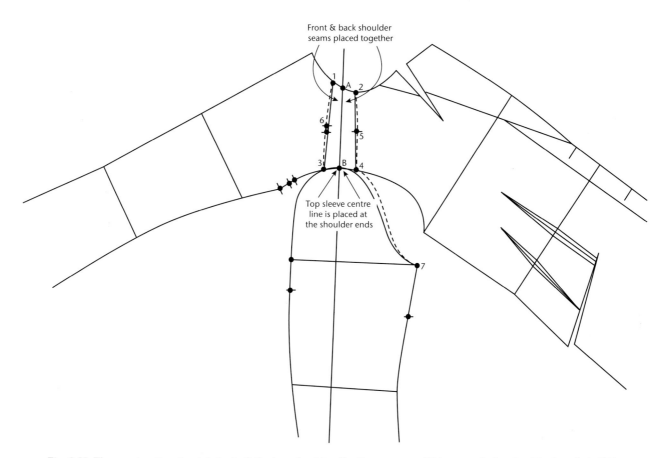

Fig. 6.58 The constructional points to draft the box shoulder. For the purpose of this example the shoulder length is 4¾".
(Not to quarter scale)

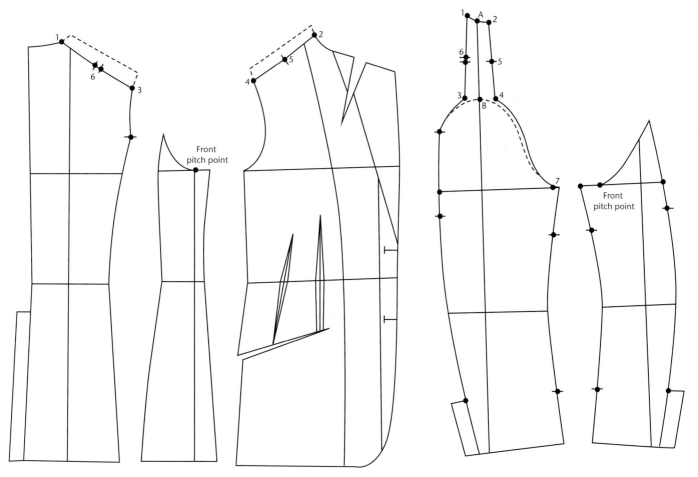

Fig. 6.59 The panels traced off as separate pieces. (Not to quarter scale)

B

Located mid-way between points 6 to 24.

C from B

Mark ⅛″ below point B. Join Point A to point 6, hollowing a curve at point C.

D from 23

The desired height at the front shoulder ends, in this case ½″.

E

Located mid-way between points 14 to 23.

F from E

Mark ⅛″ below point B. Join Point D to point 14, hollowing a curve at point F.

G from 7 (Fig. 6.62)

The crown height of the top sleeve, as previously drafted, with no extra height: 6″, to correspond with the armhole depth.

H from G

The adjusted crown height: ½″ below point G. The depth can be deepened at the underarm, which automatically creates more height at the cap of the

sleeve. Square a 90° line both ways. At the forearm seam, mark point I: ½″ below point 26.

J from 23

½″ below point 23. Place the forearm seams together and draw in the new run of the sleeve circumference. This type of shoulder and sleeve head will need ease at the sleeve head, which is already incorporated into the pattern, and a sleeve head roll will be inserted to finish the line.

On the internal body canvas, at points C and F (the centre of the front and back shoulder), a dart will need to be inserted into the horsehair cloth, sandwiched between the soft felt and canvas, then hand pad stitched together; this is then stretched with a dry, heavy iron. When hand basted in to the body of the jacket, with shoulder seams sewn and pads inserted, the tailor will hand mould the line of the shoulder from where it curves into the neck and up at the shoulder ends. These are the final touches to shaping a pagoda shoulder. The silhouette works particularly well in wools 10oz and above: the softer and heavier the weight the easier it is to shrink and mould with the iron. A 7oz (198g) lightweight suiting would bubble and show every discrepancy.

THE DARTED SLEEVE HEAD (Fig. 6.63)
The darted sleeve head was a popular sleeve head style, which originated in the Victorian era, a variation of the 'leg 'o' mutton sleeve'. This kind of sleeve acquired its name due to the incredible volume at the top of the sleeve, created by gathering the crown with tucks, which tapered from the elbow into a slim cuff. Versions were interpreted into darted sleeve heads throughout the 1930s and 1980s. To adjust the sleeve pattern to add width and height for a darted sleeve head with five parallel darts, use the following procedure.

Diagram (i) (Fig. 6.65)

Trace and use the slimmer three-quarter sleeve basic block (Fig. 5.15). Trace the net top sleeve, including all

Fig. 6.61 Bianca Jagger wearing a white suit, cut by legendary Savile Row cutter Tommy Nutter, with trademark wide lapels and wide pagoda shoulders.
(Photo: Express Newspapers/Hulton Archive/Getty Images)

balance points and centre line. Points 1 and 2 are indicated at the armhole depth line, and point 3 is at the cap of the crown on the centre line.

4 from 1, and 5 from 2

Raise the crown height by lowering the depth by ³⁄₈″. Rule a 90° horizontal line across the sleeve. Mark point 6 where it hits the centre line.

7

Located centrally between points 5 and 6. Draw a vertical dotted line to point 8.

9

Located centrally between 6 and 4. Draw a vertical dotted line to point 10.

10

Located centrally between points 3 and 12.

11

Located centrally between points 3 and 8.

13

The hind arm seam.

Diagram (ii) (Fig. 6.64)

This diagram shows the lines after they have been slashed and spread to increase the volume of the sleeve. Slash centre line points through point 3 and stop at point 6. Slash horizontally from point 6 to points 4 and 5, but not through them. Take another sheet of pattern paper and rule a vertical line. Place the centre grain line of the sleeve pattern along this line.

Decide the crown height. Crown heights vary with the desired fashion and depend on the prevailing silhouette and length of the shoulder seam. In the example, the cap height of the sleeve has been increased by 1³⁄₄″. The original crown height was 6″ (to fit a 6″ armhole depth). Therefore, it is now 7³⁄₄″. When the sleeve is made up, the cap will be filled with sponge and wadding to fill out 1³⁄₄″ thickness at the cap.

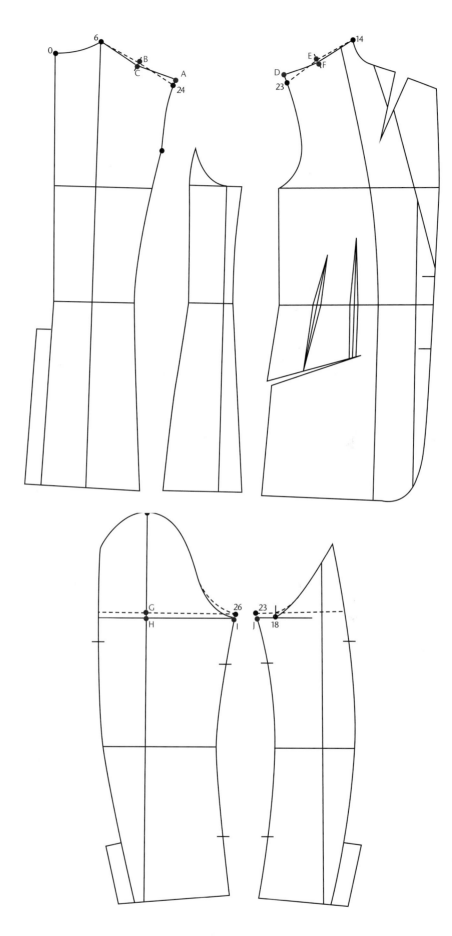

Figs 6.61 and 6.62: Adjustments to the single-breasted blazer and sleeve to accommodate a pagoda shoulder line. The shoulder length is 4 ¾″.
(Not to quarter scale)

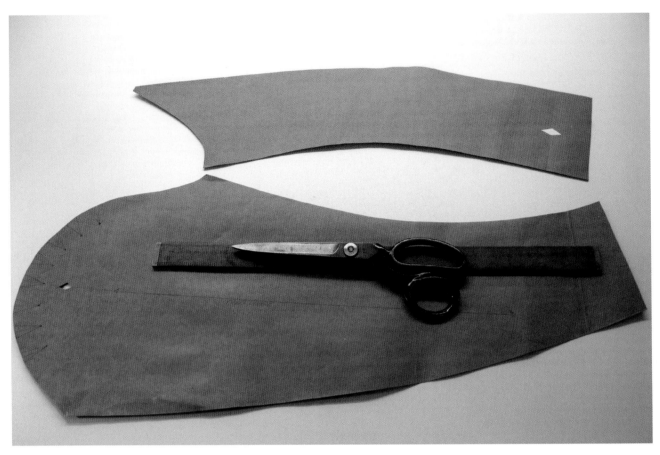

Fig. 6.63 Card pattern of traditional "Leg 'O' Mutton" sleeve, showing top and under sleeve.

14 from 6
Spread open vertical width: 1". At point 6, slash through line 12 and 8.

15 from 14
Spread open vertical width: ¾".

3A from 3
Spread horizontal width: 1½".

3B from 3
Spread horizontal width: 1½".
Use the vary form curve to re-draw the line of the hind arm seam. Points 16 and 17 replace points 1 and 4, which are now distorted due to the slash and spread procedure carried out on the pattern.

Diagram (iii) (Fig. 6.64)
This diagram shows placement of the darts.
Trace off the new sleeve shape represented in Diagram (ii).

18 from 15
Located centrally between points 2 and 16 on the crown depth line. Determine the width and number of darts. In this particular draft there are approximately six darts; styles can have between one and eight darts in the crown of the top sleeve. Styles can have between one and eight darts in the crown of the top sleeve, as the cropped Eton jacket on the mannequin shows (Fig. 6.64). Extra darts are useful to eliminate extra fullness, if the sleeve is too big or has stretched during the tailoring process, which can be added to the sleeve after the pattern has been made, if needed.

From point 3 in the centre of the top sleeve, to points 3A and 3B, there is a total spread of 3". As darted sleeve heads do not require a lot of ease at the sleeve cap, add to the 3" the amount of excess fullness/ease allowed in the basic block of the master pattern. In the foundation for the slimmer three quarter sleeve, the total ease/fullness

is 1½". This added to the spread will be 4¾", to be divided between the required number of darts. In this case the example has five darts:
4¾" ÷ 5 = ⅞", which can be rounded up to 1".
Therefore each dart width will equal 1". At point 3, draw the centre dart.

19 from 3
Length of the dart: 1⅜".

20 from 3, 21 from 3
Half the dart width: ½".
Indicate remaining central points between darts, points 3A, 3B, 10 and 11. The distance between each dart is ¾".

29 from 20
¾"

29 from 3A, 30 from 3A
Half the dart width: ½".
Mark the correct dart length at point 28: 1⅜".

Figs 6.64 An eight-dart sleeve head was applied to the sleeve pattern in this cropped bespoke 'Eton' jacket.

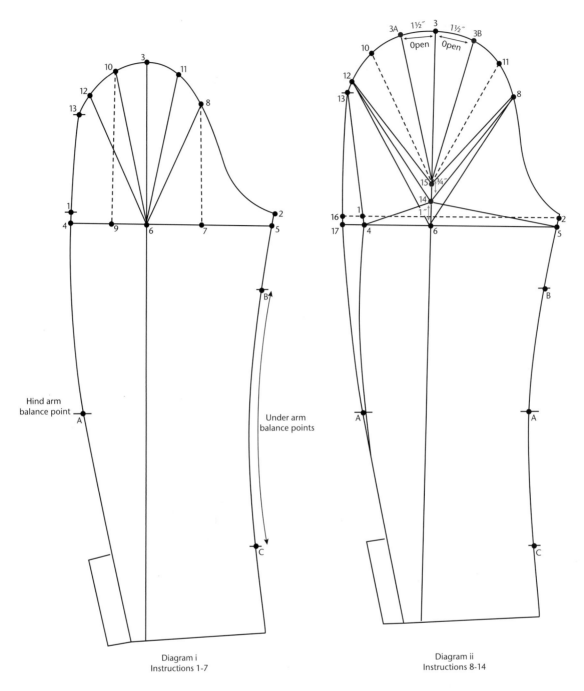

Fig. 6.65 Stages of adjustment to the top sleeve to add extra fullness to accommodate the addition of darts, and cap height.
(Not to quarter scale)

23 from 21
¾"

23 from 3B, 24 from 3B
Half the dart width: ½".
Repeat for point 24 from 3B. Mark the correct dart length at point 22: 1⅜".

32 from 30
¾"

32 from 10, 33 from 10
Half the dart width: ½".
Mark the correct dart length at point 31: 1⅜".

26 from 24
¾".

26 from 11, 27 from 11
Half the dart width: ½".
Mark the correct dart length at point 25: 1⅜".
To shape the cap edge correctly, the darts should be folded in before cutting along the sleeve cap. Trace off finished top sleeve.

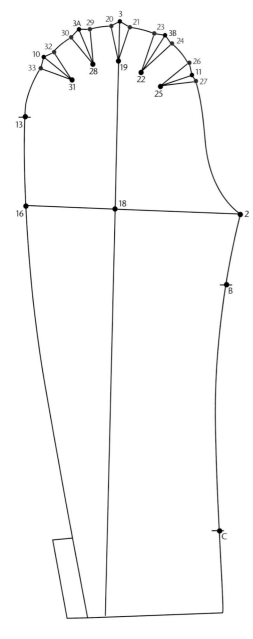

Diagram iii
Instructions 15-24

Fig. 6.66 Close-up of the eight dart sleeve-head. Note that the extra height on the sleeve-head is filled out with sponge and wadding creating the extra volume to the shoulder silhouette. Depending on the style outcome, the dart values documented in Fig. 6.65 can be amended to add between one and eight darts to the crown, simply divide 4¾″ by the number of darts required.

Chapter 7
Collars, Lapels and Templates

7

The constructional elements of the collar and lapel

To understand how to make a pattern for a collar, it is important to realize the key constructional elements, before drafting on paper.

The collar on a bespoke tailored jacket is constructed as two separate pieces, and is hand stitched onto the neck seam of the forepart and back bodice of the jacket. It consists of an under collar and a top collar; traditionally the under collar is cut on the bias in melton fabric, which should be tonal to the colour of the suiting used on the jacket body, and then pad stitched to collar canvas, which is also cut on the bias. The canvas is sandwiched between the melton under collar, and top collar.

The under collar is hand basted onto the neckline, and eventually hand felled to secure the collar in its final position.

The top collar is cut in suiting, and marked on the straight grain line at the centre back. It is also hand draped onto the under collar and basted into position. Normally, for traditional bespoke collars a generic pattern with extra inches of inlay is all that is required as a pattern piece to give to the tailor. The jacket maker will re-shape the under collar; the lines of the collar are drawn to the desired style after it has been basted to the neckline. The same process is applied to the top collar, which is cut with excess length for the purpose of draping it onto the under collar and re-cut to size.

Opposite page: Fig .7.1 Author's own jacket on the dress form; drafting style lines for collars and lapels on the pattern that translate into beautiful modern tailored jackets.

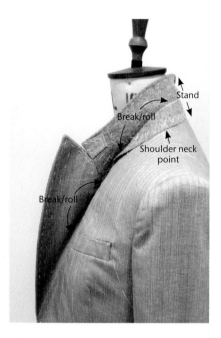

Fig. 7.2 Identifying important points of the tailored collar, at the under section of the collar and lapel.

Ready-to-wear jackets adopt similar techniques, but are simplified for mass manufacture. The under collar and top collar are cut in self-fabric, which is machine sewn onto the neckline, rather than hand stitched. The outer edges of the top collar will also be machined to the under collar, and bagged out at the corners, cutting away the excess seam allowance at its points, to reduce thickness and bulk.

Medium price point jackets (valued half way between bespoke and ready-to-wear) will adopt collar melton for the under collar, but will use machine construction techniques to blind stitch the collar to the neck seam, and fix the top collar to the melton.

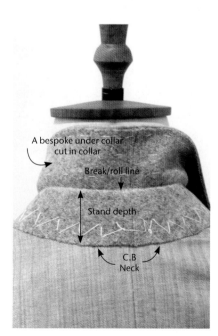

Fig. 7.3 Identifying important points of the tailored collar at the centre back.

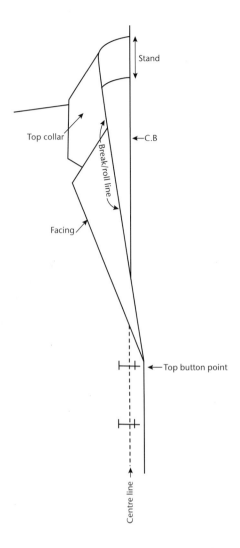

Fig. 7.4 Terminology used when constructing the top section of the collar and lapel.

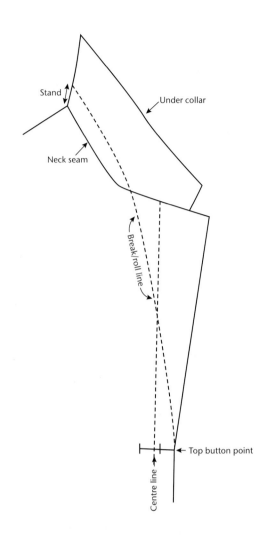

Fig. 7.5 Terminology used when constructing the under section of the collar and lapel.

Flat pattern cutting system for tailored gents' collar

Regardless of the desired constructional techniques, a collar pattern of some description will need to be drafted. The first system describes how to draft a gents' collar to the exact neck measurement and size, more suited for ready-to-wear construction techniques; the second is a generic collar block with added inlay, for the purpose of stretching, moulding and hand tailoring for a traditional tailored collar (reserved exclusively for bespoke jackets). Before starting the pattern, decide on the method of construction, and apply the instructions for the correct approach.

Drafting a classic tailored gents' collar to the exact neck measurement and size

1. CLASSIC TAILORED GENTS' COLLAR WITH NOTCH LAPEL (Fig. 7.6)

The following system demonstrates how to draft a one-piece tailored collar to the exact neck measurement, by initially drafting the under collar, with a centre back seam. The top collar pattern can be traced from the under collar pattern, and is cut on the fold at the centre back. It is adjusted to add roll, so that it does not pull the under collar too tightly when it sits on top. Suitings will shrink when pressed with an iron, and roll allows the collar to curve

under at the edges. If the collar is curling up at the point of the lapel and at the corners of the collar, more roll is needed in the pattern to compensate for the shrinkage of the suiting.

For the purpose of the exercise, the block selected is the single-breasted two-button blazer, as previously drafted. This draft has a dart in the neckline of the forepart, and it is helpful to close the neck dart temporarily, so as not to hinder the process of drafting the collar. For speed, simply pinching out the dart will suffice, or the dart can be closed and moved into the waist dart for the time being. If this is not acknowledged the value of the dart will be included

Fi. 7.6 The classic tailored gents collar applied to the two-button single-breasted Richard Nicoll blazer.

into the front neck measurement on the collar pattern and will not fit the neckline when it comes to construction.

Before starting the pattern (Fig. 7.7Ai), it is necessary to measure the half back neck (B from A): $3^1/8''$.

When drawing in the desired style lines for a classic notch lapel and collar, a useful trick can be to draw the revere onto the body of the forepart (Fig. 7.7Ai), showing the lapel when it folds back along the break line. Sometimes a pattern maker will want to check the proportions before drafting the collar; this allows the cutter to transfer the lines symmetrically, by folding the pattern paper on the break line, and

tracing the lines of the revere. Starting in this way will help to determine the correct depth of lapel from the shoulder, and the width of lapel, style lines and angles of notch, so that the appropriate adjustments can be marked at this stage.

To draft the basic block for a gents collar (Fig. 7.7ii):

D from C
Extend the front shoulder to the required stand height of the collar: $1^1/8''$.

E
This is marked at the top button. Point F is always ½" above the top buttonhole to allow spring, when

the lapel rolls after it has been pad stitched to the body canvas.

G from D
Rule a continuous line past point D. Mark point G as the half back measurement: $3^1/8''$.

H from G
Square a 90° line ¾" from point G; this is to account for collar diversion. The shorter the collar diversion the higher the collar will sit, or it will sit flatter if the diversion is longer. Join point H to point D. Line H, D, and F are the break/roll line. Square a 90° line both ways from point H.

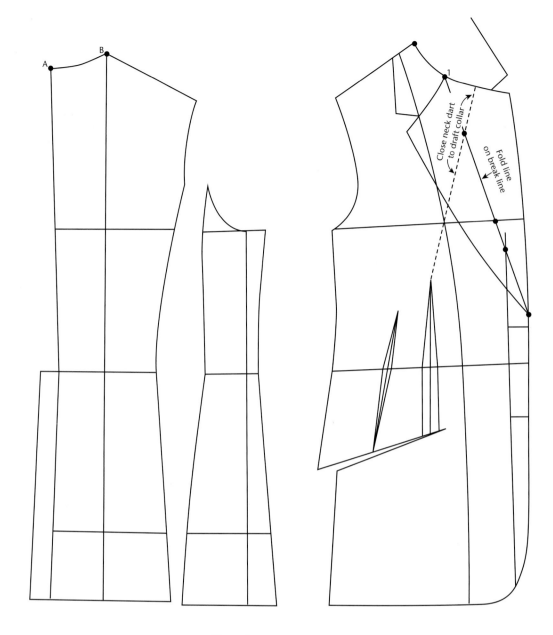

Diagram i

Fig. 7.7a Classic tailored one-piece gents' collar: constructional points.
(i) Drawing the desired style lines of revere onto the jacket front. (Not to quarter scale)

I from H
The required stand height: 1⅛".

J from H
The collar fall: 2¼" (1⅛ × 2)
Square a 90° line from point J.

L
Indicate the point of the lapel, traced from the S.B. draft, with the letter L.

M from L
The lapel notch: 1¼".

K from L
The corner of the collar is angled 1¼" from point L. If desired the revere template (see Template 1) can be used, to obtain a classic notch.

Draw the outer edge of the collar by joining point J to K with a line; depending on style, this line can be curved or straight and angular, a style preference of the cutter.

O
The waist line at the front edge.
P from O
Width of the facing: 3¼".

Square down to point Q with a straight line. Draw a curve from point P to point R with the vary form curve, ¾" in from the neck. This formulates the points for the facing pattern.

Trace off the basic block of the collar, and label as the under collar pattern piece (Fig. 7.8Biii). Indicate all balance notches, the roll/break line and shoulder balance point. The grain line will be indicated on the bias, as marked, which also helps the top collar to roll over the under collar. Cut two under collars, with a seam at the centre back. Depending on the desired finish, the under collar

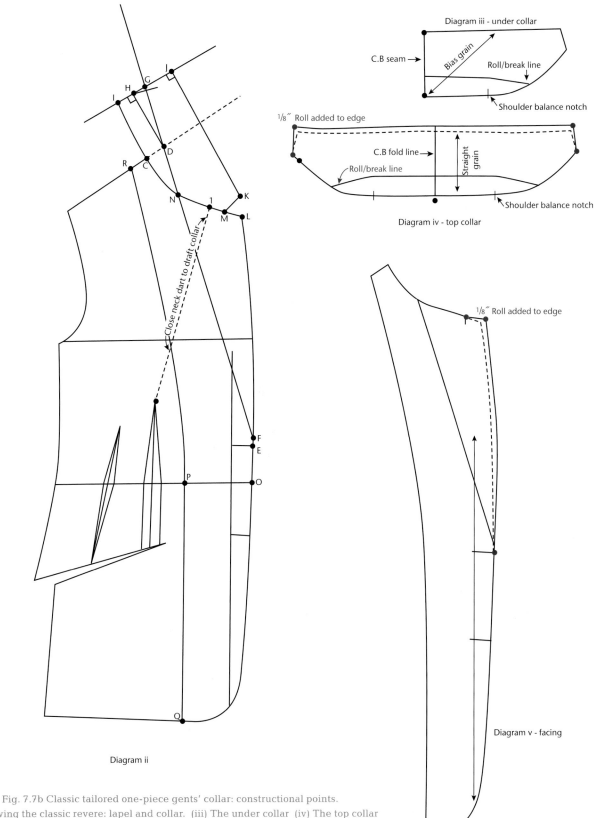

Diagram ii

Diagram iii - under collar

C.B seam →

Bias grain

Roll/break line

Shoulder balance notch

⅛″ Roll added to edge

C.B fold line →

Roll/break line

Straight grain

Shoulder balance notch

Diagram iv - top collar

⅛″ Roll added to edge

Diagram v - facing

Close neck dart to draft collar

Fig. 7.7b Classic tailored one-piece gents' collar: constructional points.
(ii) Drawing the classic revere: lapel and collar. (iii) The under collar (iv) The top collar
(v) The facing. (Not to quarter scale)

can be cut in self or in collar melton.

Use the under collar pattern to trace a top collar (Fig. 7.7Biv), cut in one piece only, with the fold at the centre back. Add ⅛″ roll around the outer edge of the collar as shown for roll allowance. The dotted line shows the original line before roll was added, and the outer line depicts the added

roll. The grain of the cloth should be straight at the centre back fold line, to match the C.B. pattern of the jacket.

The facing can be traced off as shown (Fig. 7.7Bv). As with the top collar, ⅛″ roll has been added to the edge of the lapel, from nothing at point E, curving outwards ⅛″, to nothing at point M. It is important to add roll to the

outer edge of the lapel on the facing pattern, as the lapel of the forepart is hand pad stitched to the body canvas (Fig. 7.9), to secure all internal layers. If roll is not added, the lapel points become too tight when the facing is sewn on, and the front edge will curl up, looking badly constructed, and cheapening the jacket.

133

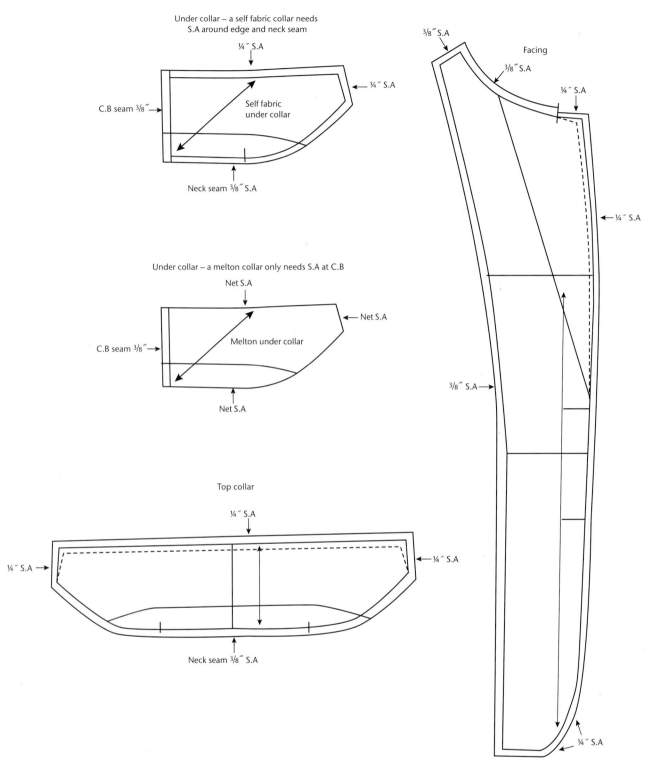

Under collar – a self fabric collar needs
S.A around edge and neck seam

¼″ S.A

¼″ S.A

C.B seam ³⁄₈″ →

Self fabric
under collar

Neck seam ³⁄₈″ S.A

³⁄₈″ S.A

Facing

³⁄₈″ S.A

¼″ S.A

¼″ S.A

Under collar – a melton collar only needs S.A at C.B

Net S.A

Net S.A

C.B seam ³⁄₈″ →

Melton under collar

Net S.A

³⁄₈″ S.A →

Top collar

¼″ S.A

¼″ S.A →

¼″ S.A →

Neck seam ³⁄₈″ S.A

¼″ S.A

Fig. 7.8 Traced off under and top collar, and facing pattern pieces with included roll, and allocated seam allowances.
(Not to quarter scale)

Fig 7.8 shows the traced off facing and collar patterns fully labeled with seam allowance and grain lines, to include allocated roll.

The under collar is depicted for two constructional methods; one is for self fabric sewn by machine: This should have ³⁄₈″ seam allowance at the centre back and neckline, and ¼″ around the outer edge of the collar; and the other one is for constructing the collar in felt melton. This under collar only requires seam ³⁄₈″ seam allowance at the centre back, due to the method of

hand application; hence the remaining seam lines are labeled net. Either process requires the under collar to always be cut on the bias grain line.

The top collar is cut on the fold at the centre back, on the straight grain. ³⁄₈″ seam allowance is added to the

Fig. 7.9 The forepart of the jacket after it has been pad stitched to the body canvas at the lapel area.

neckline, and ¼" to the outer edge of the collar, on top of the roll indicated with a dotted line.

The facing is traced and marked with ¼" seam allowance at the front edge, and ³⁄₈" at the shoulder, inside seam and part of the neckline to the notch balance point. The straight

grain line is currently marked on the centreline. This will vary dependent on the suiting selection. For stripe and check cloth, it is traditional to cut the first stripe on the suiting parallel to the front edge of the lapel between the lapel point and the buttonhole.

2. CLASSIC GENTS' COLLAR WITH SEPARATE CONCEALED STAND (Fig. 7.10i)

For ready-to-wear collars, that are machined into the neckline, it can be advantageous to cut the gents' collar with a separate concealed stand in both the under and top collar pattern. The top collar will still be on the fold and cut in one piece, and the under collar will still have a centre back seam, but will be cut in self fabric. A concealed stand can be incredibly useful to improve the fit of the collar, as it will encourage the break line to sit closer into the neck. It will also help if a wider collar stand is desired.

Repeat instructions A to K for the one –piece gents collar, with the exception of adjusting the break line on the forepart to have a stand height = 1¼", instead of 1⅛". Trace off the one-piece under collar. Indicate the roll/break line with a dotted line, marking point H at the centre back and point N at the neckline (Fig. 7.10i)

Close the lines by overlapping ⅛" along the stand seam, indicated by

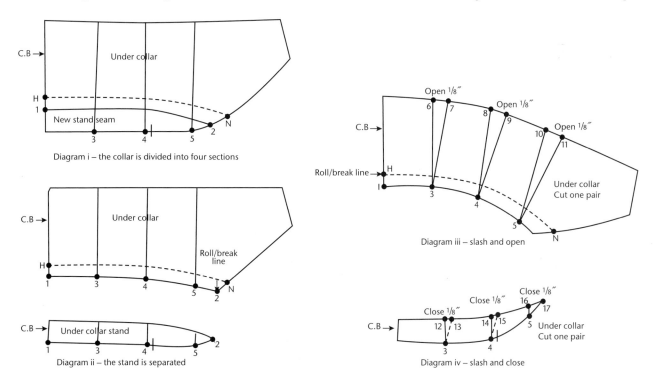

Fig. 7.10 The stages of adapting the one-piece gents' collar into a separate concealed stand. (i) A new stand seam is marked and the collar is divided into four sections. (ii) The stand is sep arated, dividing the collar into two pattern pieces. (iii and iv) Slash with scissors lines 3, 4 and 5. (Not to quarter scale)

points 12 and 13, 14 and 15, and 16 and 17.

1 from H
Draw in the stand seam, ½″ below the break line.

2 from N
Draw in the stand seam: ½″ below the break line.

Divide the collar into four equal portions, indicated by points 3, 4 and 5, by marking three vertical lines. Cut along the stand seam and separate into two parts, labelled as 'under collar stand' and 'under collar' (diagram ii).

At the under collar slash lines 3, 4 and 5 to nothing at the stand seam (diagram iii). Place onto a clean sheet of pattern paper. At points 7 from 6, 9 from 8 and 11 from 10, open ⅛″ and secure with tape. The extra width on the outer edge allows the collar to not strain when it drapes around the collarbone.

At the under collar stand, slash lines 3, 4 and 5 to nothing at the neckline (diagram iv). Close the lines by overlapping ⅛″ along the stand seam; this allows the collar to sit closer to the neck.

Trace the under collar and collar stand onto a new sheet; be certain to true the lines into a smooth run at the slash lines. Re-measure the stand seam to make sure the seam fits when constructed. Normally the total by which the seam is closed (⅜″) needs to be added back into the pattern at point 2, so it is always better to check before finishing the pattern. Remember the stand will sew back to the under collar, so the length of the stand seam must be exactly the same on both patterns.

Trace the top collar from the under collar, adding ⅛″ roll at the outer edge, and trace on the fold at the centre back. Trace a collar stand for the top collar, which is on the fold at the centre back, as well. No roll is needed for the stand pattern.

The collar system described, whether a one-piece tailored gents' collar, or gents' collar with concealed stand, will translate into all manner of style variations in jackets; the principles for drafting the collar remain the same.

Fig. 7.11A The D.B. peak lapel under side.

Fig. 7.11B The D.B. peak lapel top side.

3. CLASSIC TAILORED GENTS' COLLAR WITH PEAK LAPEL

For the one-piece gents' collar with peak lapel, the same system is applied as for a double-breasted blazer with peak lapel. All that will change is the proportion of point K in relation to the peak of the lapel.

For the purposes of this exercise, the two-button, show three double-breasted blazer (Fig.6.26) has been used to draft a collar for a peak lapel. The system to draft an under collar for a double-breasted style is exactly the same as for a single-breasted jacket.

Therefore: Repeat instructions from point A to point J as with the notch revere. Indicate points L and M at the peak of the lapel, as previously drafted (*see* Fig. 7.12).

K from M
Mark point K 1¾″ from point M. The corner of the collar should be slightly shorter than the lapel peak, as this is more pleasing to the eye, depending on the width of the lapel. The angle of line K and M sweeps ⅛″ away from the peak line L and M. It is almost parallel, but not quite.

Join point K to point J with the vary form curve.

In this example point E, which is the top buttonhole, is located approximately on the waist line. Mark in the facing.

N from E
The facing: 6″ from the front edge. Square down to point O on the hemline, and curve up to point P at the shoulder, ¾″ from the neck.

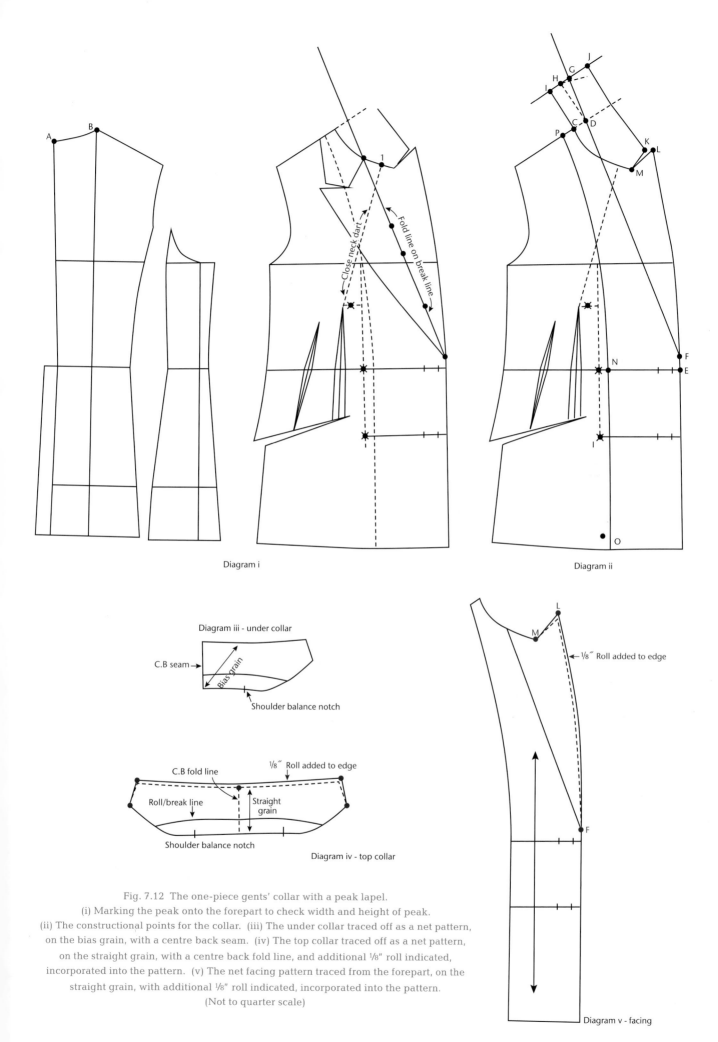

Diagram i

Diagram ii

Diagram iii - under collar

C.B seam →

Bias grain

Shoulder balance notch

C.B fold line

⅛″ Roll added to edge

Roll/break line

Straight grain

Shoulder balance notch

Diagram iv - top collar

⅛″ Roll added to edge

Diagram v - facing

Fig. 7.12 The one-piece gents' collar with a peak lapel.
(i) Marking the peak onto the forepart to check width and height of peak.
(ii) The constructional points for the collar. (iii) The under collar traced off as a net pattern,
on the bias grain, with a centre back seam. (iv) The top collar traced off as a net pattern,
on the straight grain, with a centre back fold line, and additional ⅛″ roll indicated,
incorporated into the pattern. (v) The net facing pattern traced from the forepart, on the
straight grain, with additional ⅛″ roll indicated, incorporated into the pattern.
(Not to quarter scale)

137

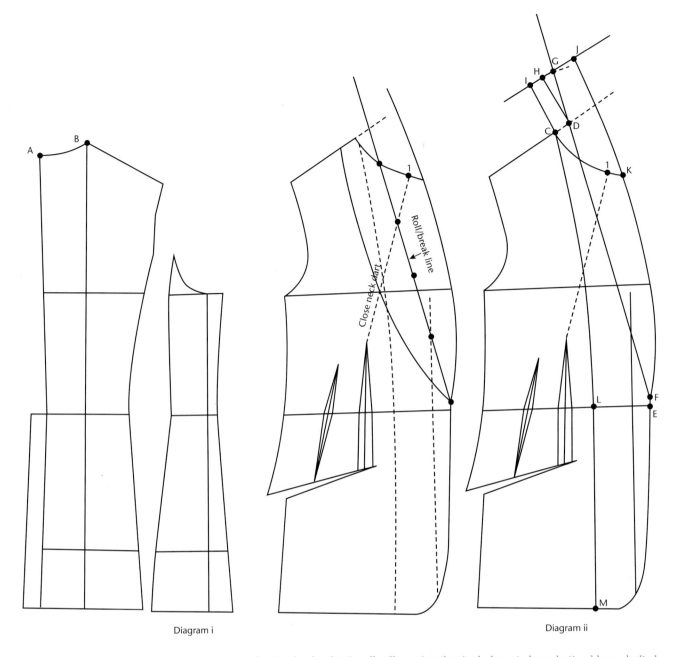

Diagram i

Diagram ii

Above& opposite: Fig. 7.13 The constructional points for the classic roll collar, using the single-breasted one-button blazer drafted previously. (i) Marking the roll/shawl onto the forepart of the blazer to the desired shape and width, then folding along the break line and tracing exactly the shape. (ii) The constructional points for the under collar, drawn in one with the lapel. (iii) The under collar is traced off as a net pattern, on the bias grain, with a centre back seam. (iv) The top collar is grown-on to the facing pattern, with ⅛″ roll indicated; added from nothing at the button position, and out around the entire edge of the roll lapel. A centre back seam is necessary, as the pattern will be too wasteful in cloth without it. (Not to quarter scale)

CLASSIC ROLL/SHAWL COLLAR – COLLAR CUT IN ONE WITH THE GARMENT

This particular style of collar is rarely seen in womenswear. It was traditionally used on smoking jackets and has occasionally been fashionable for modern women's jackets, for example in Richard Nicoll's 2009 show. It is also a popular lapel for tuxedo styles. It is known as a 'roll' or 'shawl' collar, where the collar is cut in one with the blazer, with a continuous curve.

For the purposes of this exercise the one-button single-breasted blazer has been used to apply the roll collar, cut in one with the blazer. The style lines are very different, but the system to draft the collar remains the same.

Instructions A to K are repeated as with the tailored notch revere. The line J, K, and F is joined with a French curve or vary form curve, instead of a notch or peak (Fig. 7.13 diagram ii).

In this example point E, the top buttonhole, is located approximately on the waist line.

L from E

3 ¼″. Square down to point M on the hemline. Join point L to point C with a curve; the facing at the shoulder is easier to construct if it goes directly to nothing at point C.

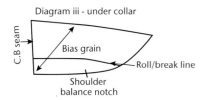

Diagram iii - under collar

C.B seam

Bias grain

Roll/break line

Shoulder
balance notch

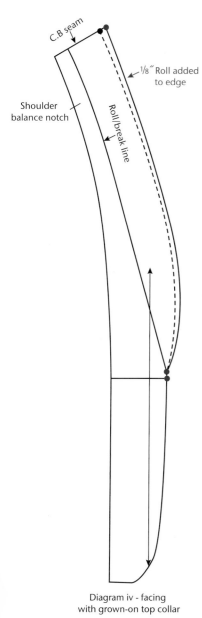

C.B seam

⅛″ Roll added
to edge

Shoulder
balance notch

Roll/break line

Diagram iv - facing
with grown-on top collar

Right: Fig. 7.14 Richard Nicoll Spring/
Summer 2009 collection jacket.

A generic collar pattern for hand tailoring techniques

For a traditional bespoke collar, the under collar should be cut several inches longer and wider, which will allow the tailor to manipulate the collar while tailoring, and shape to the desired proportion after it has been hand basted in position. There is 4″ width at the centre back seam and a minimum of 3″ extra length added to the neck size. The generic collar pattern included is not cut to an exact neck measurement. It is simply significantly longer than the neck measurement for the purpose of hand manipulation. It is not suitable for machined construction.

To construct a bespoke collar, use the full size pattern (Fig. 7.18) to cut two collars in melton fabric. Sew a seam at the centre back and press open; place the collar onto the bias grain of the French canvas and baste to secure its position. Cut out the canvas, by chopping around the melton (Fig. 7.15).

Mark a chalk line on to the melton side for the stand position, shoulder balance notches and break/roll line, machining a stitch through the break line, to secure the layers. Pad stitch the collar, adding roll between each hand stitch (Fig. 7.16).

As soon as the collar has been pad stitched to the canvas, the tailor will stretch and mould the collar with a heavy tailoring iron, to the required shape, in keeping with the length of the lapel and shoulder proportion of the wearer (Fig. 7.17).

The under collar is hand basted to the net neckline on the jacket and, when it has been secured and pressed, the shape of the collar can be drawn to the desired style lines, and excess canvas cut away. Figs. 7.19 and 7.20 demonstrate the line of the collar at the centre back neck, which runs back into the shoulder and notch of the lapel.

The generic bespoke pattern can also be used to cut the top collar in the same cloth as the body. Cut it on the fold at the centre back and on the straight grain. As with the under collar the neck edge is stretched, and the outer edge moulded into a curved shape to follow the neckline it will drape around (Fig. 7.21).

The collar is draped on to the under collar, with ¾″ allowance at the outer edge, with 1″ inlay parallel to the gorge line, and at least 1″ inlay past the notch. A pin can be used to secure at the centre back, while the collar is hand basted into position. Three baste lines secure the collar: one each side of the break line and one 1¼″ from the edge of the top collar, to leave enough

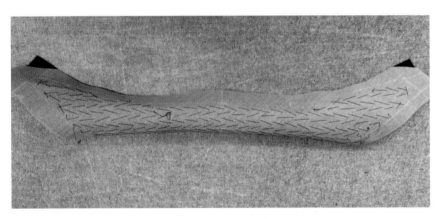

Fig. 7.15 Under collar construction: the melton is basted to the collar canvas and cut out.

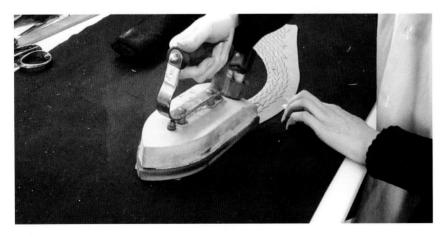

Fig. 7.16 To secure all layers the under collar is pad stitched, adding roll between each stitch.

Fig. 7.17 The pad-stitched under collar is stretched and moulded with a heavy tailoring iron.

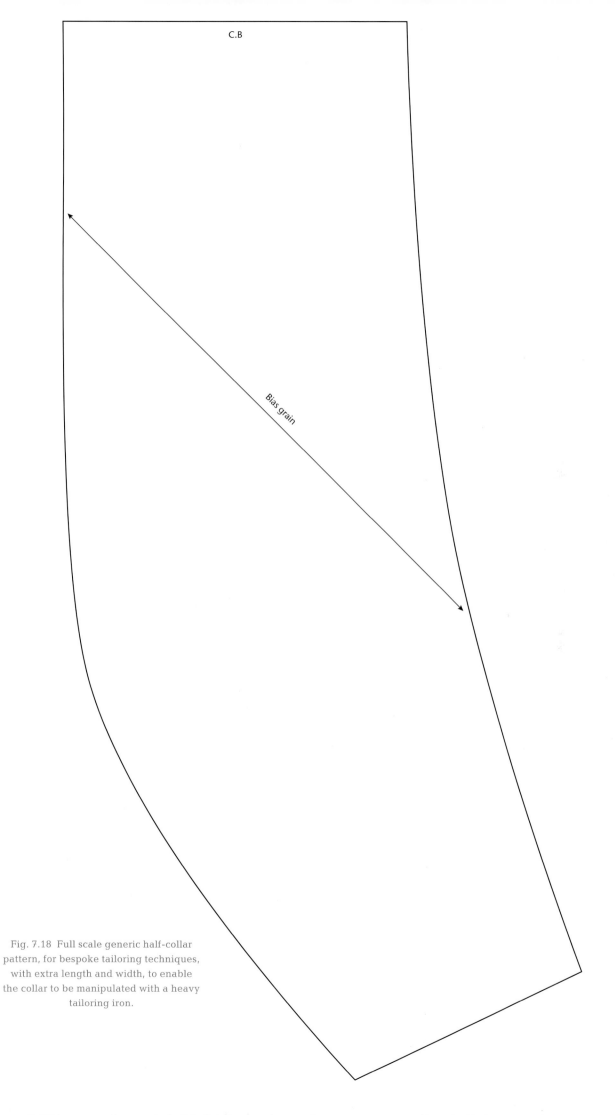

C.B

Bias grain

Fig. 7.18 Full scale generic half-collar
pattern, for bespoke tailoring techniques,
with extra length and width, to enable
the collar to be manipulated with a heavy
tailoring iron.

room to fold the inlay of the outer edge in between the canvas and melton of the under collar (Figs. 7.22 and 7.23).

Cut some of the excess inlay to be in line with the angle of the gorge. Fold in the extra inlay at the gorge line and hand baste to secure it into position.

The inlay at the outer edge of the top collar should be cut away ½" and folded in between the canvas and melton of the under collar, then secured with another row of basting stitches on the edge. The inlay at the end of the notch is folded over the corners of the under collar. (Figs. 7.24 to 7.27).

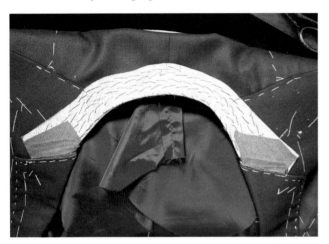

Fig. 7.19 The excess length and width of the under collar is cut away to the desired style lines, after it has been hand basted into position.

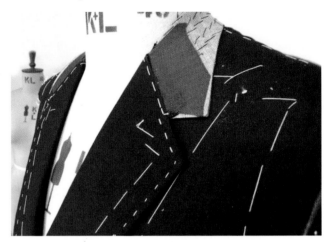

Fig. 7.20 The notch of the revere is marked directly onto the under collar and the excess cut away.

Fig. 7.21 The top collar after it has been stretched and moulded with the tailoring iron to follow the neckline it will be draped around.

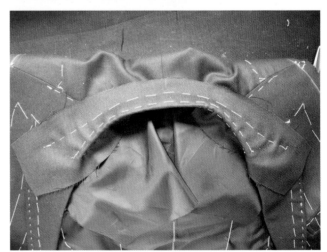

Fig. 7.22 and 7.23 The top collar is basted onto the under collar, with allowance left at the outer edge, gorge and notch.

Fig. 7.24 Inlay along the gorge line is folded inside and basted into position. The fold line is hand fell stitched.

Fig. 7.25 Inlay is basted down on the inner neck.

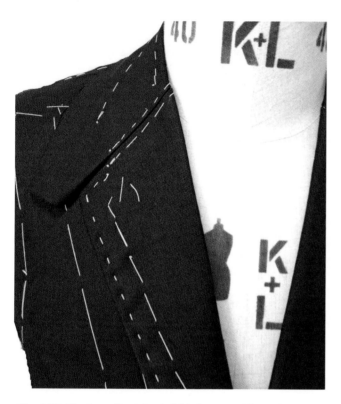

Fig. 7.26 The top collar inlay is folded over and basted down at the end of the notch.

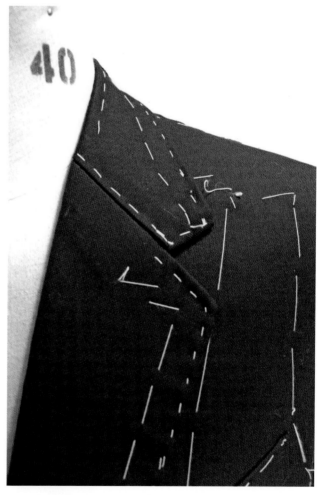

Fig. 7.27 The finished notch revere lapel.

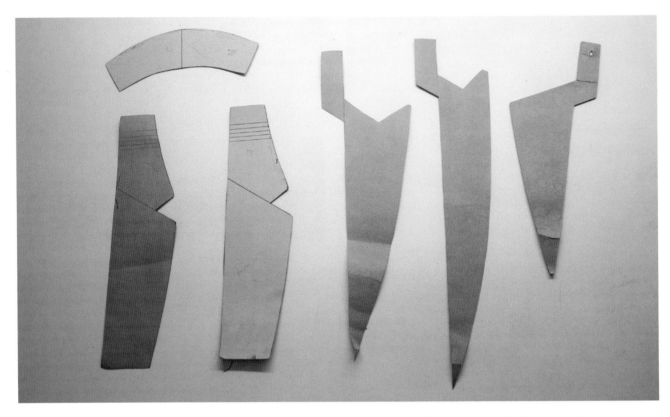

Fig. 7.28 Generic lapel shapes used to aid the pattern maker, tailor or beginner when drafting a jacket.

Templates

It is helpful to create sets of blocks for collars and lapels, which can be used to draw onto the forepart of blazer patterns when drafting new blocks. A set of two full-size lapels have been included to aid the process, which can be tedious for the inexperienced pattern maker to create from scratch.

Style lines and proportion are the trickiest elements to teach: it is something that will develop with years of training the eye through practice and experience. The shapes can be traced as a template to support all systems taught throughout the book. On the lapels a shoulder line notch has been indicated to judge the height of the lapel when it is folded back. The template can be placed as desired on the break line and the length of the lapel can be adjusted to the desired distance from the shoulder. The width can also be altered, if the template is placed to the required value from the break line.

Templates can also be made for other sections of the jacket. It is incredibly

tricky to obtain a smooth running of lines when shaping the armhole. When the shoulder seams of the front and back are placed together, check the shape of the armhole on the pattern before chopping into cloth: it should look like an egg shape. If it does not, the universal armhole template can be used to obtain smooth curves.

It is also hard to obtain a classic round corner at the front edge of the jacket; templates can be used to trace front edge style lines directly onto the pattern.

The sleeve circumference shape is another tricky line to obtain. When the under seam of the under sleeve and top sleeve are placed together, the curves should run smoothly, and follow the armhole. A sleeve template can be used to draw around onto the pattern and during construction, if the sleeve shape needs adjusting to fit the armhole.

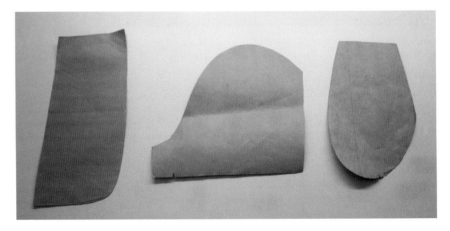

Fig. 7.29 Templates for other sections of the jacket, for use when drafting flat patterns, and during construction.

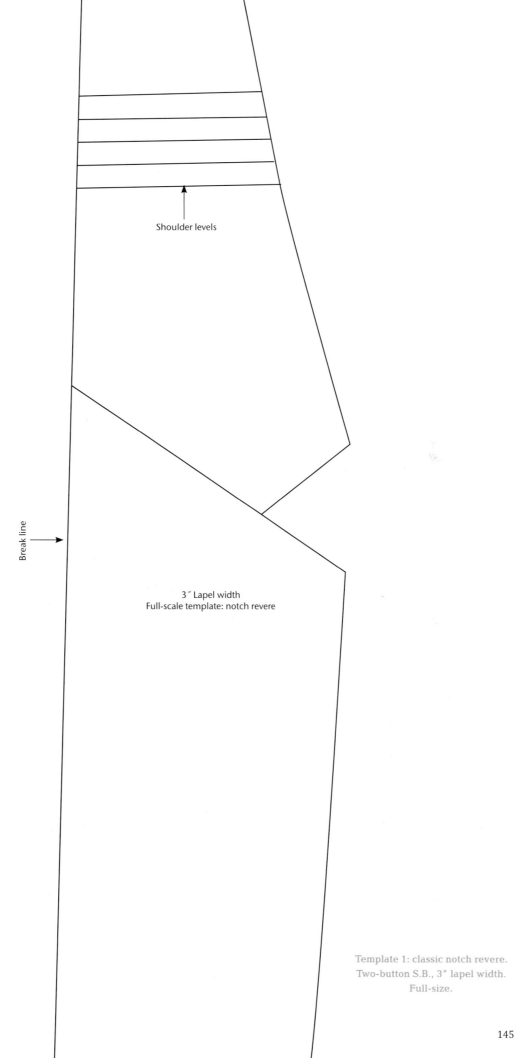

Shoulder levels

Break line

3″ Lapel width
Full-scale template: notch revere

Template 1: classic notch revere.
Two-button S.B., 3″ lapel width.
Full-size.

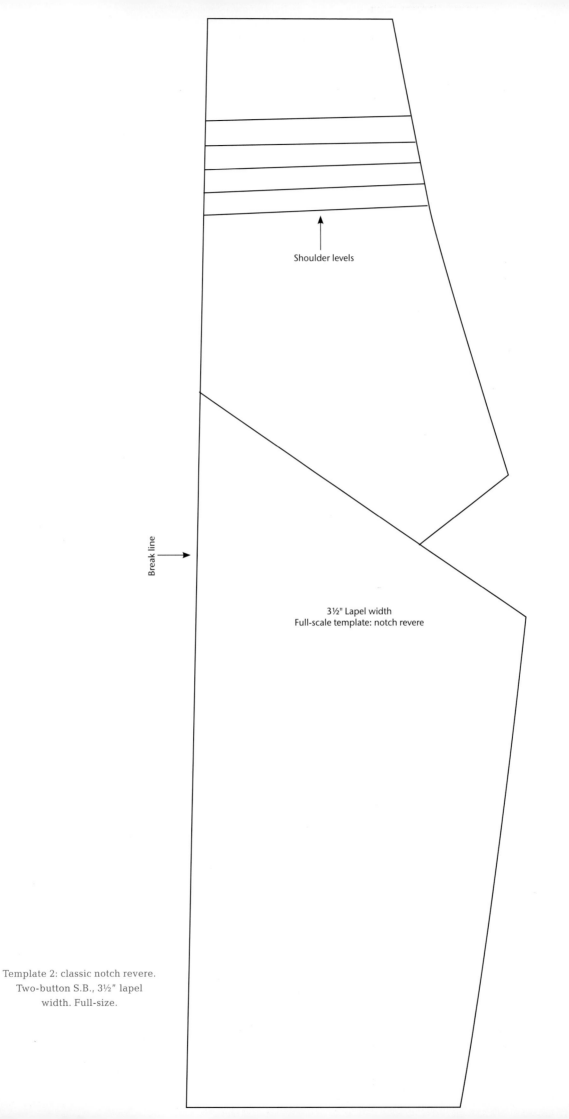

Shoulder levels

Break line

3½" Lapel width
Full-scale template: notch revere

Template 2: classic notch revere.
Two-button S.B., 3½" lapel
width. Full-size.

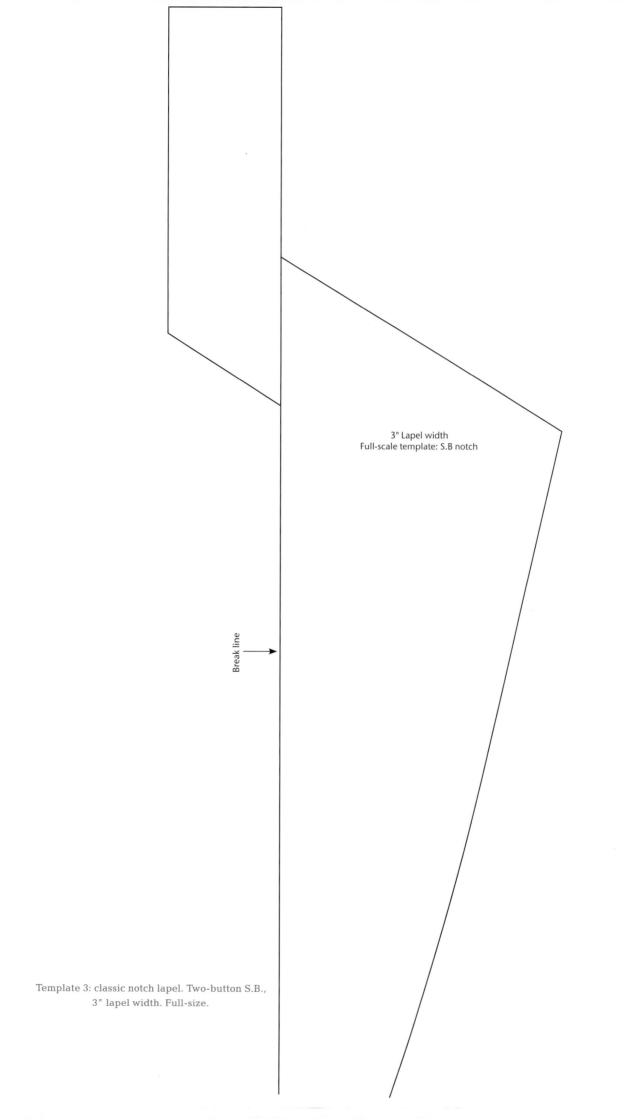

3" Lapel width
Full-scale template: S.B notch

Break line →

Template 3: classic notch lapel. Two-button S.B.,
3″ lapel width. Full-size.

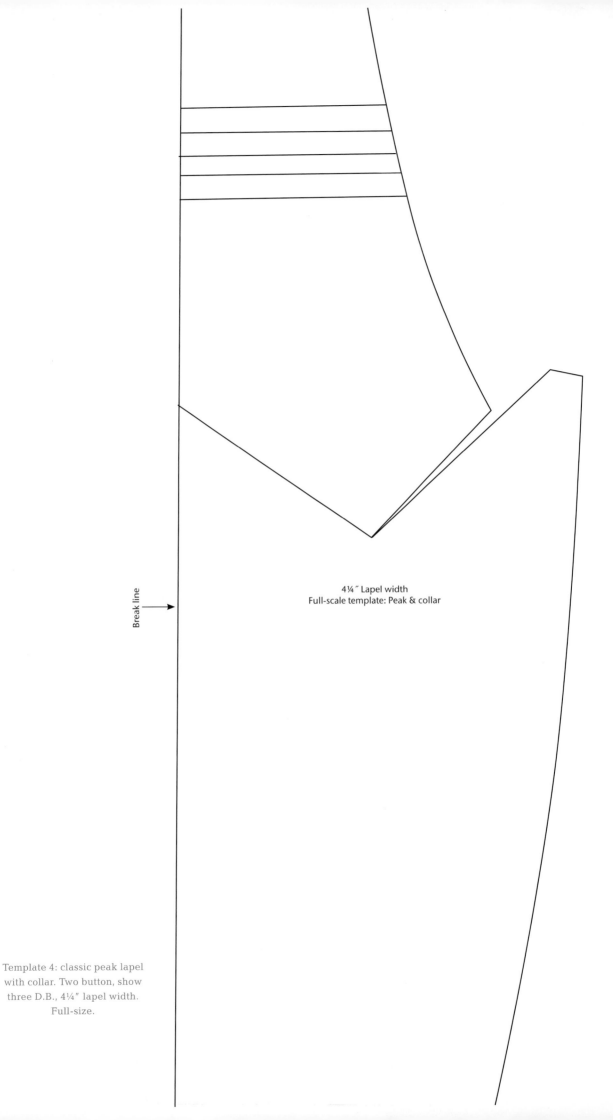

Break line →

4¼″ Lapel width
Full-scale template: Peak & collar

Template 4: classic peak lapel
with collar. Two button, show
three D.B., 4¼″ lapel width.
Full-size.

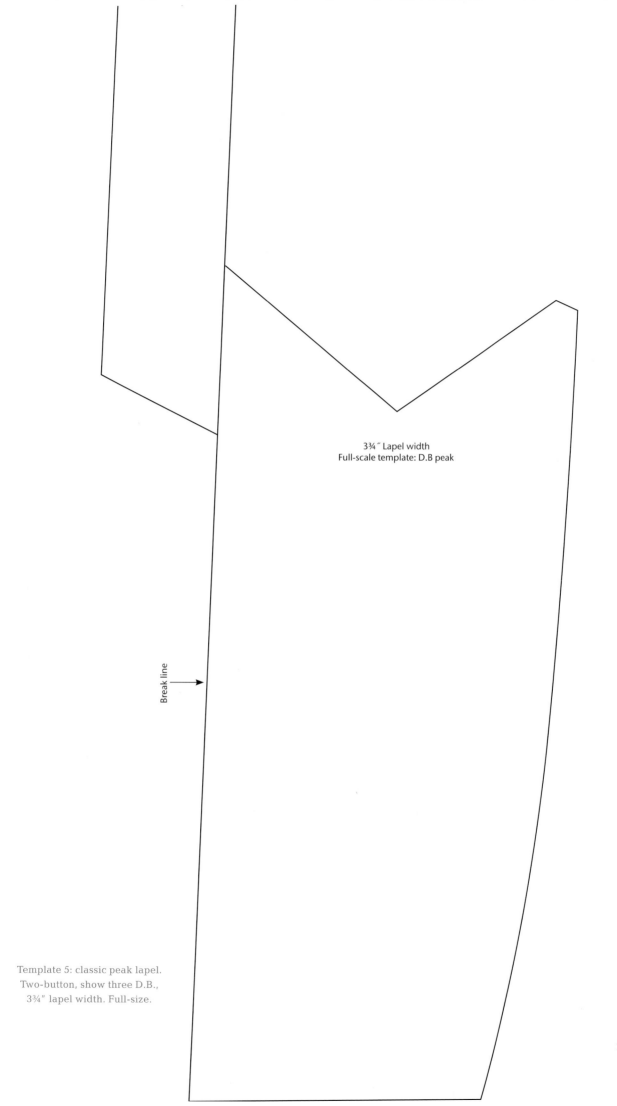

3¾″ Lapel width
Full-scale template: D.B peak

Break line

Template 5: classic peak lapel.
Two-button, show three D.B.,
3¾″ lapel width. Full-size.

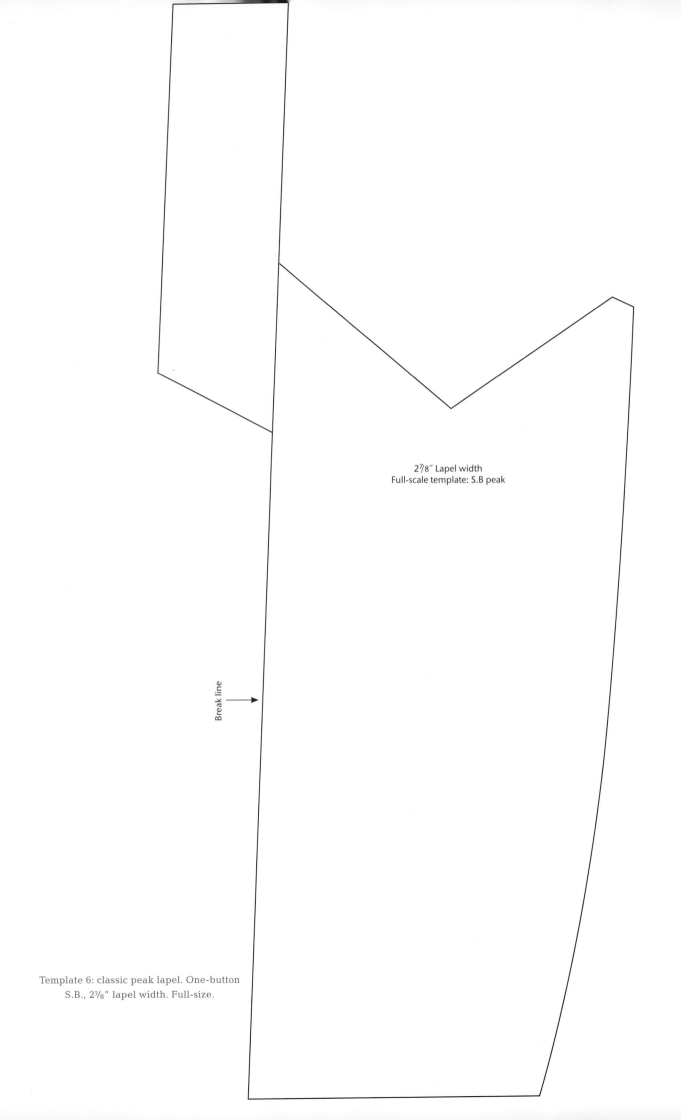

2⅞″ Lapel width
Full-scale template: S.B peak

Break line →

Template 6: classic peak lapel. One-button
S.B., 2⅞″ lapel width. Full-size.

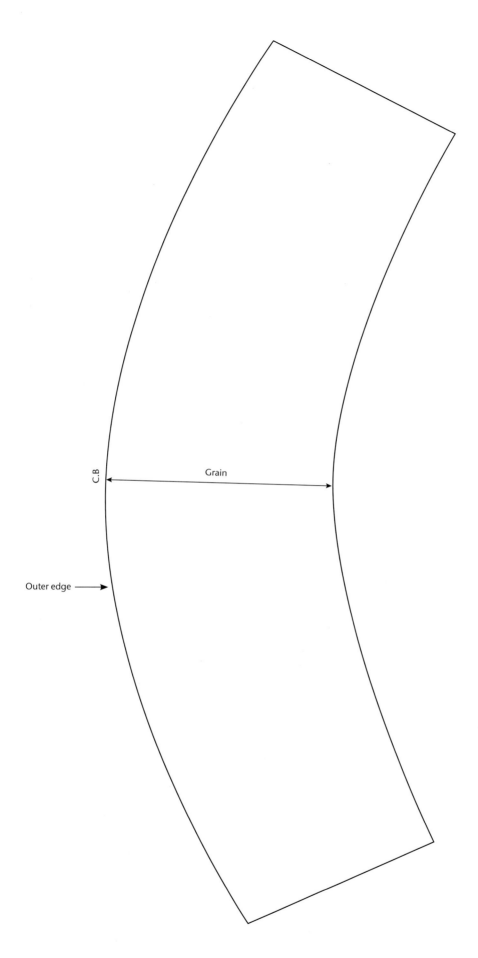

C.B

Grain

Outer edge ⟶

Template 7: back collar edge curve, to assist in drawing the collar onto the canvas when constructing a bespoke collar. Full-size.

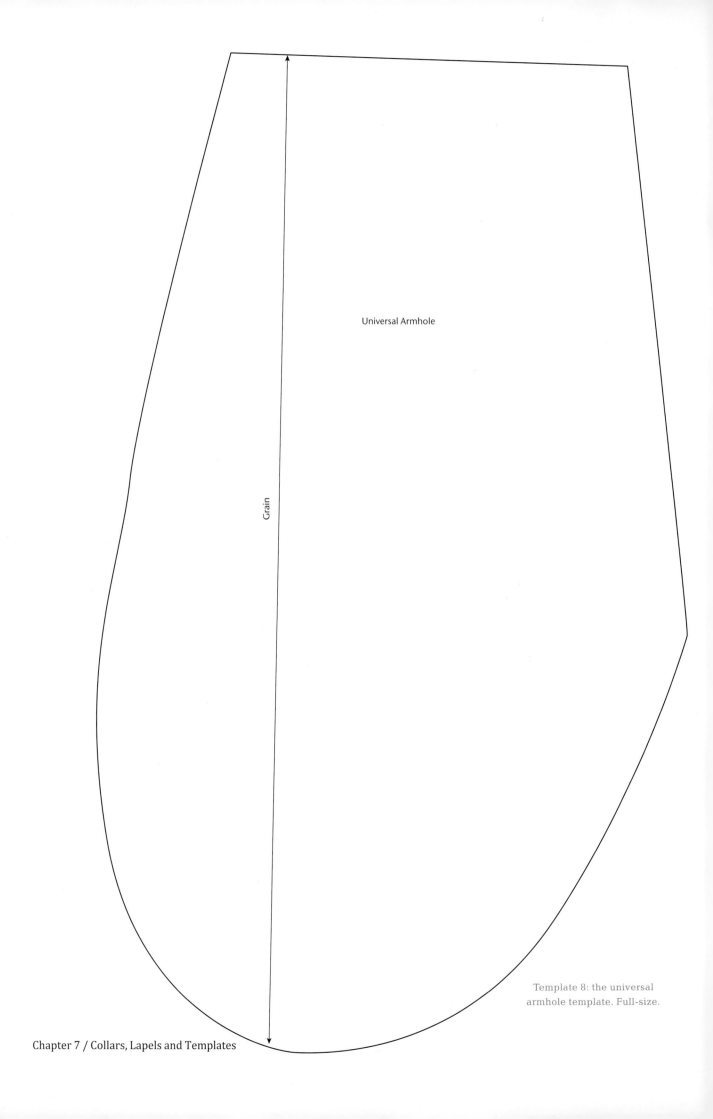

Universal Armhole

Grain

Template 8: the universal armhole template. Full-size.

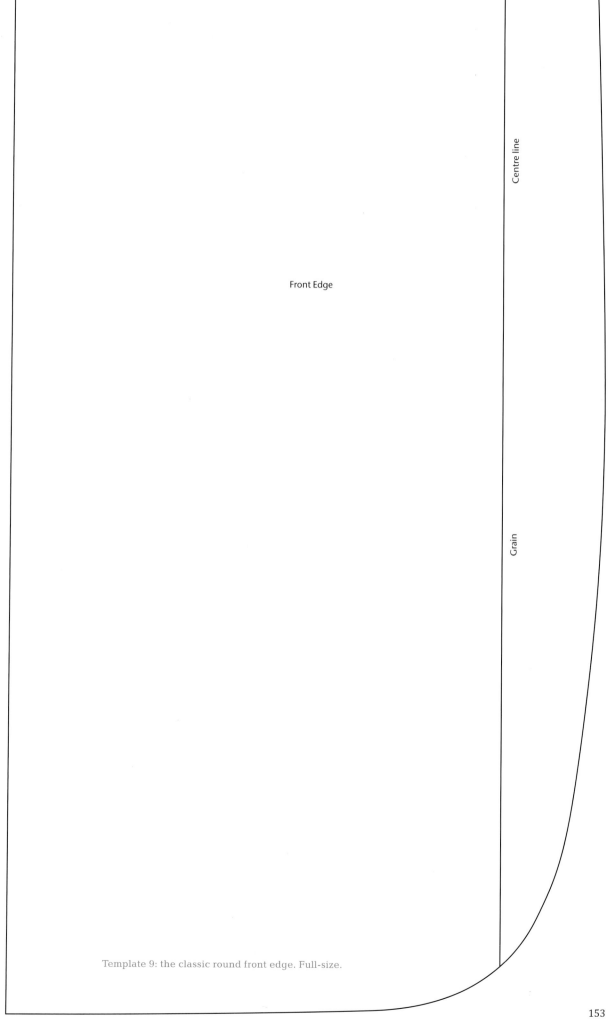

Front Edge

Centre line

Grain

Template 9: the classic round front edge. Full-size.

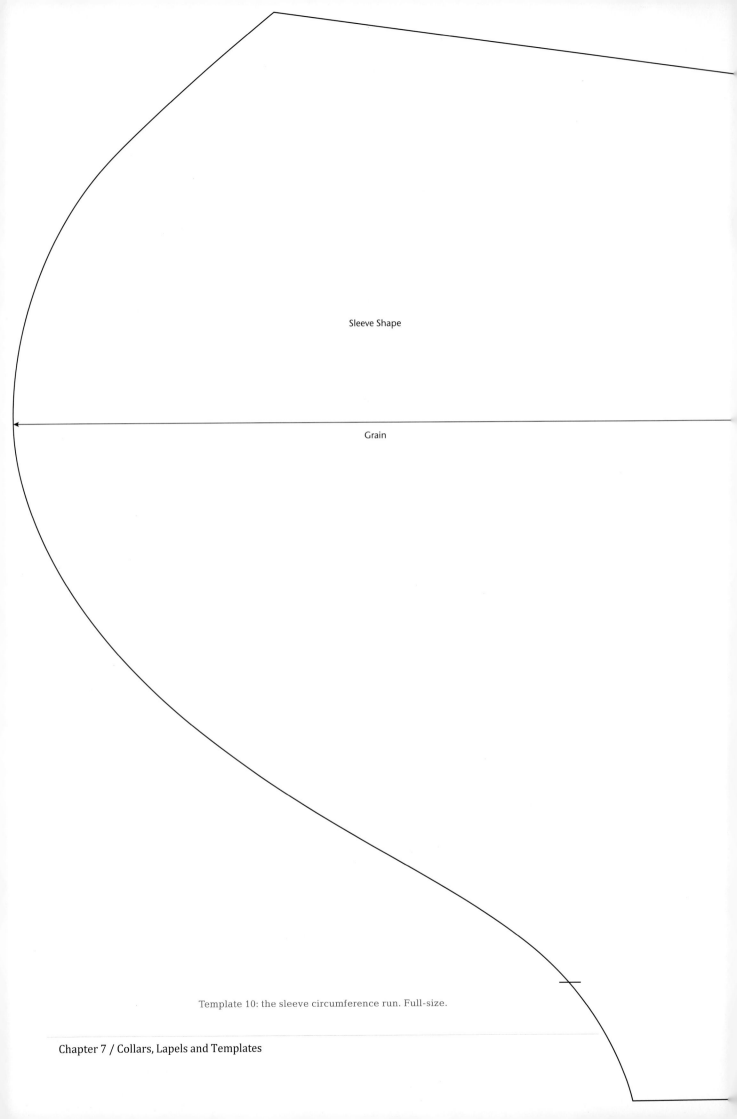

Sleeve Shape

Grain

Template 10: the sleeve circumference run. Full-size.

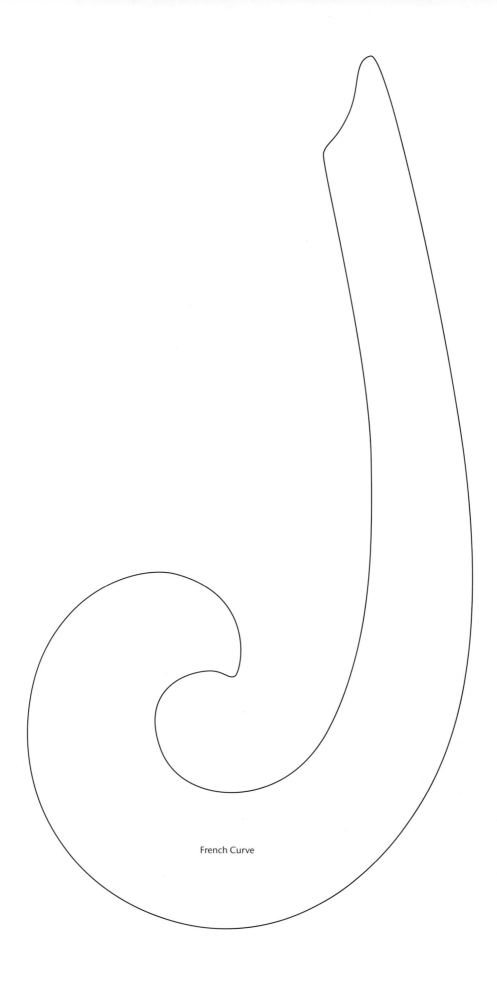

French Curve

Template 11: French curve. Quarter-scale.

Chapter 8
From a Basic Block to a Working Pattern

The purpose of this chapter is to transfer the blocks previously drafted into a functioning, workable pattern, by adding seam allowances, inlays, pocket details, linings, internal structures and interlinings. This part of the process is known as 'finishing the pattern': to prepare the pattern to be cut out into test fabric, or in cloth; to realize the jacket as a three-dimensional garment. An astonishing number of pieces make up the finished pattern of a tailored jacket; a pattern needs to be drafted for every single pocket piece, interlining, and lining.

Finishing the flat pattern

The method of construction depends greatly on how the pattern is finished off: traditional hand tailoring techniques require large inlays for the purpose of fitting and hand manipulation; machine methods require set seam allowances. The chapter describes both systems, and tricks from both practices can be combined to evolve your own procedures for developing and finishing the pattern, depending on the final outcome of the project.

For apprentices or students, it is advisable to practise as much as possible in muslin or test fabric; an experienced cutter will be able to judge at the draft stage whether the lines look true, and comprehensive, in keeping with their experience and observations of the wearer, and will adjust certain points accordingly. The divisional drafting system is a guideline after all and may need

Opposite page: Fig. 8.1 The finished patterns are placed, and the outline is marked with chalk. Wider inlays are added to the pieces for fitting and hand tailoring, and chopped in cloth.

personal adjustments for specific demands. Apprentices and students will need to prepare as much as possible by cutting calico toiles to check their lines and balance, and should avoid cutting directly into cloth until the pattern is correct. Even with plenty of inlays, sometimes this will not rescue a badly drafted pattern. Fashion-forward styles are more suited to pre-toiling, allowing more scope to try new things before committing to the real fabric, and while the systems do differ slightly, it is not unheard of to combine the two. Inlays can also be added into toiles to make small adjustments if necessary.

Adding seam allowances and inlays

The basic block should be retained as the master copy of the draft and used to trace all the pieces that make up the pattern. Once they are traced off, the pattern needs to be finished so that it can be cut out in cloth or calico, to make a jacket. The traced panels are net sewing lines, and seam allowances and inlays need to be added, so that a tailor, or sample machinist can construct the garment.

As a general rule ⅜" is the standard size for seam allowance added onto most net lines; more inches will be added where there is a hem line. At lines which are curved or edges that are machine bagged out, a ¼" seam allowance is recommended, as it will appear too thick if it is cut wider. Adding a seam allowance is easy, as all pattern masters, triangles and curves, metric or imperial, have ⅜"/1cm seam allowance indicators. Place the ⅜" line on the ruler on the net sewing line of the pattern and mark the seam.

Fig. 8.3 shows the single-breasted two-button blazer previously drafted

Fig. 8.2 Marking seam allowance with a pattern triangle, using the allowance indicator line.

with allocated seam allowances and inlays indicated. This is what transforms the draft into a working pattern that is ready to be sewn in calico as a toile, which will allow

157

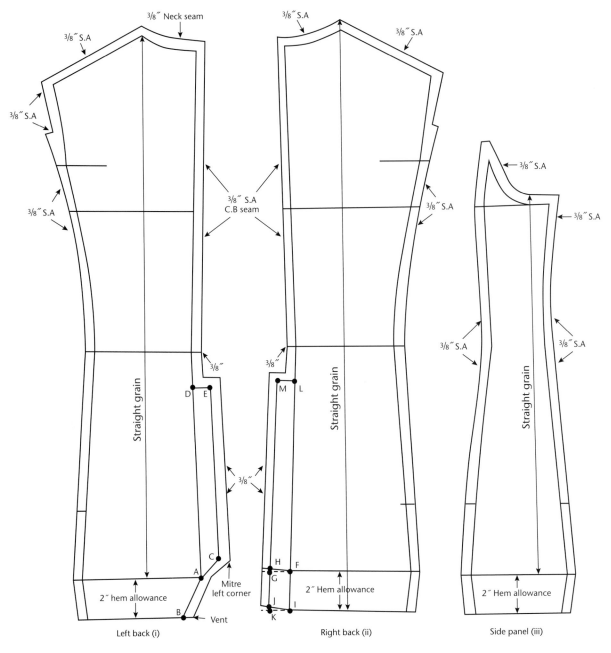

3/8″ Neck seam

3/8″ S.A

3/8″ S.A

3/8″ S.A

3/8″ S.A

3/8″ S.A
C.B seam

3/8″ S.A

3/8″ S.A

3/8″ S.A

3/8″ S.A

3/8″ S.A

Straight grain

Straight grain

Straight grain

3/8″

3/8″

D E

M L

3/8″

C

A

H F
G

Mitre
left corner

2″ hem allowance

2″ Hem allowance

2″ Hem allowance

B

J I
K

Vent

Left back (i)

Right back (ii)

Side panel (iii)

Above & Opposite page: Fig. 8.3 Traced off single-breasted blazer, with seam allowances, suited for ready-to-wear machine techniques. (i) Left back pattern. (ii) Right back pattern. (iii The side panel pattern. (iv) The forepart pattern. (v) The facing pattern. (vi) The under collar pattern. (Not to quarter scale)

the pattern maker to see the three-dimensional shape as a first prototype on a model or the dress form. It will take from one to three fittings to perfect the pattern with a series of adjustments, and is the accepted system for the more fashion-forward tailored styles.

Adding vents on the body and sleeve patterns

It is advisable for a back with a centre vent to trace a left back and a right back pattern. This can be achieved easily by flipping the back bodice

and marking the lines on both sides of the pattern, and tracing one left and one right side onto a clean sheet of paper. Depending on the cutting table being worked on, it may help to lay a clean sheet of white pattern paper underneath the draft, so the lines are more visible. Be careful to copy the lines accurately, with all balance notches and grain lines. When labelling the pattern, include 'RSU', meaning right side up, so that when the pieces are cut in cloth no mistakes are made: the right side of the pattern to be placed to the right side of the cloth.

In traditional menswear, the left side of the vent lies on top of the right side; in ladies' jackets, some pattern makers will switch the side the vent lays on, so that the right side lays on top. It is my personal style preference to keep a ladies' centre vent universal, and as androgynous as possible. Therefore, the ladies' vent follows the same direction as a man's jacket vent.

This can be observed in (Fig. 8.3) above: the left back section of the vent lies on top of the right back. On the left back, at points A, B and C, the corner of the vent and hem should be

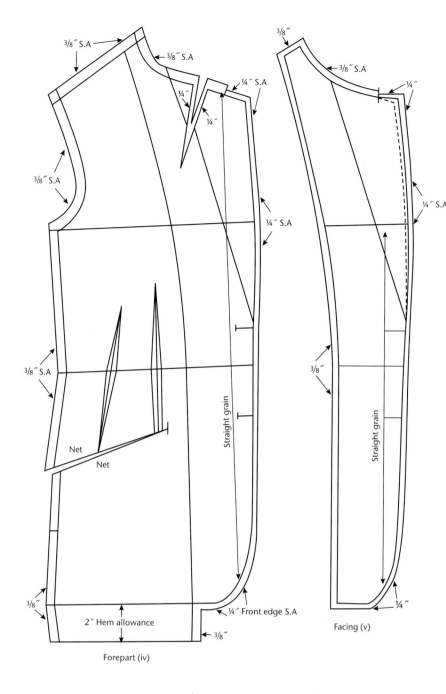

3/8″ S.A

3/8″ S.A

3/8″ S.A

1/4″

1/4″

1/4″ S.A

3/8″

3/8″ S.A

1/4″

3/8″ S.A

1/4″ S.A

1/4″ S.A

3/8″ S.A

3/8″ S.A

Straight grain

Straight grain

Net

Net

3/8″

1/4″

2″ Hem allowance

1/4″ Front edge S.A

3/8″

Forepart (iv)

Facing (v)

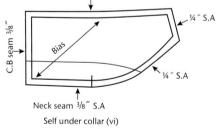

C.B seam 3/8″

Bias

1/4″ S.A

1/4″ S.A

Neck seam 3/8″ S.A

Self under collar (vi)

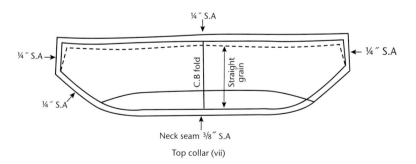

1/4″ S.A

1/4″ S.A

1/4″ S.A

1/4″ S.A

C.B fold

Straight grain

Neck seam 3/8″ S.A

Top collar (vii)

mitred to thin out the excess cloth, which can be too thick if it has not been cut away. The corner seam can be drawn directly onto the pattern, by folding back the vent and hem (points A–D), also shown in Fig. 8.5, where the corners have been folded in to mitre the left vent. This will represent the way it will be constructed, and draft a 45° seam angle from point A.

The dotted lines on Fig. 8.6 signify the corner seam, vent, and hem once the hem and vent have been folded and pressed. These lines are also necessary for drafting a lining pattern.

On the right back – Fig. 8.3 (ii) – the right side of the vent will lie under the left vent. The length will need to be raised ¼″ at points G to H and K to J, to shorten its length slightly. This is so that when the left vent lies on top of the right vent it does not peep below the hemline on the left side. This can look unsightly and cheapen the jacket.

All seams that are to be pressed open or flat require ⅜″ seam allowances. It is at the front edge of the forepart Fig. 8.3 (iv), that a ¼″ seam allowance will need to be added from the revere notch to the round of the front hem, where it meets the facing line. This is because the front edge and facing is machine bagged out during construction. Therefore the facing front edge has a ¼″ allowance.

The same applies to the outer edges of both the self-fabric under collar Fig. 8.3 (vi) and top collar (vii), also requiring a ¼″ seam allowance.

A hem allowance of 2″ for a ready-to-wear jacket is a good amount to add to the hemline. This allowance will allow the cutter to slightly adjust the length if needed, and allow the tailor to mark a smooth running hemline after the side panel seams have been machined.

As a final note, any line that is cut on the fold should be left as a net line, or cut as a full pattern, so that seam allowance is not added by mistake. For example, the top collar at the centre back line: both sides of the top collar from the C.B. have been traced off to avoid this.

As with the bodice of the blazer, the sleeves have ⅜″ seam allowances and a 2″ hem allowance.

Fig. 8.4 The centre vent construction.

Fig. 8.5 Folding the corner seam to mitre the left vent and trace through.

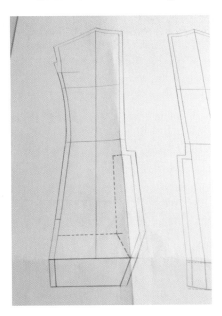

Fig. 8.6 The vent is folded back and the corners are mitred to reduce bulk when sewing.

The vent at the cuff is approached in the same manner as the centre back vent, left and right pattern. The cuff vent at the top sleeve is mitred, as it is the top side of the vent, and the cuff vent of the under sleeve is cut slightly shorter in length, as it is the under section.

Mark the position of the buttonholes, according to the number of buttons at the vent; traditionally four functioning buttons are used. The ligne size for a cuff button on tailored jackets is size 18.

To mark four buttonholes (Fig. 8.11):
The holes start ½″ back from the edge of the topside of the vent, marked parallel to this edge.
Point A: The bottom hole is marked 1½″ up from the hem; mark a line parallel to the hemline.
Point B: The distance between each hole: ⅝″.
Point C: The distance between each hole: ⅝″.
Point D: The distance between each hole: ⅝″.

The length of the buttonhole: ¾″.

Inlays for bespoke tailoring patterns

Typically for a bespoke tailored jacket a toile will not be made and it is cut directly into cloth, with several inches of inlay added to certain parts of the pattern, which will allow adjustments to be made during the fitting stages. This is because the styles are generally more classic in style, and fitting in the actual cloth directly to the wearer

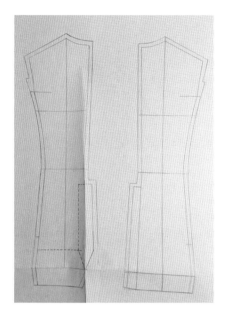

Fig. 8.7 The top side of the left vent, alongside the under section of the right vent.

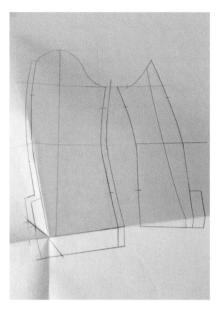

Fig. 8.8 Fold the hem and cuff of the top sleeve and mark a mitred seam.

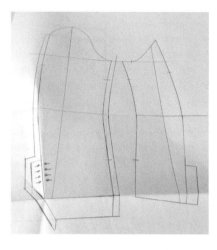

Fig. 8.9 The top sleeve with added seam allowance at the cuff vent.

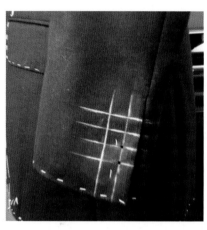

Fig. 8.10 The buttonholes marked onto the cuff of a jacket, before being sewn.

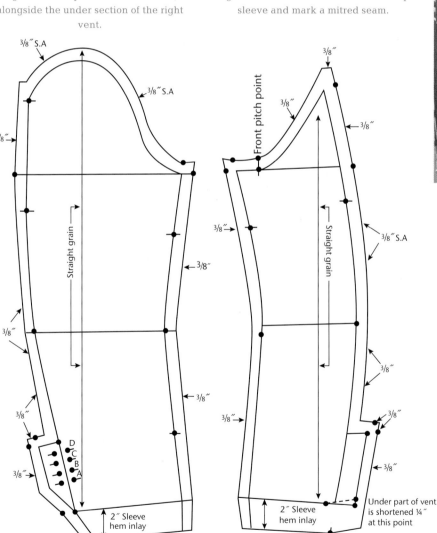

Fig. 8.11 The top sleeve and under sleeve traced off from the basic sleeve block as separate patterns, with seam allowances.

through a series of baste fittings is the preferred process practised on Savile Row, and by traditional tailors.

The inlay is cut away through a series of stages; and at the final stage a smaller inlay amount is left inside the finished jacket, so that it may be altered in time, as the wearer grows with the jacket. This allows the garment to be passed down through generations of the same family. The black dots in Fig. 8.12 represent the net sewing lines of the block before seam allowance has been added. The red dots indicate where a ³⁄₈″ seam allowance has been added and the blue dots show the inlay added.

For the purposes of this exercise, inlay has been shown on the pattern draft to indicate placement; usually it is marked directly onto the cloth, when cutting out, and is marked in chalk. It can be marked onto each pattern; it just makes it more difficult to mark the net sewing lines on the cloth. If

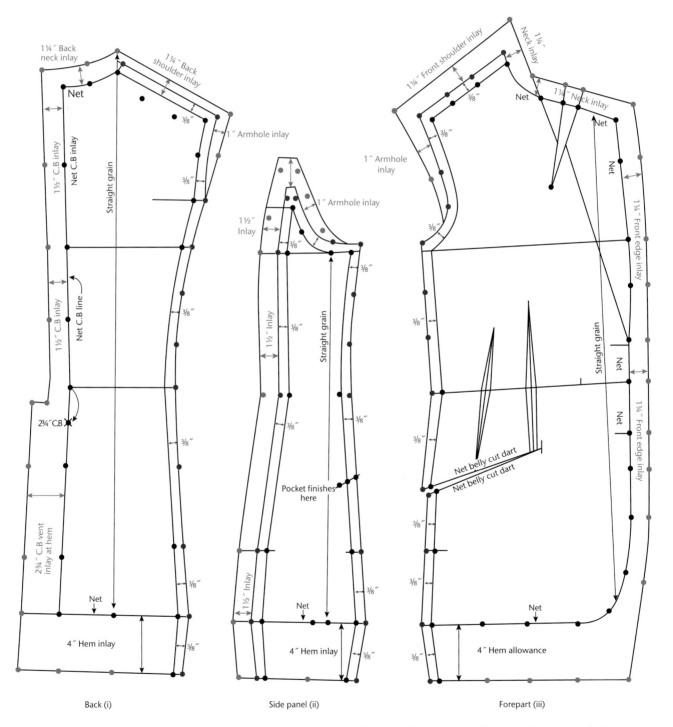

Fig. 8.12a Traced off single-breasted blazer with seam allowances and added inlays for bespoke tailoring techniques. (i) Back pattern. (ii) Side panel pattern. (iii) Forepart.

Chapter 8 / From a Basic Block to a Working Pattern

preferred, small holes can be punched along the sewing lines of the pattern for the purpose of making chalk marks, when chopping in fabric.

THE BACK PATTERN (Fig. 8.12 i)

On the back vent, it is not necessary to have separate right and left patterns; one pattern is used to cut one pair. This allows the tailor to re-cut the vents to their desired method of construction. At the centre back and back neck, no seam allowance is required; inlay is added directly on to the net line: 1½" at the C.B., to allow the back to be let out. If it is not utilized during the fitting stages it is re-cut to 1" by the tailor when the jacket is finished and remains inside.

At the back neck 1¼" inlay is applied and if not used up in the fitting is re-cut to ¾" at the finishing stage, as it supports the weight of the under collar canvas and melton helping the tailor to hand baste the collar onto the neckline; a series of vertical cuts in the inlay will allow the width to sit around the curve of the neckline.

At the back shoulder, in addition to the ⅜" seam allowance an extra 1¼" should be added. This is so that the shoulder balance can be adjusted, and once again, if it is not used up during fit stages, should be cut back to the ⅜" seam allowance edge at the finishing stage, so that the back shoulder can be eased into the front shoulder.

1" inlay is added to the ⅜" seam allowance at the armhole. This will also be cut away once the sleeve has been hand basted into the armhole, before inserting the sleeve head roll.

A regular ⅜" seam allowance is added to the side back; no inlay is needed at this point, as it is included onto the side panel.

Finally, the back hemline requires 4" inlay to allow the cutter to adjust the length. The final width is 2", which should be cut away at the very end, if the jacket is not lengthened throughout the fit stages.

THE SIDE PANEL (Fig. 8.12 ii)

The back seam of the side panel has ⅜" seam allowance and 1½" inlay to allow the blazer to be let out at the waist and hip area through the fitting stages. This inlay should be stretched at the waist with a heavy tailoring iron so that it does not distort the appearance of the waist with draglines. This is especially important for more fitted styles, and a small cut may need to be applied at the waist point. The finished inlay is ¾/1", if not used in fit stages, and will be left inside the final finished jacket, to allow it to still be let out if needed. The value depends on the waist suppression: for straighter styles 1" is fine; the more fitted the style is at the waist, the harder it is for the inlay to sit clean over the waist, so ¾" is advised.

At the front side seam only ⅜" is needed, since the hip pockets will be machined onto this seam, rendering it impossible to let out or take in.

A further 1" inlay on top of the seam allowance at the armhole assists the tailor to mark a smooth running armhole after the side seams have

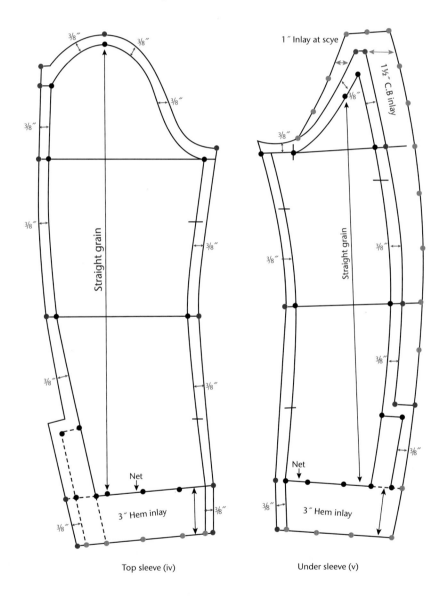

- ● = **Net lines of the pattern (taken from the basic block)**
- ● = **⅜ Seam allowance added to net lines**
- ● = **Inlay added to both net lines and seam allowance**

Fig. 8.12b Traced off sleeve patterns with seam allowances and inlays
(iv) Top Sleeve. (v) Under Sleeve.

been sewn. The inlay can be cut away after the sleeves go in.

Side panel hem inlay: 4″, to adjust the length.

THE FOREPART (Fig. 8.12 iii)

At the front edge of the forepart, the edge is net with 1¼″ inlay added so that the coat waist can be adjusted, and the width or height of the lapel can be determined in the fittings. This inlay is cut down to ¼″ when the jacket is ready to be finished and machined to the facing, after completion of all fit stages.

The front neckline is also net with 1¼″ inlay, which is helpful for altering the balance and supporting the weight of the under collar. The centre of the neck dart should be cut up after it has been chopped out in cloth.

At the front shoulder a ⅜″ seam allowance is included, with 1¼″ shoulder inlay to adjust the front balance if needed.

The armhole has 1″ inlay on top of a ⅜″ seam allowance, which smoothens to nothing where the curve of the armhole graduates in at the chest.

At the side of the forepart, which sews to the side panel, a ⅜″ seam allowance is added, but no inlay, as there is a pocket machined at the hip. The dart in the pocket, also known as the belly cut, is left as a net line with no seam allowance. When chopping in cloth, cut directly on those lines and up the centre of the first dart, leaving the closed dart as marked.

The hem, as with the other pieces is net with a 4″ inlay.

THE UNDER SLEEVE (Fig. 8.12 iv)

At the underarm seam ⅜″ seam allowance is added; no inlay is required, to make it easier to seam the underarm of the top sleeve and ease in the fullness, which is pre-stretched with the tailoring iron.

On the hind arm seam a regular ⅜″ seam allowance is added, plus 1½″. This is necessary to adjust the size of the sleeve, with a further 1″ inlay around the scye allowing the sleeve to be let out or taken in accordingly.

The hem allowance is 3″, in case extra sleeve length is needed, and will be re-cut to 2″ at the finishing stage.

THE TOP SLEEVE (Fig. 8.12 v)

The underarm seam has ⅜″ seam allowance. As this seam is stretched with the iron before sewing, inlay would render this task impossible.

At the hind arm, a ⅜″ seam allowance is added, and no inlay is required; it can be added if the cutter is unsure the pattern will fit well enough.

There is no inlay applied at the sleeve circumference, as it would be unpractical to sew the top sleeve with a wide inlay, so the regular ⅜″ seam allowance is all that is required.

The hem allowance is 3″, in case extra sleeve length is needed, and will be re-cut to 2″ at the finishing stage.

Internal linings

The jacket should have an internal lining to cover the seam allowances, body canvas and internal trimmings. Normally cut in shiny silk or twill lining, the colour will be tonal to the suiting, or it may contrast, as desired.

There are several ways to construct a lining, depending on the method of construction for the market level.

A bespoke lining pattern will be cut with extra inches in length and width added to the back, side panel and forepart pattern, so that is not too tight, then hand basted onto the jacket panel by panel. Extra fullness, so that the lining is not too tight, is hand tacked through the waist area.

Ready-to-wear linings are machined into the jacket, and smaller values are added in width and length. The pattern is always taken from the master draft of the jacket pattern.

Bespoke tailors will not need to make a pattern of the lining, they will simply place lining and cut around the forepart, side panel, back and sleeves.

Fig. 8.13a shows the forepart already seamed to the side panel, and placed by the tailor directly onto the pre-shrunken lining, which should be on the double. This requires experience, and I would recommend placing the pieces without seaming the side or darts, if trying out this method.

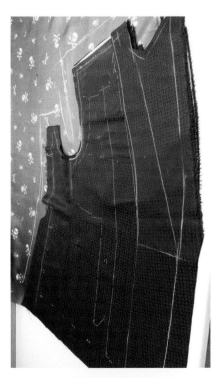

Figs 8.13a & b Creating a bespoke lining does not require a pattern. Tailors place the pieces of a wool forepart and side panel directly onto pre-shrunken lining and uses these as a template to mark the outline of the body and facing, in chalk.

Inlays, and seam lines are then chalked around the outline of the body and front edge, to mark a separate facing in cloth. All darts, balance points, chest

Fig. 8.14 The facing and lining outlines as previously marked are then chopped with shears.

Fig. 8.15 The back body placed onto lining and cut around with additional widths of inlay.

Fig. 8.16 Theback lining pieces.

pleat and in-breast pockets are also indicated; before removing the outer layer of the jacket (Fig. 8.13b) to reveal the outline of the pieces, which are then chopped using the tailoring shears (Fig. 8.14).

At least 1½" extra inlay is included onto the shoulder inlay already included on to the body, and 2" at the side panel back seam, so that it can also be amended throughout the bespoke fitting process, and recut where needed. The hem can be cut in line with the 4" hem inlay.

The back body is also treated in the same way (Figs. 8.15 and 8.16), placed onto the lining at the fold line on the centre back. 1½" is also added at the shoulder, centre back seam for the inclusion of a back pleat, and at the vent, whether it be on the side or centrally.

Repeat the instructions for the under sleeve, and top sleeve (Figs 8.17 and 8.18), allowing extra height at at the crown (¾") and through the hind arm seams (¾").

Adding inlays into the lining allows the tailor to manipulate the lining by hand (fig 8.19), and recut after basting together. This method of construction is only suitable for bespoke tailoring/

Left: Fig. 8.18 The top sleeve is placed onto the lining and extra inlay is added at the hem and crown.

Right: Fig. 8.18 The top sleeve in cloth and sleeve lining placed side by side.

Fig. 8.19 Bespoke linings are hand basted into position.

haute couture methods using hand construction only, not machine. Machined internal linings are appropriate for ready-to-wear techniques and the lining requires an exact pattern taken from the basic block.

The excess inlay helps the tailor to hand baste the lining into the body with extra length in the waist, which stops the lining from shrinking too much, avoiding tightness. The lining is hand stitched into the jacket before attaching the shoulder seam. The seams are hand felled, and white bastes removed when the jacket is finished, shown in Fig. 8.13.

TRACING AN EXACT LINING PATTERN FROM THE S.B. DRAFT (Fig. 8.20)

For ready-to-wear techniques an exact lining pattern should be drafted, and the basic block is used to construct the new pattern. A pattern can be made using this system for a bespoke jacket as well. The principles of drafting a bespoke or ready-to-wear lining is based on the same theory: linings are functional and should conceal the internal construction. Their insertion should not hinder or distort the balance of the jacket, or movements of the wearer. The pieces of the lining are machined into the jacket.

The system described is intended for ready-to-wear machined linings that are pre-shrunk using an industrial steam iron; if the lining is not steamed before inserting into the jacket, it will shrink, and will be too tight for the body of the jacket. The lining increase values documented are a guideline – they can be adjusted to increase the size and width, if the lining is not steamed before insertion – but as a rule, all linings should be shrunk using the steam iron, whether the construction is by hand or machine.

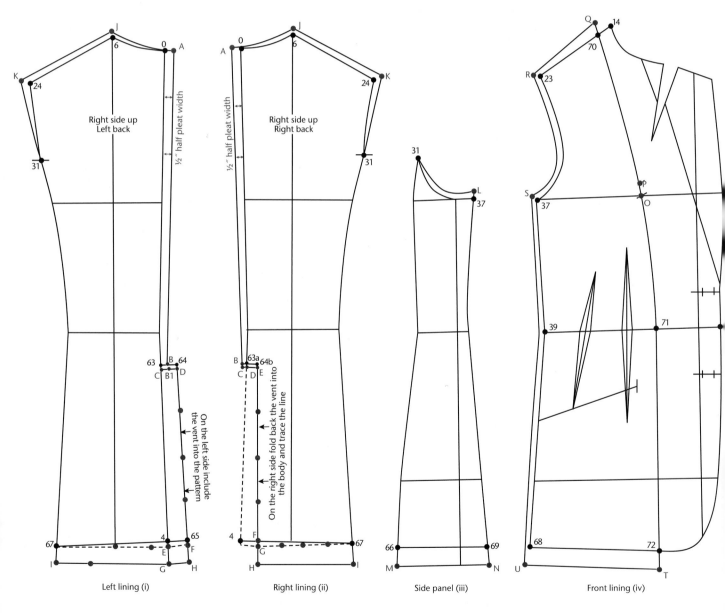

Above & Opposite: Fig. 8.20 Plotting the points of a lining pattern using the draft of the single-breasted blazer. Points of the lining are indicated with red dots, and the original lines of the block with black dots. (i) Left back lining pattern. (ii) Right back lining pattern. (iii) The side panel lining pattern. (iv) The forepart lining pattern.

For the purposes of this example, a lining pattern has been drafted from the S.B. two-button jacket pattern, with a centre vent.

THE BACK LINING

At the centre back of the lining a 1″ total pleat should always be added to aid movement of the shoulder blades, and shrinkage of the lining. If this is not added, the lining can hinder movement while wearing the jacket. Sometimes the outer shell will even distort if the lining is too tight, therefore a C.B. pleat is absolutely necessary. How this is applied depends greatly on the style of back.

BACK LINING WITH CENTRE VENT

The left back lining (Fig. 8.20i)

A back with a centre vent is a little more complicated and requires a left and right back lining pattern. To draft the left back, see diagram (i) on Fig. 8.20. Trace the reverse side of the original net S.B. back, with added centre vent to acquire the left side.

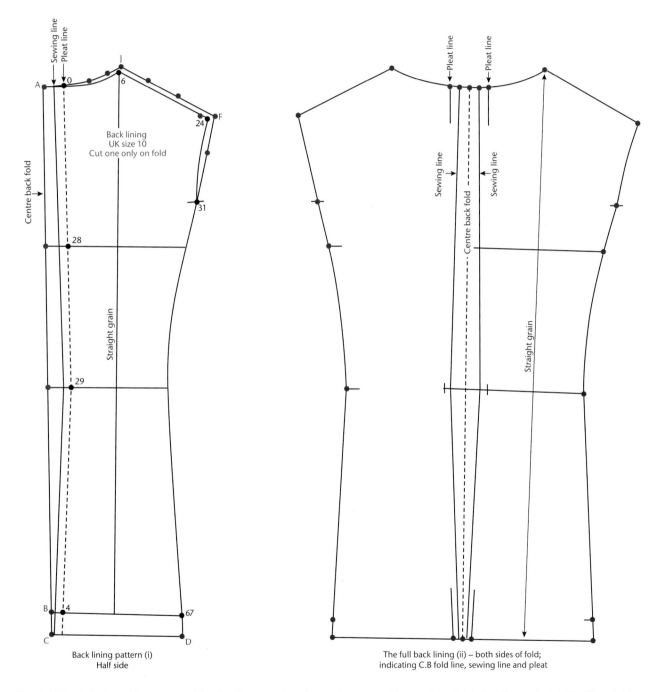

Back lining pattern (i)
Half side

The full back lining (ii) – both sides of fold;
indicating C.B fold line, sewing line and pleat

Fig. 8.21 Back lining with no vents. A back with no vents only requires one pattern, cut on the fold at the centre back with a pleat running the entire length of the seam. (i) The back lining pattern. (ii) The back lining, showing both sides of the fold.

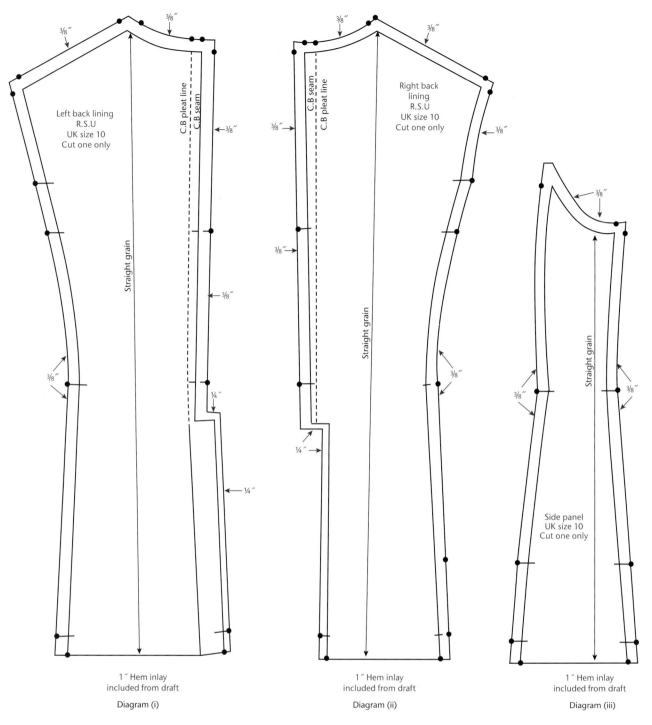

Diagram (i)

Left back lining
R.S.U
UK size 10
Cut one only

Straight grain

C.B pleat line
C.B seam

3/8″
3/8″
3/8″
3/8″
1/4″
1/4″
1/4″

1″ Hem inlay
included from draft

Diagram (ii)

C.B seam
C.B pleat line

Right back
lining
R.S.U
UK size 10
Cut one only

Straight grain

3/8″
3/8″
3/8″
3/8″
1/4″

1″ Hem inlay
included from draft

Diagram (iii)

Side panel
UK size 10
Cut one only

Straight grain

3/8″
3/8″
3/8″

1″ Hem inlay
included from draft

Above & Opposite: Fig. 8.22 Traced off full body lining patterns with added seam allowances.
(i) Left back lining. (ii) Right back lining. (iii) The side panel lining. (iv) The front lining.

A from 0

At the centre back of the neck, mark
half the pleat width: ½".

B from 63

At the top of the centre back vent
mark ¼", the half pleat width. Rule a
line from A to B.

Lining a vent to look clean from the
outside can be tricky, and if length is
not added into the lining pattern, it will
twist the balance of the vent, making
it appear unsightly on the wearer.

Points C from 63, Bi from B and D from
64 represent where ¼" length has
been added to address this common
problem.

This will add ¼" length through the
centre back lining seam, so that it will
not pull too tight. A further ¼" is added
at points E from 4 and F from 65.

The net hemline is identified by point
67, and newly lengthened points E and F.
Extra inlay should be added to the hem
– a value between 1" and 3" will suffice
– and the tailor will re-mark and cut the

hem of the lining, when the final hem
length of the blazer has been determined.
In the example 1" inlay has been added
to G from E, H from F, I from 67.

At the back shoulder extra height
is added to allow ease of movement
across the shoulder blades. Therefore,
points J from 6 and K from 24 are 3/8".
Re-draw the back shoulder between
K and J, and the back neck between J
and A, and back armhole from nothing
at point 31 to point K.

The pattern should be labelled as

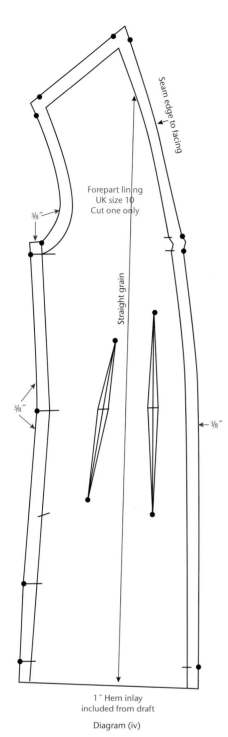

Seam edge to facing

Forepart lining
UK size 10
Cut one only

3/8"

3/8"

Straight grain

3/8"

3/8"

1" Hem inlay
included from draft

Diagram (iv)

A from 0
At the centre back of the neck mark
half the pleat width: ½".

B from 63
Mark ¼", the half pleat width. Rule a
line from A to B.
Fold back the vent along the centre
back seam at points 63a and 64b.
Trace the line onto the body.
Points C, D and E are where ¼" added
length has been included.

G from F
¼" added length at the net hem.
Re-draw the net hem from nothing at
point 67 to point G.

H from G, and I from 67
1" inlay.

J from 6 and K from 24
3/8". Re-draw the back shoulder
between points K and J; the back neck
between points J and A; and back
armhole from nothing at point 31 to
point K.
Label the pattern as 'right side up'.

BACK LINING WITH NO VENTS
(Fig. 8.21)
A back with no vents only requires
one pattern, and is straightforward to
draft and construct. The pattern is cut
on the fold at the centre back.

To draft the back lining without a vent:
Trace the back from the S.B. two-
button jacket draft. The black dots
indicate the key points from the
original draft. Mark the 1" pleat width
at the centre back neck (A from 0) to
½" at the hem (B from 4).

1" extra length is applied at the
hem (points C from B and D from 67),
and extra height through the shoulder
(3/8"), so that the lining is not too tight,
allowing ease of movement.

Diagram (ii) shows the full back
lining pattern, cut on the fold,
indicated by the dotted line in the
centre. Only one piece of lining is
required. It also indicates the sewing
line and balance points for where to
crease the pleat.

THE SIDE PANEL (Fig. 8.20iii)
To draft the side panel trace the net
S.B. side panel jacket pattern and indi-
cate original key points and numbers.

L from 37
Add 3/8" at the underarm point and
re-draw the armhole back to nothing
at point 31.

M from 66, and N from 69.
1" hem inlay.

No extra width is added to the seams;
however, for larger sizes, add ¼"
between each size code increase, at
line 66 and 31. This is not necessary
for smaller sizes, as the excess will
crease the lining, making it look
unsightly.

THE FOREPART (Fig. 8.20iv)
To draft the forepart lining, trace off
the net forepart pattern and indicate
original key points. It helps to simplify
the front pattern as much as possible.
Therefore, remove the dart in the belly
cut of the pocket position, and convert
the first dart closest to the front edge
to a closed dart as shown.
Point O is identified on the bust line
where it crosses the facing. In the
general area of the bust point it is
advisable to add a bust pleat.

P from O
1" bust pleat.

Q from 70
1" length added to compensate for the
added bust pleat.

R from 23
Add 3/8" at the shoulder ends.

S from 37
Add 3/8" at the front underarm point.
Add an additional 3/8" at the side seam.

T from 72, and U from 68
1" hem inlay.

To finish the lining pattern trace off
the individual pattern pieces and
add seam allowance. Fig. 8.22 shows
allocation of seam allowances.

'right side up', to avoid confusion when
cutting the pattern into lining. Mistakes
can happen in a busy cutting room, and
it helps to identify the right side of the
pattern (meaning right side of pattern
to be placed to right side of fabric).

The right back lining (Fig. 8.20ii)
To draft the right back lining.
Trace off the original net S.B. back
jacket pattern, with centre vent folded
inside, and key landmark points
indicated as shown in (ii).

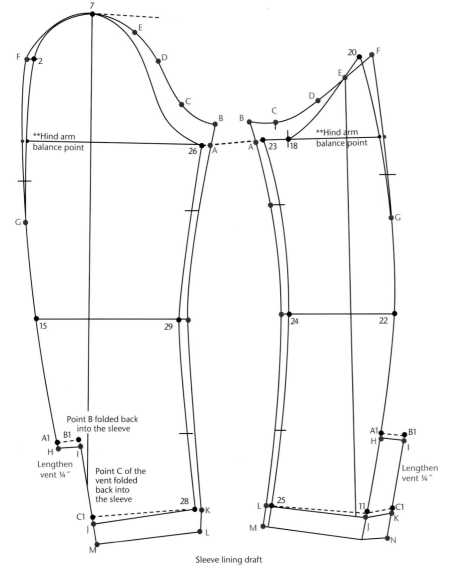

F from 2
Square out from point 2 in a 90° line: ⅛" width. Smooth the line with a vary form curve back into the hind arm seam to nothing at point G, 6" below the hind arm balance point.

A1
Fold in the placket extension, where the cuff vent will start, and trace the cuff line (B1 and C1), repeating the same instructions as with the centre vent on the back lining pattern, and continue the line down to the hem.

H from A1
Extra length through the vent lining needs to be added, to prevent the lining from being too tight: ¼"

I from B1, and J from C1
¼" added vent length.

K from 28
Cuff width: ⅛". Re-draw the underarm seam with the vary form curve back to points A and B.

L from K and M from J
Added extra length: 1".

The under sleeve
Start at point 23 at the underarm point and extend out a 90° line by ¼" to point A.

B from A
Raise the underarm point, to allow ease of movement of the arm: 1", to match what was drafted on the top sleeve.
Smooth the curve of the circumference run through points C, D and E, and extending out to point F, past point 20 if needed. At this point it is advisable to re-measure the new sleeve circumference, starting at point F on the top sleeve to point B; then from point B on the under sleeve (mark point C as the exact front pitch measurement: 1¼") and to point 20. Only extend past point 20 if the sleeve is too small for the armhole.
Measure the line from the hind arm balance level, to point F on the top sleeve; this measurement must be the

Fig. 8.23 The sleeve lining pattern. The lining points plotted with red dots on the original draft of the top and under sleeve.

The principles for creating the sleeve lining are similar to that of the front, side panel and back lining.

The top sleeve
Trace a copy from the original draft of the top sleeve and under sleeve onto a large sheet of pattern paper. The original number points have been indicated with black dots, and the lining points are represented with red dots. At the top sleeve, start at point 26 at the underarm point and extend out a 90° line by ¼" to point A.

B from A
Raise the underarm point, to allow ease of movement of the arm: 1". Raising at point B will also reduce the depth of the sleeve height, helping to minimize the ease value. Smooth the curve of the circumference through points C, D and E, back into point 7 at the centre of the top sleeve. The sleeve template (template 10) can be used to re-draw the top sleeve shape. The new fullness value for the top sleeve lining is 1".

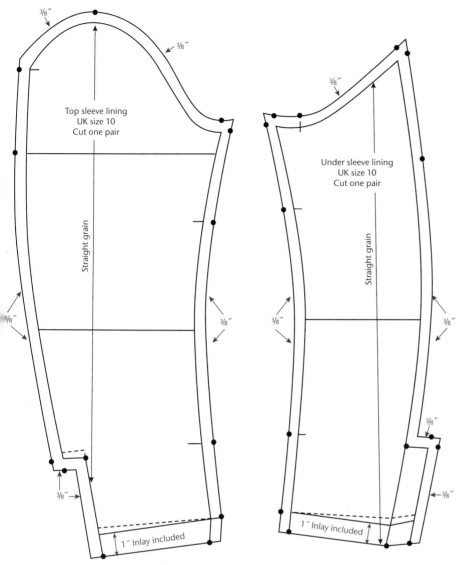

Traced off sleeve lining with seam allowances

Fig. 8.24 The sleeve lining pattern. The top sleeve and under sleeve lining are traced with seam allowances.

construction, and to prevent wear and tear over time, maintaining the longevity of the blazer. Canvases are always cut into body canvas, with horsehair chest piece and covered with soft felt. A body canvas can be full body, meaning it is cut the entire length of the front blazer, or a floating canvas, where it is inserted at the shoulder and finishes above the chest. For a softer looking blazer a floating canvas is better, and for a more structured front use a full-length canvas with horsehair at the chest.

THE STRUCTURED FULL BODY CANVAS

The full body canvas is sandwiched between the lining and the suiting. The purpose is to retain the structure of the forepart of the jacket, which is not always the shape of the wearer; clever pattern making and hand moulding can transform a person's shape. With the addition of an extra dart the bust will appear fuller, and an extra layer at the shoulder will create a stronger shoulder line: thus the canvas is the foundation of the desired silhouette.

Fig. 8.25 Jacket forepart with hand basted internal canvas.

same on the under sleeve, which will also determine the location of point F. Smooth point F with a vary form curve back into the hind arm seam to nothing at point G, 6″ below the hind arm balance point.

H from A1
Extra length through the vent lining needs to be added, to prevent the lining from being too tight: ¼″.

I from B1
¼″ added vent length.

J from 11, and K from C1
¼″ added vent length.

L from 25
Extra cuff width: ⅛″.

M from L, and N from K
Added extra hem length: 1″.
Trace the patterns (Fig. 8.23) and add ⅜″ seam allowances. No additional hem allowance is needed, as 1″ inlay has already been included while drafting the lining pattern.

The internal support of the blazer: body canvas and interlinings

Body canvas and interlinings are essential to reinforce the jacket, to maintain its structure during

Full body canvas (i)

(iii) Soft felt chest piece

(ii) Hair cloth chest piece

Fig. 8.26 The full body canvas is essential to reinforce the jacket, and is cut into several layers of canvas and hair -cloth to maintain structure through wear and tear.
(i) Full body canvas - covers the full length of the blazer.

Fig. 8.27 Internal canvas layers: (ii) Hair cloth used for the chest piece and shoulder support. (iii) Soft felt to cover the hair cloth in the chest. For darker cloths the felt covering is black; for paler cloths the felt is white.

Fig. 8.28 The tailor makes up the layers of body canvas, fixing them together with hand pad stitching, for a softer chest; or machined zig zag embroidery stitch for a firm chest. The darts are closed with linen pieces, and the shape of the bust is then moulded using a heavy tailoring iron.

Fig. 8.29 The tailor hand bastes the canvas into the forepart of the jacket, with a series of uniformed rows of stitching, in white basting cotton.

KEY COMPONENTS
OF A FULL BODY CANVAS

Hair canvas covers the full length of the front of the jacket, and is softer in hand feel than the hair cloth. Hair cloth is firm, and covers the chest area to add extra support. Both hair cloth and hair canvas contain hairs from the manes and tails of horses; making them agreeable and easily shaped by hand and pressure applied from a heavy tailoring iron.

The difference between the hair cloth and hair canvas is the amount of hair in the fabric: hair cloth has significantly more hair interwoven than the hair canvas. An extra piecing is cut to support the shoulder, also in the hair cloth. As horsehair fabrics can be uncomfortable and scratchy for the wearer, due to the coarse and wiry hair texture, the chest piece is covered with soft felt, and as long as the hair cloth is cut ¼" from the edge, it will be

encased within the felt. Over time, some hairs may wear through the felt and poke through the lining. When this happens it is best to undo the front lining to get back inside and trim the hair short; some tailors will burn the ends with a cigarette lighter! But this should be exercised with extreme caution, and should not be carried out as recommended practice to remove the hairs.

Four separate pattern pieces make up the canvas (Fig. 8.30). Piece 1 is the

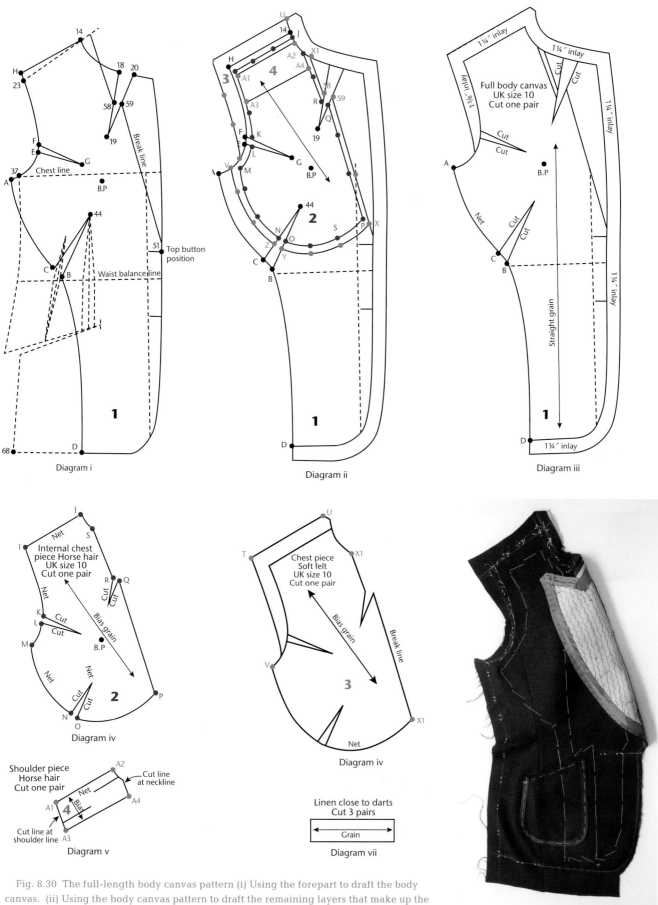

Fig. 8.30 The full-length body canvas pattern (i) Using the forepart to draft the body canvas. (ii) Using the body canvas pattern to draft the remaining layers that make up the canvas. (iii) Full body canvas pattern. (iv) Internal horse hair chest pattern piece. (v) Internal horse hair shoulder pattern piece. (vi) Chest pattern piece for felt covering. (vii) Linen strip pattern piece.

Fig. 8.31a The forepart of a tailored jacket with canvas basted into position.

Fig. 8.31b The tailor will secure and shape the lapel by hand pad stitching roll between each row of stitching.

foundation of the canvas, and should be marked on the straight grain of the fabric. To draft the canvas pattern, trace the forepart of the S.B. two-button blazer (Fig. 8.30 i) and mark the following pivotal points.

PLOTTING THE LINES OF THE FULL CANVAS, USING THE S.B. (Fig. 8.30i) TWO-BUTTON DRAFT (i)
Draw in the net front edge, neckline, neck dart, shoulder, armhole and hem. The dotted line indicates the net sewing lines of the forepart pattern. Designate all key balance points:

waist, break line, button positions and bust point. These will also need to be transferred onto the hair canvas in chalk, when it is eventually cut out.

A from 37
Mark ½" past the front seam.
Point B is suggested ¼" above the waist balance line next to the second dart.

C from B
The value of both waist darts added together at the exact waist balance line is 1".
Draw in the new waist dart and joint to point 44 (the original end of the front dart point).

D from 68
The canvas should not cover the entire front. On the example, measure 5" from 68 along the hemline. Join point D to C with the vary form curve. Begin at point D with a 90° straight angle and gradually curve a smooth line. Continue the line from points C to A, curving outward.

E from 37
Optional armhole dart. Adding an additional dart can create a more structured chest, giving the illusion of a fuller bust. It is important to have the bust point of the canvas positioned perfectly on the bust point of the wearer, otherwise this can create the illusion of a wide bust, almost barrel-like in appearance if it is positioned incorrectly. The standard size of the dart is ⅜". Add

⅛" for every larger size above the standard UK 10 (US size 6).

E from G and F from G
Length of the dart: 3⅛". Point G should be positioned centrally between the dart ends 44 and 19. It can also can be calculated by measuring ½" above the chest line.

H from 23
Extend past the shoulder vertically by the value of the armhole dart, ⅜". If this is not done the canvas will be ⅜" shorter than the shoulder end when the dart is closed with linen.

TRACE OFF THE FULL CANVAS; USE TO DRAFT THE CHEST, SHOULDER, AND FELT PIECES (Fig. 8.30ii)
Trace off the net lines of the body canvas. Inlay needs to be included at the following seams:

- Front edge continuing into point D at the hem: 1¼"
- Front neck: 1¼"
- Front shoulder: 1¼"
- Front armhole: 1⅜" at the shoulder end to nothing before armhole curves in at the chest line.

The canvas inlays will be cut back to the net lines, after it has been hand basted into the fronts of the blazer and secured with rows and rows of pad stitching at the lapel, and at the pocket bag.

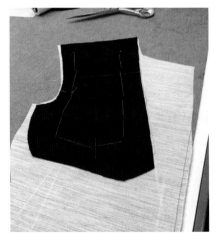

Figs. 8.32a and 8.32b An example of the floating chest canvas, with all layers hand basted together. This differs as it is cut higher above the waist.

Fig. 8.33 Hand pad stitched canvas.

Draft the points that will be piece 2: the hair cloth chest piece, represented by red dots.

I from H and J from 14

The hair cloth should sit ⅜″ below the net shoulder line and inside of the net armhole, this so that the hairs will not scratch the wearer. Mark the new shoulder line.

K from F and L from E

Dart ends on the hair cloth: ⅜″ inside of the net armhole.

M from A

The hair cloth is cut 1⅝″ inside of the underarm point at A. Mark the new armscye through points M, L, K and I. From point M, re-draw the outer curve of the chest piece.

N from C, and O from B

2″ from the outer edge of the body canvas.
Join point O to N and M.

P

Approximately ⅜″ back from the break line and 2″ above the top button position.

S from X1, and Q from 59 and R from 58

The chest canvas sits ⅜″ inside the break line at the neck darts. Draw in the new break line for piece 2 between points S, R, Q and P.

Plot the points for piece 3 – the soft felt, indicated with blue dots. The idea is to cut the pattern slightly bigger than the hair cloth chest piece, so that it does not finish edge to edge and irritate the skin of the wearer. Points T and U are marked on the edge of the 1¼″ inlay at the shoulder ends.

V from A

At the underarm point V is marked ¾″ in from A. Follow the curve of the armscye around the armhole and edge of the armhole inlay back into point T at the shoulder inlay edge.

X from 51

1″ above the top button position.

Y from B and Z from C

1⅛″. Join points V, Z, Y and X with a curved line.

Re-draw the break line between points X and X1 with a straight line, still including the value of the darts. Mark a shoulder support (piece 4), indicated with yellow dots.

A1 from I, and A2 from J

Step the edge of the shoulder piece from the edge of the chest piece: ⅜″. Draw in the shoulder line between points A1 and A2.

A3 from A1, and A4 from A2

The width of the shoulder piece: approximately 2″.

THE CANVAS PIECES TRACED OFF AS SEPARATE PATTERNS (Fig. 8.30iii-vii)
Trace off the four individual pattern pieces as separate patterns. On piece 4 (diagram v), two cut lines have been added in to the shoulder piece to allow ease of movement over the shoulder bone and at the cut line. These cuts are then spread open, when basted to piece 2 (iv).

All layers are hand basted together with the shoulder piece, and covered with the soft felt on top (piece 3vi).

Rows of hand pad stitching are stitched to secure all layers for a softer feeling chest; machine stitching with a zig zag embroidery stitch will also work if preferred and this creates a firmer bust line.

The darts in the hair cloth and hair canvas are cut open to the end of the darts, after all layers have been stitched. They are then closed with pieces of rectangular linen, and stitched back and forward over the linen to secure.

The size of the linen pieces should be 6″× 1½″ (Fig. 8.30vii), and are cut away once machined and closed.

A bridle is also required (Fig. 8.36a), and is stitched along the break line for extra support. The piece is cut in lining on the straight grain and should be cut from the top of the break line and finish about 1″ above the top button position. In the example the bridle measures 12⅜″ × 1½″. Indicate points A, B and C along the break line and top buttonhole.

E from D

1½″. Rule across from point A to E (¾″) and to point D (¾″).

F from C

½″. A total of 1″ above the top buttonhole, indicated as point B.

G from F

¾″. Join points D and G and E and F with a straight line parallel to the break line.

Trace the bridle pattern as a net pattern. No seam allowance is required.

Another canvas enforcement is sandwiched in between the fabric of the forepart lapel and canvas to support the point of the lapel shape, (Fig. 8.36b). The piece is cut in cotton silesia or linen, depending on the desired firmness of the lapel. The

Fig. 8.34 Darts are cut and closed. With linen. Inside view.

Fig. 8.35 Darts are closed with strips of linen and stitched over. Outer view.

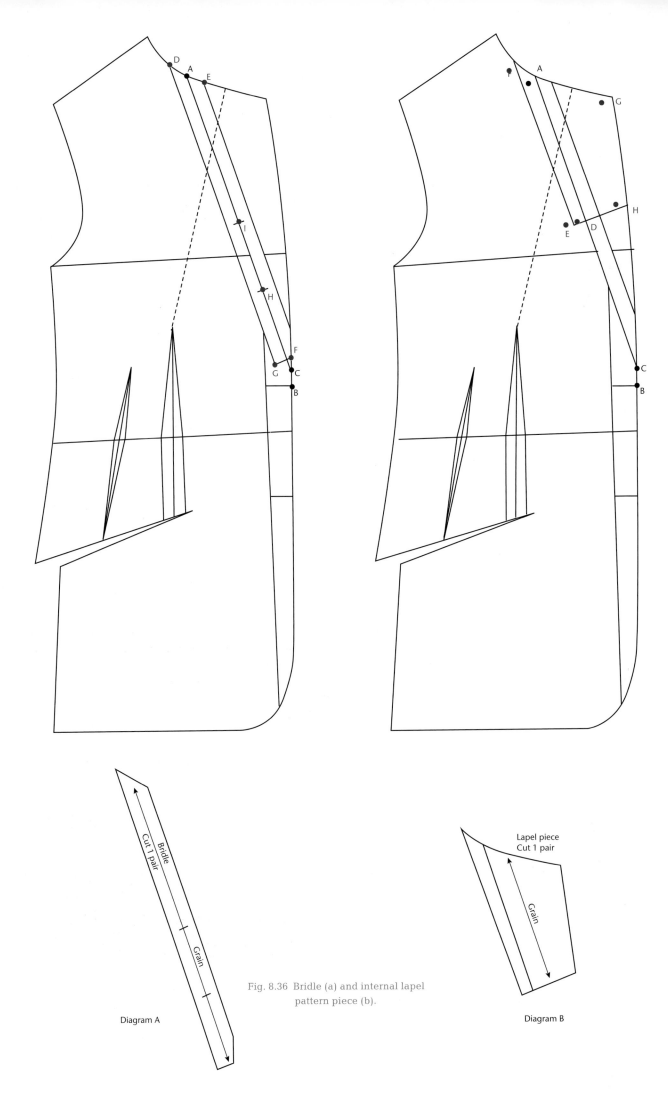

Fig. 8.36 Bridle (a) and internal lapel
pattern piece (b).

Diagram A

Diagram B

break line is cut on the bias, to allow it to roll more easily over the lapel.

D from A

This is located centrally in the middle of the break line. Square across from point D and out to the lapel edge at point H.

E from D

¾".

F from A

¾".

Trace the lapel piece as a net pattern. No seam allowance is required.

To compensate for canvas shrinkage, the hair cloth and hair canvas still needs to be pre-washed before cutting out the pattern. This is sometimes not enough and further shrinkage can happen when steam is applied. This is why it is advisable to have extra inlay when basting a canvas into a front; the excess is cut away as soon as it has been secured into position. Also, the top layer of the jacket front should be basted on to the canvas tight, causing the canvas to underneath to have a small amount of fullness, which shrinks under the iron.

Internal supports

Internal supports are necessary to re-enforce areas of weakness on the jacket, which can stretch during construction. Interlinings can be pieces of lining, linen, or silesia cotton that are sewn in at certain locations as extra support. Fusible, or fusing, can also be applied with the iron, which gives a cleaner finish. Patterns for these pieces can be traced from the master copy and used during construction. The pieces needed are listed below:

Back neck piece (Fig. 8.37i) A, B, C and D

One pair.

The back neck of the jacket can stretch out of shape before the collar is applied, so a piece of linen covering the area is hand stitched on to the seam allowance for hand construction; or a piece of fusible can be applied instead,

for ready-to-wear construction. Mark point A, the centre back neck and measure 1" down to point C.

At point B measure slightly less (¾"), so that it does not interfere with the ease in the back shoulder. Trace the piece as a net pattern.

Back armhole piece (ii)

One pair, cut in fusing.

F from E

¾" from the shoulder end.

H from G

¾".

Join F and H with a parallel curved line. Trace as a net pattern.

Back vent piece (Fig. 8.37iii)

One pair, cut in fusing.

The centre vent also needs extra support: a fusible is a cleaner option, to allow the vent to lay steady. Mark points M and N at the top of the vent and square out from N to O: ¾". Rule up to points P and Q, ½" above the top of the vent.

Trace as a net pattern (M, K, Q, P & R).

Back hem piece (Fig. 8.37iv)

Cut one pair, cut in fusing or backed with cotton silesia, which is hand inserted.

A 4" hem interlining should also be added, as it will help hide the blind stitches when the hem is turned up at the finishing stage. Trace as a net pattern.

Side armhole piece (v)

One pair, cut in fusing.

C from A, D from B

¾".

Join D and C with a parallel curved line.

Trace off as a net pattern.

Side hem piece (Fig. 8.37 vi)

One pair, cut in fusing, or silesia cotton. A 4" hem interlining to the hem should also be added, and it will help hide the blind stitches when the hem is turned up at the finishing stage, represented by points E, F, G and H.

Front hem piece (Fig. 8.37vii)

One pair, cut in fusing, or cotton silesia. A 4" hem interlining to compress the hem should also be added, and it will help hide the blind stitches when the hem is turned up at the finishing stage. Trace as a net pattern, represented by points A, B, C and D.

Top sleeve hem piece (Fig. 8.37i)

One Pair, cut in fusing.

B from A

2". Rule a line across to point C.

D

2" above net hemline, rule across to point E.

G from H

½".

F from G

1".

Trace off the piece as a net pattern.

Under sleeve hem piece (Fig. 8.37 ii)

One pair, cut in fusing.

J and K

2" below net hemline.

L and M

2" above net hemline.

O from P

½"

N from O

¾"

Trace off the piece as a net pattern, including points J and Q.

Fig. 8.37 Fusible can be used as an interlining, to bond the hem of the sleeve, adding support.

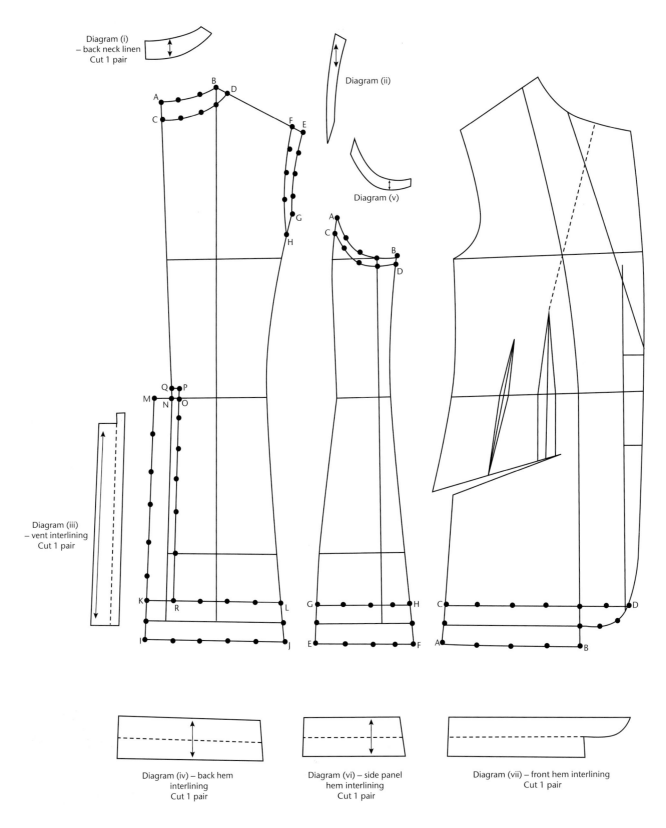

Diagram (i)
– back neck linen
Cut 1 pair

Diagram (ii)

Diagram (v)

Diagram (iii)
– vent interlining
Cut 1 pair

Diagram (iv) – back hem
interlining
Cut 1 pair

Diagram (vi) – side panel
hem interlining
Cut 1 pair

Diagram (vii) – front hem interlining
Cut 1 pair

Fig. 8.38 Plotting pattern pieces for interlinings on the jacket pattern, to be cut in fusing, linen, or selisia. (i) Back neck linen.
(ii) Back armhole piece. (iii) Back vent Interlining. (iv) Back hem support. (v) Side armhole piece. (vi) Side panel hem support.
(vii) Front hem support.

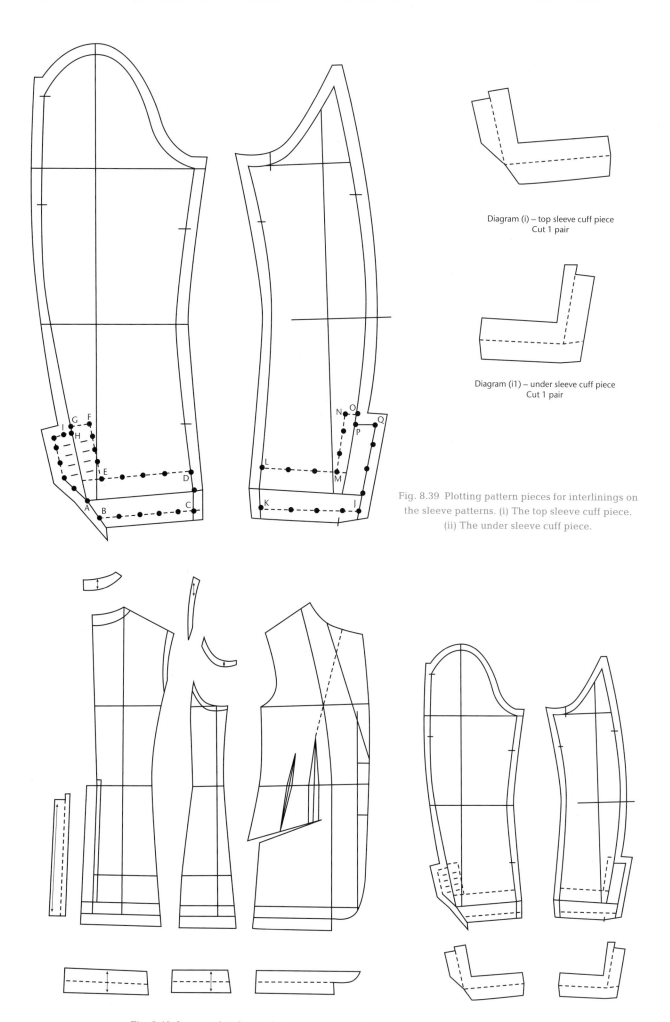

Diagram (i) – top sleeve cuff piece
Cut 1 pair

Diagram (i1) – under sleeve cuff piece
Cut 1 pair

Fig. 8.39 Plotting pattern pieces for interlinings on the sleeve patterns. (i) The top sleeve cuff piece. (ii) The under sleeve cuff piece.

Fig. 8.40 Layout of jacket and sleeve patterns with key interlining pieces traced off.

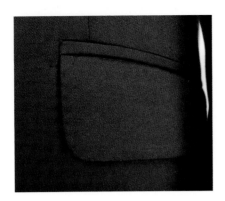

Fig. 8.41 The jet and flap pocket.

Pockets

There are several options that can be explored when deciding the style of pockets to add to a ladies' jacket. Most have a variety of pockets: an in-breast pocket and two main pockets located on the hip.

Sometimes for more masculine styles, an outer breast welt can be added to the chest. Tailored pockets can be double jetted, have a jet with a flap, single welts or patch pockets.

All pockets drafted throughout this section have been developed for the S.B. one-button jacket pattern.

THE JET AND FLAP POCKET

The 'jet and flap' is a classic hip pocket, with a small jet framing the edge of the flap, and an inner jet, on the inside of the pocket opening. The jet and flap are cut in the cloth used on the body of the jacket, and lined with the same fabric as the internal lining. The flap is also fused for extra support.

Traditionally the flap was created to protect the contents of the inner pocket, with the option

of tucking it in to reveal the double jets. However, this is never acknowledged and the flap is seen as a traditional design detail of a tailored jacket pocket.

Fig. 8.42 (i) represents the drafting lines of the pieces that will make up the pocket, marked directly onto the forepart pattern, from the pocket angle. The angle is essentially the pocket opening and is identified by points A and B. Diagrams (ii) – (ix) show the traced off individual pattern pieces with seam allowance.

PATTERN PIECES REQUIRED FOR A JET AND FLAP POCKET

The flap

The pocket angle from the forepart pattern can be used to mark the net flap pattern. It is helpful to remember not

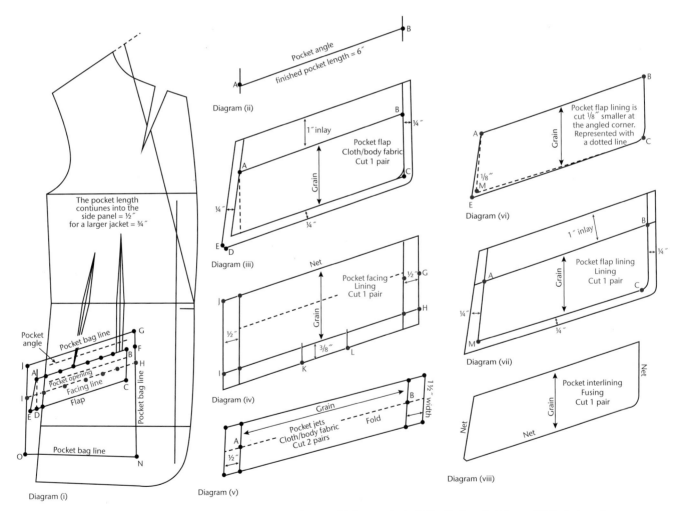

Above and Opposite: Fig. 8.42 Drafting the pieces of a jet with flap pocket. (i) Draft of pocket lines. (ii) Pocket angle. (iii) Pocket flap. (iv) Facing. (v) Jet. (vi) Flap lining draft. (vii) Flap lining traced off. (viii) Pocket interlining. (ix) Pocket bag. (Not to quarter scale)

to include the dart width in the pocket length and that the pocket will continue ½" into the side panel, and ½" past the first front dart. Fig. 8.40 (ii) indicates the slanted pocket angle traced from the forepart, 5¾" (the length of the pocket minus the front dart width). The angle can be used to check the slant on all pattern pieces, to be correct and consistent with this line, otherwise the patterns will not match properly.

To draft the flap (Fig. 8.40 iii):

Trace the angle from the forepart from point B to point A, which extends ½" past the forepart to the exact pocket length.

A from B

The length of the pocket: 5¾".

C from B

The width of the flap: 2".
Square a 90° line parallel to the grain from point B to C: 2". The grain should

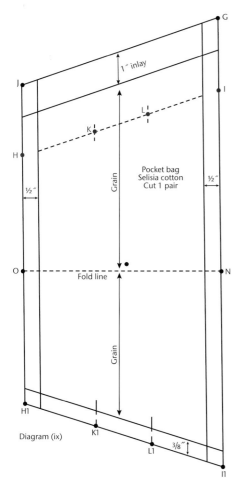

Diagram (ix)

be transferred from the forepart pattern onto the flap. The grain of the flap must match the grain of the forepart. If they do not, this can be very apparent when cutting out into a stripe or check suiting. The stripe on the flap must match the stripe on the front jacket. The corner at point C should be rounded to a slight curve.

D from A

Square down from A: 2", the width of the flap parallel to the grain line.

E from D

The slant of the flap = ¾". This is a more flattering line for the flap, due to its position on the hip. Join E to A. That completes the net outline of the flap. A ¼" seam allowance should be added at the edges, as it is bagged out to a lining, and a 1" inlay should be included along the top edge, to allow the flap to be inserted easily through the pocket opening during construction.

The facing (Fig. 8.40 iv)

The facing pattern (iv) is seamed to the pocket bag on the inside of the pocket opening. It is normally cut in lining, the same as the internal body lining; and it is used to cover up the pocket bag at the entry. The lining facing is considered aesthetically more appealing to see than the silesia cotton of the bag.

To draft the facing:
F from B (i)

Added width: ½". The facing and pocket bag should be wider than the pocket length by ½" both sides.
G from F

1" inlay above the pocket opening.

H from G

Width of the facing: 2½".
Draw an angled line from G to J, parallel to the pocket angle. J from G: 6¾".
Draw an angled line from H to I, parallel to the pocket angle. I from H: 6¾".
Add ⅜" seam allowance to the line H and I. Two balance notches can be marked at points K and L to indicate where to sew to the pocket bag.

The jet (Fig. 8.40 v)

The jet (v) is a 1½" wide strip, which is folded in half, to construct the frame of the pocket. One pair is required for one pocket. In other words, two pairs should be cut in total.

To draft the jet pattern:

Trace the pocket angle from A to B adding ½" each side of A and B.
Square up and down from A by ¾", totalling 1½".
Square up and down from B by ¾", totalling 1½".
A ¼" seam allowance is included in the 1½" jet width, to sew the seam onto the pocket opening.

The flap lining (Fig. 8.40 vi)

The flap lining (vi) is taken from the flap pattern (iii).

To draft:

Trace a net copy of the flap, indicating points A, B, C, and E.

M from E

The corner of the flap should be cut slightly smaller: a small ⅛" from nothing at points A and E. This is so that when the lining is bagged out to the flap, it aids the machinist to sew without adding excess in to the lining piece, which can pleat under the flap when pressed and finished, and will imprint on to the flap.
Trace a new net copy of the flap (Fig. 8.40 vii) adding ¼" around the bottom and side edges and 1" inlay at the top edge.

Flap fusing (Fig. 8.40 viii)

Interlining is added to the pocket flap (viii) in the form of light wool fusing to retain the structure of the flap. The pattern piece is very simple: trace a net version from the pocket flap (iii). No seam allowance is required, as the fusing should not be cut edge to edge with the seam allowance; it becomes too bulky.

The pocket bag (Fig. 8.40 ix)

The pocket bag pattern (ix) is cut in cotton, known as silesia. It is drafted on the fold, and one bag is required for each pocket, which is sewn to the pocket facing. To draft:

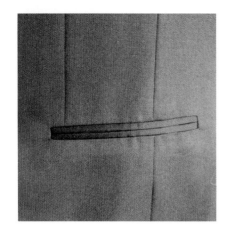

Fig. 8.43 Double-jet pocket.

indicate G and J (i) 1″ above the pocket opening and ½″ wider than the pocket length. Square down from points G to N and J to O. The length of the bag should sit 2″ above the net hemline. Rule a line across from points N and O. This is also the pocket bag fold line.

Trace a copy of the outline of J, G, N and O, to include the facing line (points H to I), and including the balance notches K and L from the pocket facing.

Flip from the fold line (N and O) to transfer the pocket bag pattern and facing line; indicated by points H1, K1, L1 and I1. This line requires a ³⁄₈″ seam allowance, and will seam to the pocket facing.

Fig. 8.44 Contemporary jet pocket: the top jet is trapped in the dart showing a variation in construction.

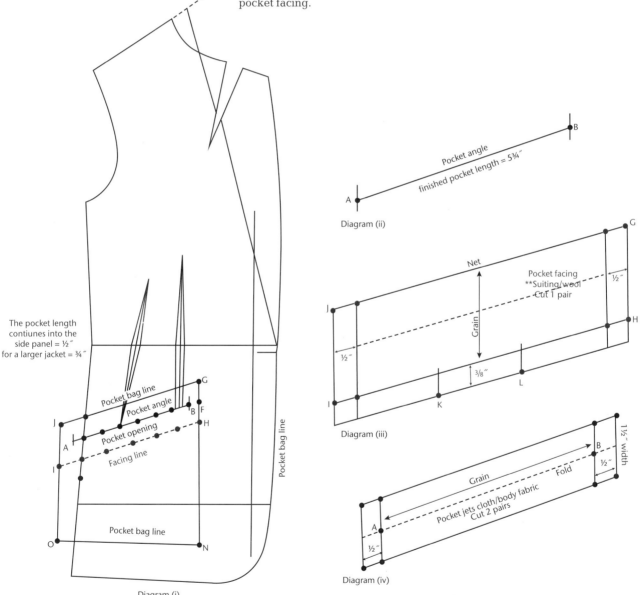

Above & opposite page: Fig. 8.45 Drafting the pieces of a double-jet pocket. Not to quarter scale.
(i) Pocket lines drafted onto forepart pocket angle. (ii) Pocket angle. (iii) Pocket facing. (iv) Jet pieces. (v) Pocket bag.

THE DOUBLE-JET POCKET

The double-jet pocket can be used internally as in-breast pockets, or as a ticket pocket, and externally as an option for the hip pocket. Traditionally double jets are more formal, suited for tuxedo styles when cut in silk; however, it is more common now to see jet pockets on classic jacket styles, as a minimal preference, minus the flap.

Fig. 8.43 diagram (i) represents the lines of the pieces that will make up the pocket, marked directly onto the forepart pattern, from the pocket angle. The system is exactly the same as for the jet with flap pocket, minus the flap.

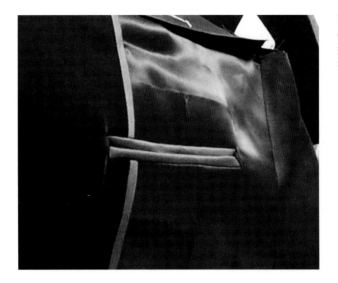

Fig. 8.46 In-breast double-jet pocket, positioned on the facing and lining.

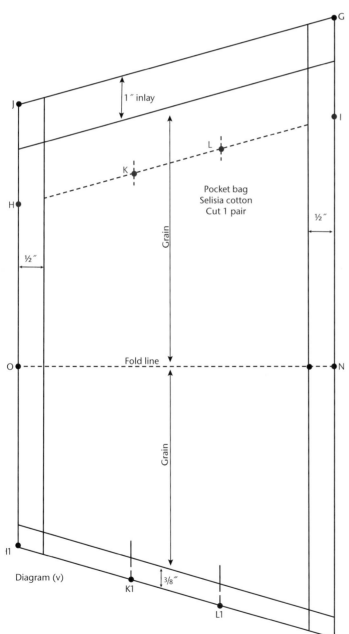

1″ inlay

L

K

Pocket bag
Selisia cotton
Cut 1 pair

½″

Grain

½″

Fold line

Grain

3/8″

K1

L1

Diagram (v)

PATTERN PIECES REQUIRED FOR A DOUBLE-JET POCKET

Pocket facing (Fig. 8.45 iii)

For double jetted pockets the facing is cut in cloth, the same used for the jacket, as it is exposed, due to the subtraction of the flap. The system to draft the facing is the same as with the facing on the jet and flap instructions. The only difference is the fabric quality that it is cut from.

The jet (Fig. 8.45 iv)

Cut two pairs in cloth and repeat the same instructions described as for the jet and flap. The jets should be interlined with fusing to support the jets.

The pocket bag (Fig. 8.45 v)

Cut one pair on the fold in silesia cotton, and repeat instructions described previously for the jet and flap pocket.

THE OUTER BREAST WELT

The outer breast welt pocket, abbreviated to 'OBW', is traditionally a chest pocket essential for a man's jacket on the left side. It is not always necessary to include this on a ladies' jacket, as it is considered a masculine additional pocket. On very fitted jackets, adding an OBW will distort the silhouette of the bust, giving the appearance that one side of the bust looks flatter than the other. For less feminine, androgynous styles of jacket, the addition of the welt will be a sounder style decision.

Fig. 8.48 diagram (i) shows the right side of the jacket and the left side

Fig. 8.47 Outer breast welt chest pocket detail.

of the jacket, which is traditionally where the outer breast welt would be added, and they are labelled as right side up, to avoid confusion when cutting out in cloth. The welt should not be added on to both sides of the jacket. The left side of the forepart represents the lines of the pieces that will make up the pocket, marked directly onto the forepart pattern, from the pocket angle.

PATTERN PIECES REQUIRED FOR AN OUTER BREAST WELT
The welt (Fig. 8.48 ii)
The welt measurementss:
Length: 4″
Width: 1″

Firstly draw the pocket angle of the welt directly onto the left side of the forepart. This can be judged by using the bust line as a guide and the first dart. Square up to the bust line from the first dart in the forepart and indicate point A.

B from A
Two-thirds of the welt pocket length: $(2 \div 3) \times 4 = 2\frac{3}{4}″$. Square 90° up and down.

C from A
One-third of the welt pocket length: $4 \div 3 = 1\frac{1}{4}″$
Square 90° up and down.

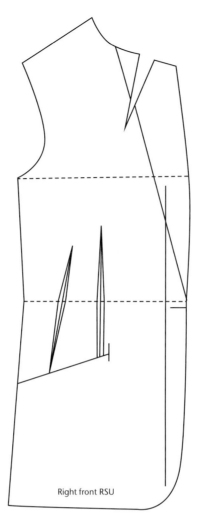

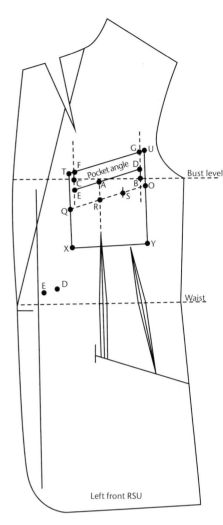

Diagram (i)

Above & Opposite: Fig. 8.48 Drafting the pieces of an outer-breast welt pocket. (Not to quarter scale). (i) Pocket lines drafted onto the left front forepart, at the chest. (ii) The welt pattern. (iii) Welt interlining. (iv) Draft lines for pocket bag and facing. (v) Facing (vi) Pocket Bag.

This positions the welt off-centre towards the back armhole. Some cutters may prefer the welt to be positioned centrally at point A; this is a style choice, and if this is preferred, point B from A will be 2″, and point C from A will be 2″ (half the length of the welt). For the purposes of this exercise the welt is positioned two-thirds back from the dart and one-third into the front from the dart.

D from B
The pocket angle slants ½″ up from the bust line.

E from C
The pocket angle slants down ½″ from the bust line.

F from E, G from D
The width of the welt is 1″.

G from F
Join G and F with a straight line. Trace the welt as a net pattern piece (ii). The top of the welt (line G and F) becomes the fold line, and another welt is traced from the fold. ½″ inlay is added at the sides of the welt and ¼″ seam allowance at the edge, which seams on at the pocket angle.

The welt interlining (Fig. 8.48 iii)
Trace another copy of the welt as a single layer (iii), as only one side of the welt needs interlining. It should also be cut as a net pattern with no seam allowance, to avoid adding bulkiness to the seam allowance.

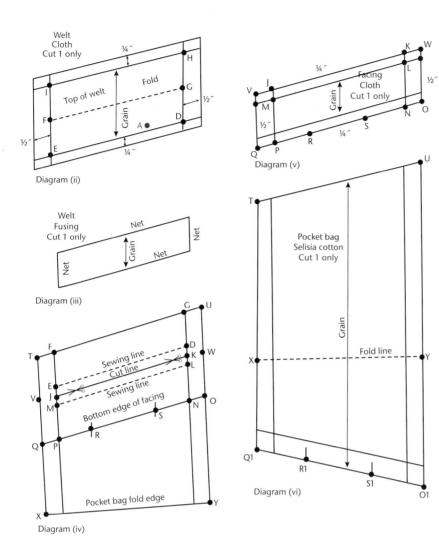

Diagram (ii)

Welt
Cloth
Cut 1 only

¼"

H

Fold

Top of welt

Grain

G

½"

I

F

A

D

½"

E

¼"

Diagram (iii)

Welt
Fusing
Cut 1 only

Net

Net

Grain

Net

Net

Diagram (v)

K W

¼"

Facing
Cloth
Cut 1 only

½"

J

V

L

M

Grain

N

O

½"

S

¼"

Q

P

R

Diagram (iv)

G U

F

D

T

K W

Sewing line

Cut line

L

E

Sewing line

V

J

N

O

M

Bottom edge of facing

S

R

Q

P

Pocket bag fold edge

X

Y

Diagram (vi)

U

T

Pocket bag
Selisia cotton
Cut 1 only

Grain

Fold line

X

Y

Q1

R1

S1

O1

Fusing can be used to bond to one side of the welt with an iron, which is a softer interlining; or a piece of collar canvas can be hand stitched into the welt, which is a more structured interlining.

The facing (Fig. 8.48 iv and v)

When constructing the welt pocket line E and D of the welt is the sewing line. The cut line is the line which cuts through the forepart ¼" below line E and D, indicated by points J and K (iv). The facing is traced from the cut line (J and K), and the sewing line is ¼" below, represented with a dotted line at points L and M.

N from L
Width of the facing: 1".

O from N
Inlay: ½".

P from M
Width of the facing: 1".

Q from P
Inlay: ½".

R and S
Balance notches, marked by dividing line Q and O into three equal parts. Trace the facing (diagram v), indicating

Fig. 8.49 Machining the welt and facing onto the pocket line of the forepart.

---

points J, K, L, M, N, P, R and S with ½" inlay at the sides O, Q, W and V. To assemble the welt pieces during the construction process, the welt is sewn along the bottom of the line M and L, and the facing is sewn along the line D and E as shown in Fig. 8.49. Once the welt and facing are stitched in position, line J to K is cut and mitred at the corners, and the facing is pulled on the inside of the forepart. The welt folds up over the cut line and the sides are machined down.

The pocket bag (Fig. 8.48 vi)

The pocket bag is cut in silesia pocketing and on the fold as with the jet and flap pocket.

To draft:
U from G
Inlay: ½". Square a 90° line down to point Y.

T from F
Inlay: ½". Square a 90° line down to X. Join point U with point T.

Y from U
The pocket bag length: 5". The length should be several inches above the waist line, any longer and it will interfere with the waist suppression. In the example it is 3 ½" above the waist.

X from T
Pocket length: 4¼".
Square across from line Y to point X. This is the fold line.
Trace lines T, U, X and Y (vi) and on the fold flip the shape and mark the balance notches R1 and S1 to stitch to the facing, and points Q1 and O1. This line then requires ⅜" seam allowance.

THE PATCH POCKET (Fig. 8.50)

The patch pocket is a single piece of cloth sewn directly onto the front of the jacket. Traditionally seen on sports blazers, or informal styles.

Before drafting a pattern for a patch pocket on a jacket style, the position of the pocket angle/belly cut must first be moved lower, towards the hem of the jacket (i). This is so that when the dart is cut through, it will be

185

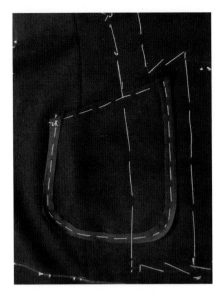

Fig. 8.50 The patch pocket is
traditionally seen on sports blazers,
or informal styles.

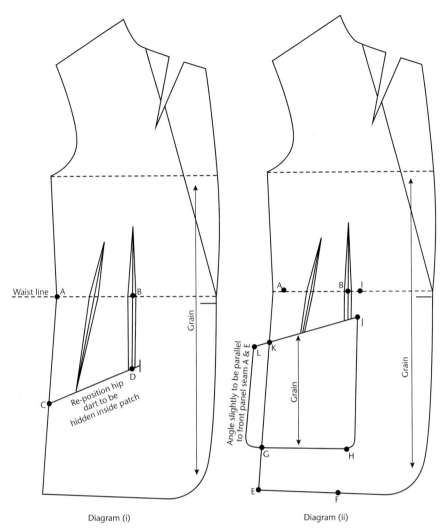

Diagram (i)   Diagram (ii)

Fig. 8.51 The process for drafting a patch blazer pocket.
(i) Moving the hip dart. (ii) The patch on the forepart. (iii) Patch pocket, with seam
allowances. (iv) Patch fusing piece. (v) Cotton backing for patch.

concealed inside the patch. If it is left
in-line with the top edge of the patch,
the edges of the cut will be visible,
and look unsightly on the wearer. To
move the belly cut on the forepart,
indicate point A at the side waist, and
point at B the centre of the front dart.

C from A
The new pocket angle from the side
waist line: 6½".

D from B
The new pocket angle from the centre
of the front dart: 4¾".
A helpful tip to remember is that the
new pocket angle should be 1½"
below the top edge of the intended
placement of the patch. It is helpful
to draw the patch on to the forepart
(diagram ii), to check the position.
Indicate point E at the side hem of the
forepart and point F on the hemline:
½" forward of the front hip dart.

G from E, H from F
The bottom edge of the patch (ii) is
2½" from the hemline of the jacket,
due to the longer length. This distance
should be reduced to 1½" for shorter
length jacket styles.
   Join points G and H with a straight
line parallel to the hem.

I from B
Half the width of the dart (¼") plus
½" = ¾". Square a 90° line to point
J (the front corner of the patch)
approximately 2" below the waist line.

K from A
The top angle of the patch: 4" from the
waist line.

J from I = 2"
If it is desired the top edge can be drafted
straight, not slanted. To draft a straight
top edge, the distance from Point K and
A will = 2", the same as J from I.
Rule the top angle from points J,
through K to point L.

L from K
½". The patch will continue into
the side body past the forepart
side seam. Rule a line from point
L parallel to the angle of the front
side seam, and curve to the desired
shape back into point G, and from

point H curve straight line back into
point J.
   Certain coins can be used to achieve
the rounded corner of the patch; a UK
two-pence piece is a useful template;
or specific drawing rulers can be
sourced with various spheres and
circles to create circular curves. When
traced off the patch will serve as a
template for future use, when making
patterns for patch pockets.
   Copy a pattern piece for the patch
(iii), tracing exactly the net lines plotted
on the forepart in diagram (ii). Transfer
the correct grain line to match the
forepart grain line, as this will be cut in
the same cloth as the body fabric. Only
one patch is required for each hip, so
cut one pair in cloth/suiting.

O from L
Add ½" inlay around the outside edge.
At the bottom curves, the allowance
will be cut back to ¼" when it is
machined to the silesia cotton.

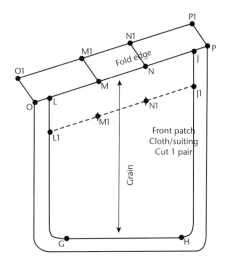

Diagram (iii)

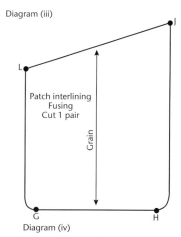

Diagram (iv)

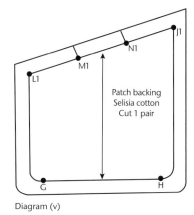

Diagram (v)

P from J

½″ inlay.

Add 1″ inlay along the top edge (lines J and L). Add two balance notches (M and N), by dividing the length of line J and L into three equal parts.

Turn back the top edge (line J and L) and cut around the seam allowance of the patch; this will give the correct mitred angle from O to O1 and P to P1. Trace with a dotted line the edge of the inlay, into the patch, for the purpose of drafting the inner cotton lining. Indicate points L1 and J1 and transfer the balance notches indicated by points M1 and N1.

The cloth patch itself also needs to be fused with interlining. A light wool fusing will suffice, and a net pattern can be traced with no seam allowance/ inlay (iv). One pair only is required: one for each patch.

Silesia cotton is used to back the patch, to add extra support and help keep its shape (v). The pattern is traced from the finished patch pattern (iii), using the points L1, G, H, J1, N1 and M1. Add ⅜″ seam allowance from points J1 and L1, to seam to the inlay of the cloth patch, and ½″ around the side and bottom edge.

Labelling the finished pattern

On completion of each pattern, the pieces should be labelled with size, description and instructions, and prepared for marking into cloth. The customer's name should be written first, followed by the size of the block, a description of what piece of the jacket the pattern is, and cutting instruction. It can be labelled in the following order.

- Name: Jo Baker Waters
- Description: forepart pattern
- Size: UK size 10 (US 6)
- Cutting instruction: cut one pair
- Fabric: cloth/suiting

For patterns with a bust seam, where the forepart is divided into two separate panels, they can be described as 'forepart panel 1' and 'forepart panel 2'.

All straight grain lines, centre line and landmark balance lines should be labelled.

Final balance marks are notched into the pattern, with notchers. These notches are the sewing language to tailors; they identify the waist, high hip, and seam allowances. Be sure not to cut too far into the seam allowance: only a tiny notch is needed. The tailor will match the notches when sewing; they should be checked on the pattern to match the same position on each panel. As an example, the true waist at the forepart seam sews to the side panel; therefore the notches should measure exactly at the true waist, and

so forth for all the other pieces.

When the jacket is cut in cloth all chalk marks will be mark stitched in white thread, to identify all darts, the bust point, true waist and the net edges inside the inlay. This is why it is necessary to transfer all landmark points from the master copy onto the traced off pattern, and to label each piece.

Finished measurements

A final set of measurements should be taken, on completion of the pattern to be given to the tailor or sample machinist. Once the pattern is cut into cloth and is tailored, some fabrics can shrink a lot or stretch out of shape, so it is necessary to have the following measures at hand, while the jacket is being made. The finished measures required are listed below:

- Jacket length
- Half cross back
- Shoulder width
- Lapel width
- Half jacket waist
- Sleeve length
- Cuff width

These measures need to be referenced while tailoring to ensure accuracy of the garment. If the measures have changed, then adjust accordingly to fit with the intended pattern.

After the body of the jacket has been sewn together, the armhole depth and armhole will be measured and checked in cloth by the tailor before sewing the outside seam of the top sleeve and under sleeve. This is because certain tailors will like to add more fullness than others in the sleeve head and will use the inlay added by pattern makers to the under sleeve as a means to amend the sleeve to their preferred method of construction. Only include pattern measurements for the armhole depth, armhole measurement, and sleeve circumference if it is requested. The pattern will be adjusted after each stage of fit, and a new set of finished measurements will be made and communicated to the tailor.

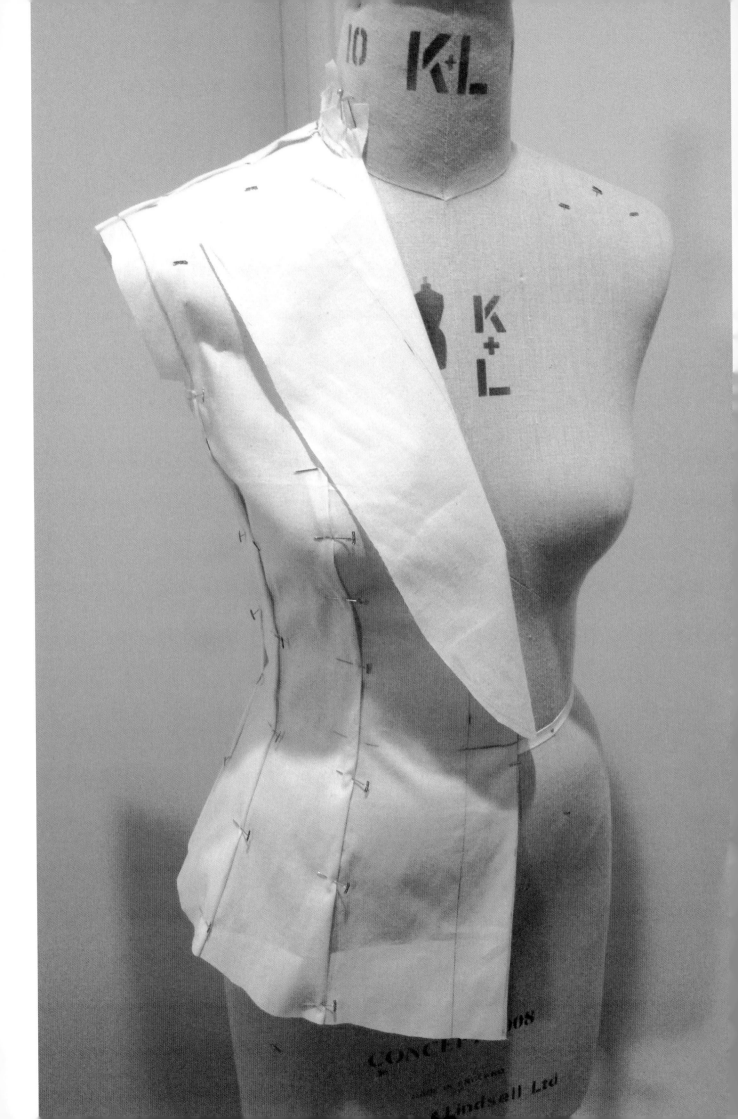

Chapter 9
Draping on the Mannequin

The splendour of this chapter is that it re-introduces vintage modelling techniques used in haute couture, lost to the modern flat pattern cutter. The style of jacket modelled on the form is draped from pre-cut squares and rectangular lengths of calico, which when hand applied to the stand, form the required shape.

Draping is an alternative way to obtain a pattern for a jacket. The mannequin can be manipulated and used to replace the customer, and should be as realistic as possible in terms of stance, figure type and proportion. Shoulder pads can be pinned to the shoulders if desired, and for disproportionate shoulders,

Opposite page: Fig. 9.1 Calico pinned on the stand, hand draped into a half jacket bodice, minus the collar and reverse shape.

wadding in the pads can be thinned out, and slopes manipulated with wadding, or built up as desired. It can also be helpful to borrow a bra from the client to clip on to the stand to obtain an accurate bust posture – full, pointed, or round – although it helps if you have worked with the client previously, or can judge if the client seems personable, before requesting to borrow undergarments. Alternatively, wadding can be pinned or tacked over the bust, to imitate the correct bust posture. Waist lines can be filled out, layers can even be added to grade to a higher dress size. Therefore, the mannequin can be developed to incorporate the disproportions of the client.

The modelling stand can be purchased in all industrial sizes; however, the standard size in couture workshops varies from US sizes 4–6, and UK 8–10. For the aid of

PROCEDURE FOR DRAPING THE HALF JACKET

- Prepare muslin/calico fabric to be draped
- Drape the front bodice
- Drape the back bodice
- Drape the collar & shape the lines of revere lapel
- Drape the sleeve
- Check accuracy, adjust if necessary & mark style lines/details in pencil
- Mark grain lines and balance points on the toile
- Use the half toile to create a paper pattern
- High right hip

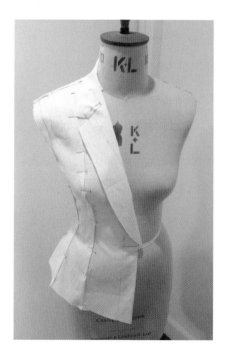
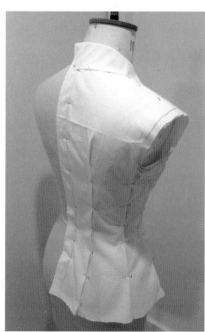
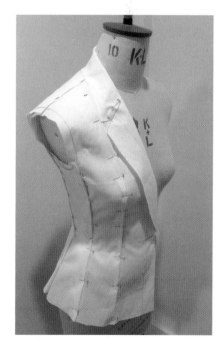

Fig. 9.2 Half-toile example jacket, pinned to the contours of the stand, front, side and back angle, with collar and reverse lapel.

apprentices miniature mannequins can be purchased to practise modelling fabric on a smaller scale. The following draping techniques can be applied to any size stand.

To drape a tailored jacket, the toile should always be draped the right side of the stand, rather than the left, as the right side is often slightly bigger in size; it is safer to make a pattern from a right side toile. In fittings, a rule to remember, it is easier to fit a bigger toile than it is a smaller one.

The half jacket on the stand is a single breasted one-button jacket, extremely fitted, to be cinched in at the waist, with front and back princess seams, side panel and a regular notch lapel and collar. It will require a tailored pad to be pinned onto the stand prior to draping.

Draping the forepart

It helps to have more cloth to drape with, as it is easier to cut away the excess fabric during the draping procedure, than to pin in extra cloth if there is not enough. Therefore, the measurements used are generous with extra width.

Cut a rectangular piece of calico. Length: the required jacket length (23″) plus 7″ inlays.

Width: half chest measurement (17″) plus 19″ extra inlays for allowances and modelling excess to drape with.

In the example on the mannequin these measurements are therefore 30″ by 36″.

It can also be helpful to block fuse the piece with interlining to help support the calico, and create a smoother looking muslin.

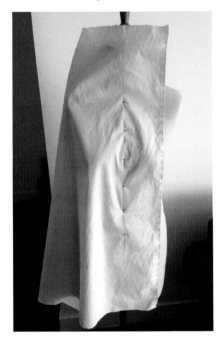

1. Mark a centre line in pencil onto the calico, parallel to the selvedge, 4″ from the edge (Fig. 9.3). This line will be pinned directly onto the front centre line of the mannequin. Start by placing a pin at the waist, at the neck point and the bust line, then place pins roughly every 2″, to prevent the fabric from dragging. Never stretch the calico when draping on the mannequin, as this will cause distortions. The fabric should be placed gradually, but firmly. Be sure to leave excess above the neckline of the stand and at the hem. Place temporary pins at the front overlap above the left bust point, at the neck point where it meets the shoulder and at the back, to secure the weight of the cloth, so it does not slip off the stand.

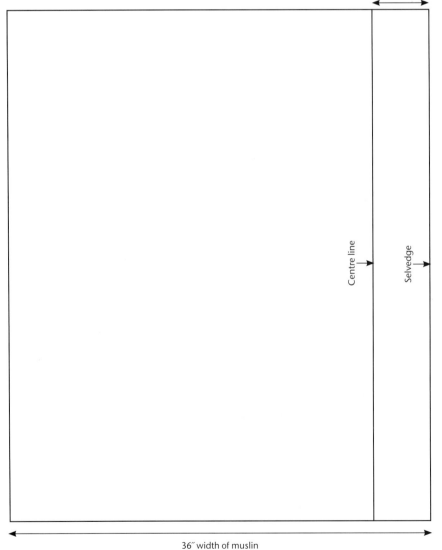

Mark a centre line
4″ from selvedge

Centre line

Selvedge

36″ width of muslin

Fig. 9.3 Calico dimensions required to drape the front bodice of the jacket.

2. The neck seam: using shears, cut away some of the excess calico and use the ends of the scissors to cut into the neck seam, to release the tension around the upper neck. This will help to mould the calico smoothly around the neck area.

3. The bust suppression (bust seam): in the toile, a seam over the bust has been pinned; the entire bust suppression will be pinned out of this seam. Start at the shoulder by pinning the excess fabric between the neck and shoulder; position the seam centrally between the two. The cloth should be smoothed across from the shoulder, without drags, and pinned carefully to follow the contour of the form. Pin in and bring down to the bust

point, make a pencil mark at the bust point, and fold over, facing towards the centre line.

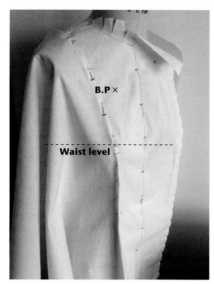

4. The waist suppression (bust seam): from the bust point, use the back of the hand to smooth down to the waist and pinch the excess fabric together, then pin through the fullness to secure the suppression, as in the image. Make another balance pencil mark for the waist level.

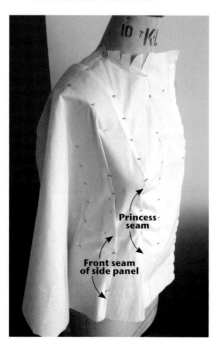

5. Front seam of side panel: pin the contours of a second seam; this seam will be the front part

of the side panel. The placement is positioned back from the bust seam, with the side seam of the mannequin positioned centrally in the side panel. Place temporary pins at the exact side seam on the cloth to the support the weight of the front.

6. Left front view: cut away some of the excess length at the hem (not all). In the example it has been chopped away to the hip circumference level. On a dress stand this can be measured approximately 8″ from the true waist level, which is indicated with white twill tape.

7. Front edge button wrap. Mark the button position on the waist line indicated on the mannequin,

as the style will be a one-button centre font closure. Measure 1½″ from the centre line and cut away from the hem up to the button position, squaring out at an angle at the button line.

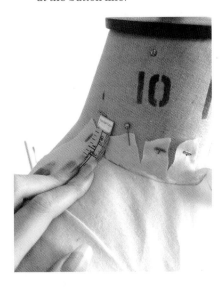

8.   Mark the stand height for the break line at the shoulder. Draw a neckline in pencil. Measure 1⅛″ from the neck point where it meets the shoulder, mark with a temporary pin placed in the neck on the mannequin.

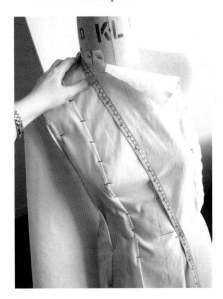

9.   Mark the break line over the bust with a pencil. It is easier to use a tape measure rather than a ruler; place it at the temporary pin in the neck to line up ½″ above the buttonhole.

10.   The break line marked with a pencil.

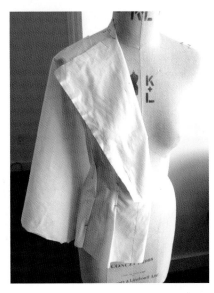

11.   Take out the temporary pin on the left side bust point, and fold the excess calico back on the break line that was previously marked. This will form the basic lapel.

12.   Mark a basic lapel shape for now and cut away the excess. Be careful not to cut away too much, as once the collar has been draped on it is easier to shape the notch collar and lapel together. There should still be at least 4–5″ of width at the top of the lapel. Depending on the style of the jacket it can be curved slightly into the buttonhole. It is advisable to return to the front edges at the end when working on the collar.

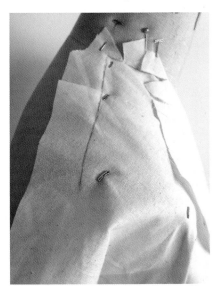

13.   Mark with a pencil the desired shoulder position (the line on the mannequin will act as a guideline). Leave at least 1″ inlay into the back.

the draglines in the image: the calico should drape smooth over the body. To reduce the symptoms of strain the seams need to be cut up the centre of the fold.

calico across the contours of the form. Where it is needed add longer cuts in the excess, until the lines of stress disappear.

14. At this stage observe the toile, cut away any excess at the side seam, still leaving plenty of inlay past the side line on the mannequin (5″), then reduce the stress lines gradually by adding a cut exactly on the side waist level.

16. Cut up the fold line of the front side panel seam, from the hem to underarm. Add a horizontal cut at the waist line.

18. Remove temporary pins and place back the side panel into the front. Fold in the edge from the waist cut down to the hem, and pin, allowing some flare at the hip. This is judged 'by eye' as it is a style decision. Continue to pin above the waist and stop at the underarm.

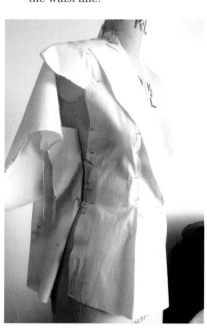

15. Once the toile is scrutinized, it becomes evident that the waist is under stress throughout the front, as the calico will not lay flat over the form due to the pinned out suppression in the seams. Observe

17. Use temporary pins to secure the side panel, which folds back towards the back of the mannequin. Add horizontal cuts into the excess and use pins to secure, using the back of your hand to smooth the

19. Cut through the fold of the bust/ princess seam, from the hem to the waist first, then above the waist, through the bust point to the shoulder, adding a cut at the

193

waist. Bust panel 1 is the side closer to the centre line; peel back bust panel 2 and secure with temporary pins. Add several cuts on the excess inlay of panel 1.

20. Remove temporary pins from panel 2, add cuts in the inlay and fold over onto panel 1, as shown. Secure into position, until the draglines smooth away.

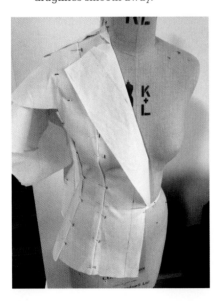

21. Front toile pinned correctly to the contours of the mannequin.

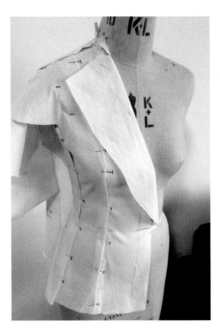

22. Side front toile showing stress symptoms that have been alleviated.

Draping the back bodice

Cut a square piece of calico.
Length: the required jacket length (23″) plus 7″ inlays.
Width: half chest measurement (17″) plus 13″ extra inlays for allowances and modelling excess to drape with.
In the example on the mannequin these measurements are 30″ × 30″ (Fig. 9.4).

23. Mark a back centre line in pencil 1½″ from selvedge. This line will be pinned directly onto the back centre line of the mannequin.

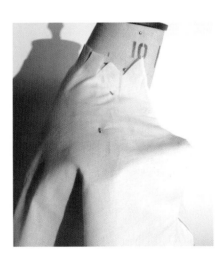

24. Be sure to leave excess above the neckline and shoulder of the mannequin, and below the hem. Secure at shoulders with temporary pins.

25. The neck seam: using shears cut away some of the excess calico and use the ends of the scissors to cut into the neck seam, to release the tension around the upper neck. This will help to mould the calico smoothly around the neck area.

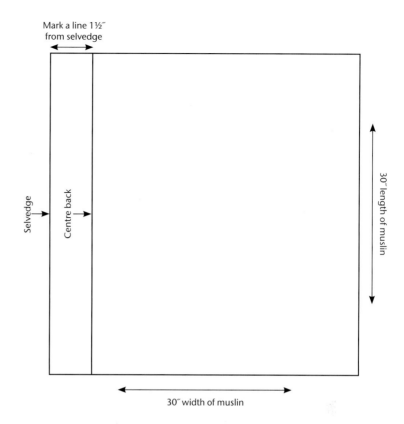

Mark a line 1½″ from selvedge

Selvedge

Centre back

30″ length of muslin

30″ width of muslin

Fig. 9.4 The diagram shows how much calico is required to drape the back bodice of the jacket.

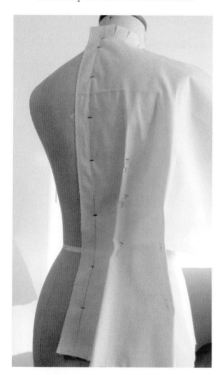

26. Pinch out the dart that will run through the middle of the back panel. Place pins at the waist from the hem, and the true waist, then to nothing at the back shoulder blades. This can also be turned into a seam, if preferred, and it will divide the toile into two panels. To turn the dart into a seam, at the end of the dart draw a pencil line running to the middle of the shoulder. Cut up the centre of the dart and through the pencil line, then when tracing off, add seam allowance.

27. In preparation to pinch in the seam that will overlap onto the side panel, add a horizontal cut at the waist line and cut away any excess inlay.

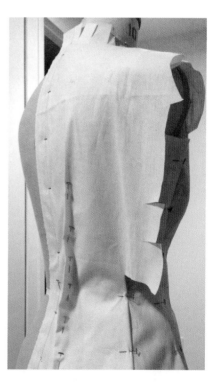

28. Fold in the inlay from the waist down to them hem, adding flare at the hip, as shown. Tip: the side seam on the mannequin should sit in the middle of the side panel, so keep that in sight when pinning

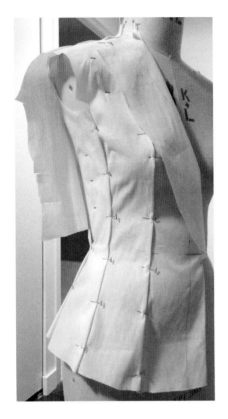

mark the armhole line in later steps. Fold and pin excess inlay at the shoulder to indicate the shoulder seam.

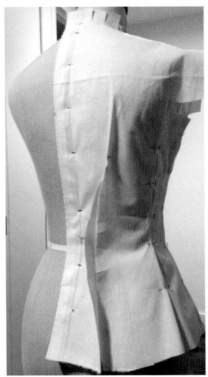

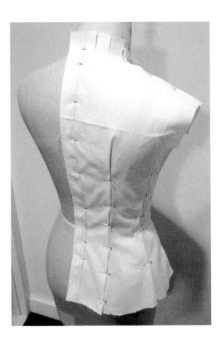

32. Back panel with dart.

this seam. The image above shows the procedure from the front view.

30. Cut up the centre of the back dart, and add cuts into the excess calico.

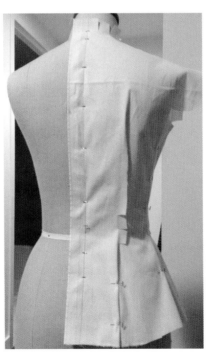

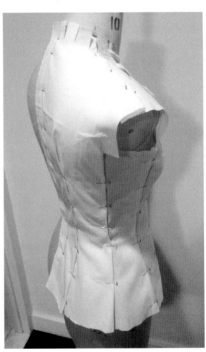

33. Side panel.

29. Pin in the remainder of the seam from the waist to the armhole, placing another horizontal cut, folding out the excess cloth to

31. Re-pin the dart, smoothing away all stress symptoms.

Drawing in the neckline, armhole and pocket position

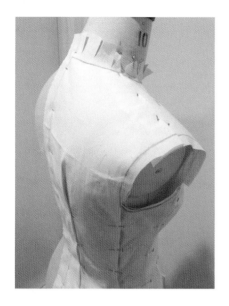

34. Back neckline: draw in the back neckline in pencil, using the mannequin as a guideline.

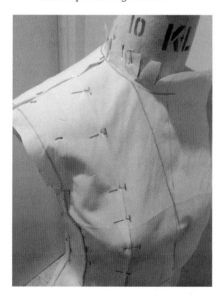

35. Front neckline: join the line from the back neckline to the front neckline.

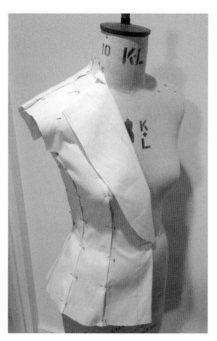

36. Measure the desired shoulder width. Place the tape measure at the neck point, where it touches the shoulder seam, and pass the tape along the shoulder, and mark the length, plus $^3/_8$" seam allowance in pencil. Trim the excess calico. Leave roughly 1½" inlay past the pencil mark.

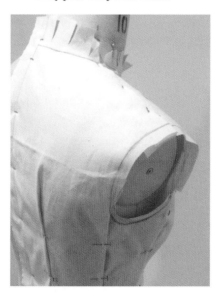

37. Draw in the back armhole run.

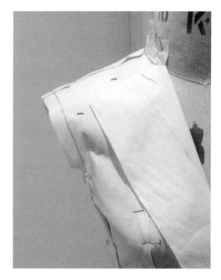

38. Draw in the font armhole run.

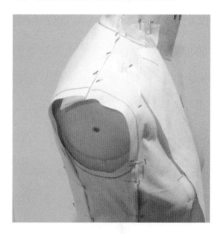

39. The side armhole; at this angle it should resemble the shape of an egg.

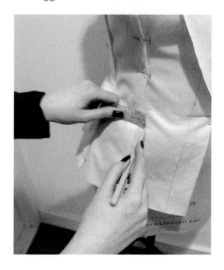

40. Mark the desired hip pocket position. On the muslin the pocket angle is slanted below the waist line.

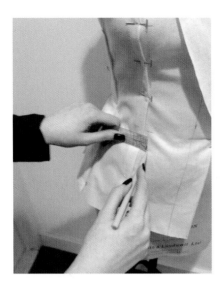

41. A ruler can be used to mark the line and also help decide the position.

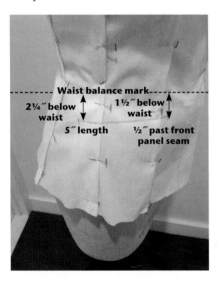

42. The pocket should be marked ½″ past the first front seam and not too far back into the side panel. Pocket length is 5″.

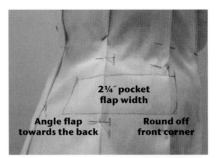

2¼″ pocket flap width

Angle flap towards the back — Round off front corner

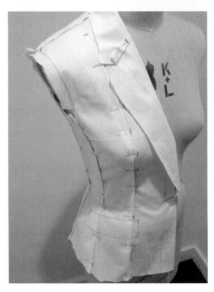

43. Draw in a flap, which can be traced as a pattern when the muslin is taken off the mannequin. The width is 2¼″ wide and angles towards the back as shown.

Draping the collar and shaping the lapel

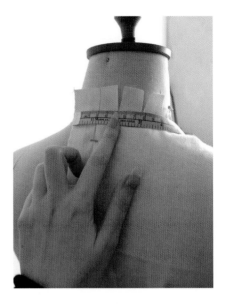

44. Measure the half back neck, including the inlay at the centre back, with a tape measure.

45. Continue from the shoulder point into the front neck, including inlay. Record the measurement.

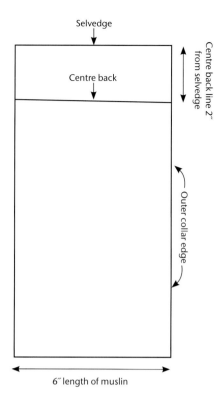

Selvedge

Centre back

Centre back line 2″ from selvedge

Outer collar edge

6″ length of muslin

Fig. 9.5 The dimensions of the calico collar to be draped.

C.B.

46. Cut a rectangular piece of calico measuring 12″ × 6″. Measure 1½″ from the selvedge and rule a line; this will be the centre back line of the collar.

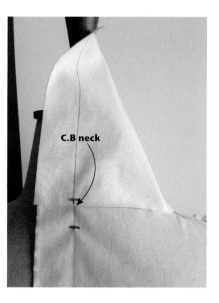

C.B neck

47. Position the C.B. line of the collar to the C.B. point of the neckline on the back bodice, and secure with a pin.

48. Side view of collar draped onto the neckline.

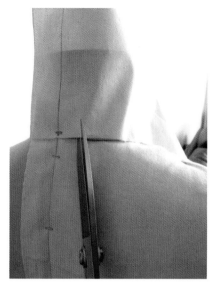

49. Use the points of shears to add vertical cuts at the neck edge of the collar, about 1″ between each one, to ease the symptoms of strain, as the collar is draped around the curve of the neckline.

50. Pin the collar to secure to the back neckline of the half toile, opening the cuts where needed to aid draping the collar smoothly.

51. The side front: continue to pin the collar onto the neckline from the shoulder point into the front neckline to the break-line.

52. Secure the collar onto the lapel. Check the length of the lapel. Make sure that the spring is not too long past the buttonhole or too short above: about ½″ roll above the button position is fine.

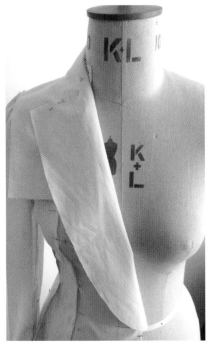

53. Re-pin the collar accordingly to obtain the desired length of lapel.

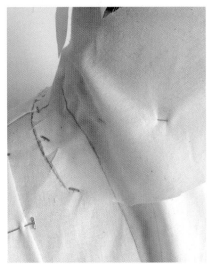

54. Fold the collar up. If necessary, pin and adjust the collar in accordance with the length of the lapel; when the desired length is achieved, mark the new front neckline, smoothing into the back neckline. Mark the stand of the collar: at the centre back it should be 1½″. At the shoulder point the stand of the collar should be marked 1⅜″. Draw in the stand and mark into the break-line of the lapel.

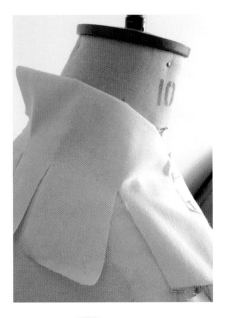

55. Fold the collar over on the breakline. Add cuts into the excess width of the collar to help it sit around the neck.

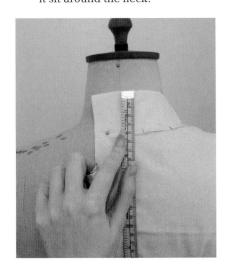

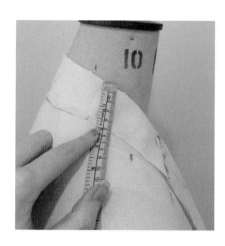

56. Mark the width of the fall: starting at the centre back break line (indicated with a pin with an orange head), measure 2″ and make a pencil mark. Measure the fall at the side neck, 1 ″, and make another mark.

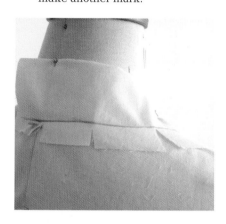

57. Cut away some of the excess width of the collar.

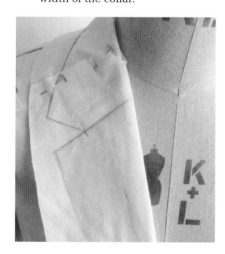

58. Draw in the notch of the lapel and collar according to desired width and style. For a classic

tailored revere lapel, observe the following images on how to measure the notch, this will assist when marking a lapel.

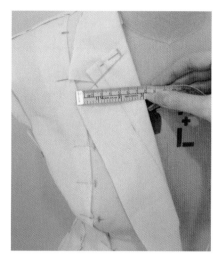

59. The lapel width: 3″, squared across from the break line.

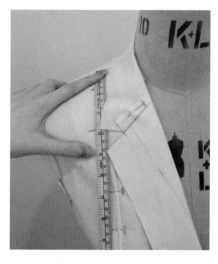

60. The lapel depth from the shoulder: 4¾″.

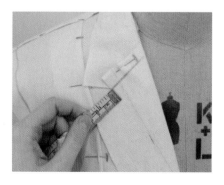

61. Mark the lapel notch balance point: 1⅜″ from lapel edge.

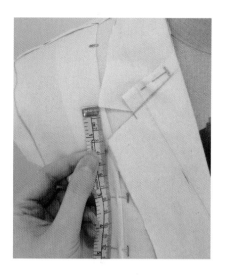

62. Measure between lapel point and collar point: 1⅜″.

63. Measure collar point from lapel balance point: 1⅜″.

64. Cut along pencil line of back collar.

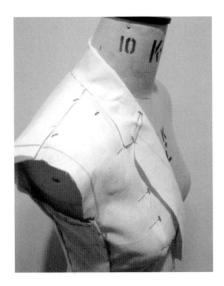

65. Side view of collar excess, which has been cut away.

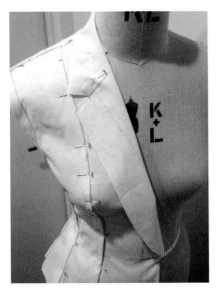

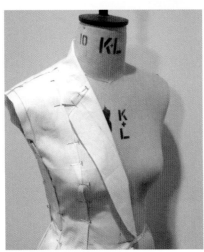

66. Front view of notch collar, with excess trimmed away.

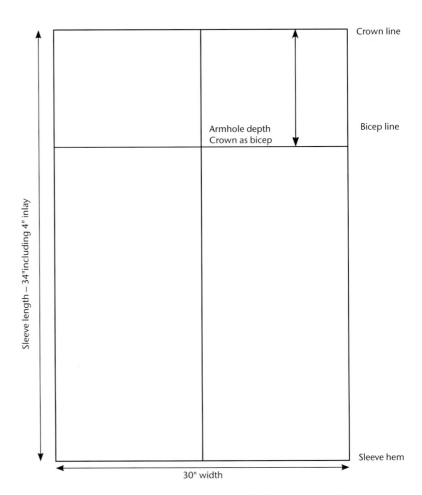

Fig. 9.7 The dimensions of the calico to be draped for the sleeve.

Draping the one-piece sleeve

67. Prepare a rectangular piece of calico, 34″ × 30″.
Length: the sleeve length plus inlays.
Width: the bicep plus inlays and extra width for draping.

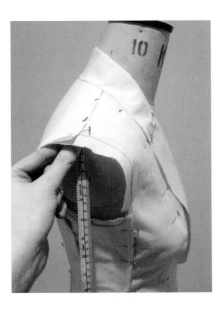

68. Measure the crown height vertically on the muslin plus 1″: 4½″. This is obtained from measuring the armhole depth on the pinned calico toile.

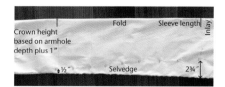

Crown height based on armhole depth plus 1"
Fold
Sleeve length
Inlay
½
Selvedge
2¾

69. Rule a 90° square horizontal line across from the crown height. Rule a vertical line down the centre of the piece and place on the fold.

70. Cut an angle from the armhole depth landmark point, angling in 1". Pin underarm seam as shown.

71. The sleeve before draping and pinning into the armhole.

72. Position the underarm seam directly into the front armhole. It is easier to line the seam up with the sideline of the mannequin as a start.

73. Add horizontal cuts in the front and back sections of the sleeve.

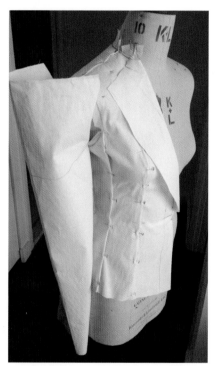

74. Side view: check the general balance of the sleeve by observing the front pitch.

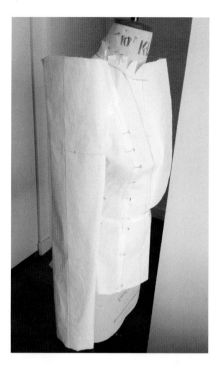

75. The correct sleeve balance: pin the front and back scye, 4" below the shoulder. The sleeve centre line should hang perfectly straight alongside the mannequin.

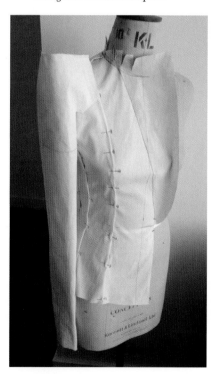

76. At the last pin on the sleeve 4" below shoulder seam of toile, add a horizontal cut and fold out excess calico on the front section of the sleeve.

77. Repeat for the back of the sleeve.

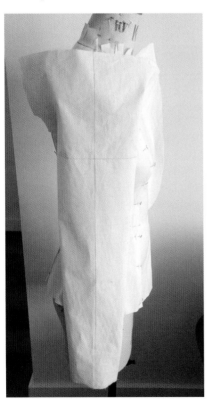

78. Side view showing the correct balance of the sleeve.

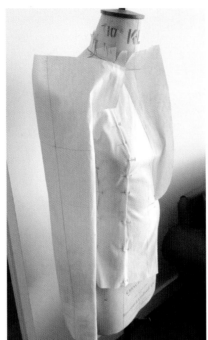

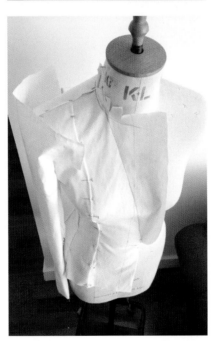

79. Aerial view.

80. Re-cut some of the excess calico into an oval shape; make sure there is at least 1″ of inlay over the armhole marked in pencil.

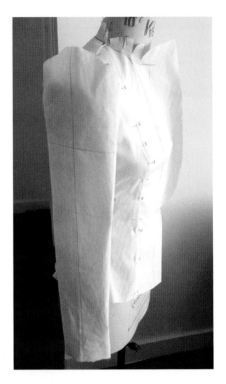

81. Pin the centre line of the sleeve to the shoulder seam, 3/8″ inside the armhole pencil line.

82. Pin the top part of the sleeve onto the armhole, easing the excess fullness evenly between each pin as shown above. As the toile will eventually be cut in wool suiting, extra fullness has been included between each pin, for the purpose of shrinking and adding sleeve roll.

83. The fullness should be concentrated at the crown area at the centre of the sleeve, where the

sleeve roll will eventually fill out the ease. In the lower back armhole the sleeve ease reduces to nothing.

84 .Draw in the net sleeve circumference line.

85. The correctly balanced draped sleeve. As it is currently pinned, the fullness at the crown is plentiful, with a high roll, which will shrink away under the iron. For different fabrics the fullness

in the crown will need to be adjusted from what is shown; to reduce the ease for lightweight cloth, the sleeve circumference can be reduced by re-shaping the sleeve to reduce the crown height. It can also be taken in at the underarm, then re-positioned into the armhole with less ease between each pin.

86. The desired sleeve length can be measured with a tape measure from the crown to the cuff, and the cuff inlay can be pinned up to the correct length.

From toile to pattern

To create a pattern from the draped shape, the bodice must first be unpinned from the mannequin. Before removing, all balance points, net sewing lines and details must be clearly marked in pencil.

THE SLEEVE

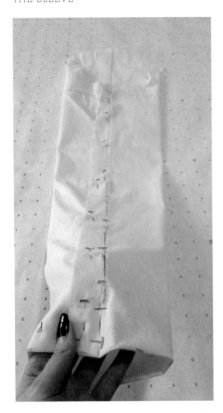

87. Begin by unpinning the sleeve, remembering to mark the front pitch point at the underarm and front and back balance notches. The unpinned sleeve is shown.

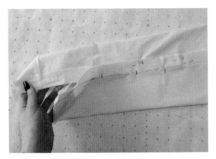

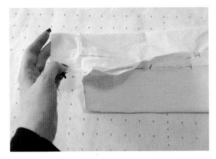

88. Mark in pencil a rough line at both sides of the underarm and at the hem of the sleeve. Remove the pins folding the hem up and at the underarm seam.

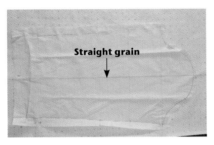

Straight grain

89. Draw a straight grain line on the paper. Square across for the

crown depth line. Pin the calico sleeve onto the lines. Open out the calico and lay flat onto pattern paper. The calico sleeve is smoothed out and laid onto paper to make a pattern. All marks are recorded onto the paper pattern.

90. Use a bodkin or tracing wheel to plot the net points of the cuff line.

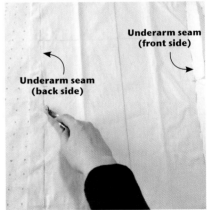

Underarm seam (front side)

Underarm seam (back side)

91. Trace the underarm seams and sleeve head circumference,

transferring marks for the balance notches. Take off the fabric sleeve and use the pierced holes to draw in the shape of the net sleeve.

Once all the lines have been copied onto the paper, remove the muslin sleeve and re-trace onto a clean sheet of pattern paper. Add 2½" inlay at the cuff and ³⁄₈" seam allowance at the underarm seams and around the sleeve head.

THE COLLAR

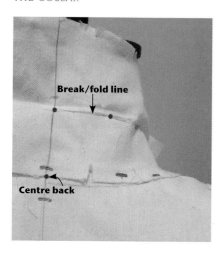

92. Before unpinning the collar, mark the front and back neckline, and the break/fold line, which has ¼" incorporated for the roll and fall of the collar.

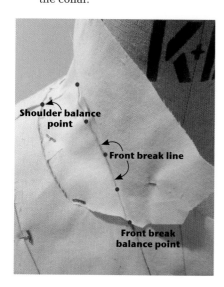

93. Mark balance notches at the shoulder seam and front break line.

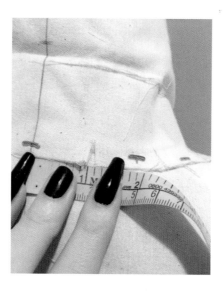

94. Measure the cuts in the collar neck edge and add them together to obtain the amount the collar neck will need to be stretched with a tailoring iron before basting onto the neckline. On the muslin each cut measures ¹⁄₈", and there are five cuts, therefore needing to be stretched by a total of ⁵⁄₈". Repeat for the outside edge as well.

   Unpin the collar and remove from the stand; double-check that the balance points for the centre back, shoulder and front break-line have been marked, and the neckline is drawn onto the front and back bodice.

95. Mark a grain line onto pattern paper, and pin the centre back of the collar to the paper, and smooth the collar flat across the paper with the use of your hands. Pin down all corners, or use a weight to hold the collar in place.

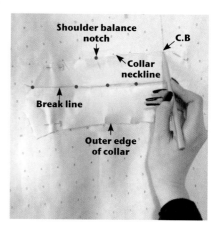

96. Draw around the edge of the collar, starting with the neck edge, transferring all balance points as shown. Use a bodkin or tracing wheel to trace through the break line.

97. Draw around the outer edge of the collar.

   After the lines have been transferred onto the paper, remove the pinned collar and trace a further two copies: one will be the under collar, the second the top collar.

   Mark a bias grain line on the under collar and add seam allowance.

   Mark a straight grain on the top collar, add ¼" roll into the pattern, and add required seam allowances to finish the pattern.

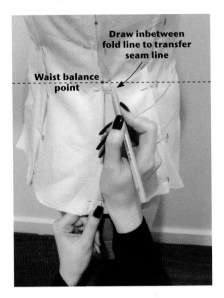

98. Before unpinning the back bodice, mark the waist balance points, and draw in the line from where the back folds on to the side panel. At the shoulder seam, a line near the fold of the back shoulder should also be marked onto the front bodice.

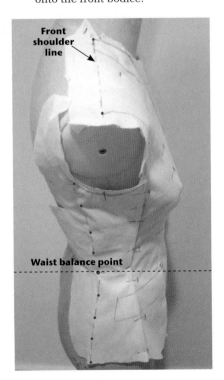

99. Unpin the centre back from the C.B. line, and at the shoulder, leaving the dart pinned in. The photo shows the back bodice

removed from the stand and the seam line drawn in at the side panel and front shoulder.
Draw in both sides of the pinned dart, and remove the pins. Flatten and smooth the back bodice flat.

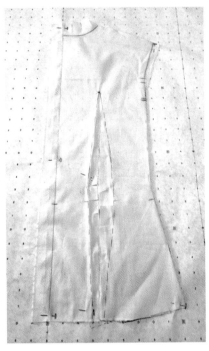

100. Mark a centre back grain line on to pattern paper, square across for a waist line, and pin the centre back pencil line on the muslin to the grain line on the paper.

101. Fold in the shoulder and side back excess calico and draw around the side, hem and shoulder net lines.

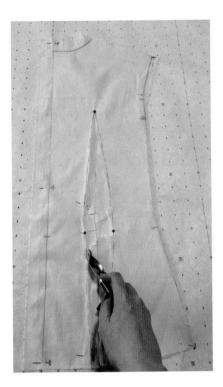

102. Use a tracing wheel or bodkin to trace the lines of the dart, the back neckline and armhole. Re-trace onto another piece of pattern paper, adding 4″ inlay onto the hem, 1½″ at the centre back, 1″ at the back neck, and ³⁄₈″ seam allowance at the remaining seams. At the dart add ³⁄₈″ seam allowance which stops 1½″ below the end of the dart.

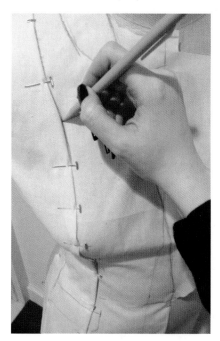

103. Mark in between the fold line through the bust. This will be the bust seam, which will divide the front panels into two separate pattern pieces. Draw a mark for the bust point and waist balance points. Repeat for the side panel seams.

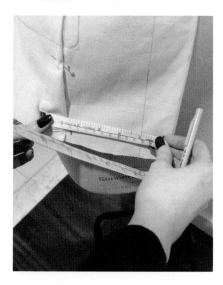

104. On the first front panel the centre line will be used as the straight grain line; this line needs to be transferred onto the second front panel and side panel before removing from the mannequin. The grain can be transferred onto

front panel 2 by measuring across from the centre line; add one mark just above the hem, 5" from the centre line; add another mark at the true waist level.

105. At the waist line measure 5" from the centre line and make a mark. Repeat for the side panel grain line. When the pieces are removed from the stand, rule a straight line through the marks. Release the pins at the centre line and unpin the front bodice from the mannequin, leaving the bust seam pinned in.

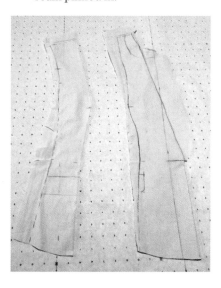

106. Rule two straight lines on spot and cross paper and allow enough space in between the lines for the

front muslin pieces. Remove the pins from the bust seam on the muslin and separate the two front bust panels. Pin the centre line of front panel 1 onto the line marked on spot and cross. Repeat for front panel 2.

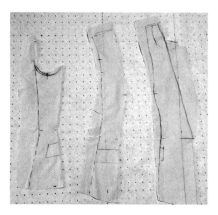

107. Repeat for side panel. Trace through all pencil lines, around edges and mark all balance points. Be sure to true all lines when making the pattern, so that they run smoothly. Re-trace a second version from the master copy and add inlays and seam allowances. Follow instructions given in Chapter 8: From block to pattern, in the section on seam allowances and inlays, for the added values.

Chapter 10
The importance of the fitting process

10

*This chapter introduces the importance
of the fitting process, as flat pattern
cutting cannot be based only upon
mathematical formulae, no more than
draping can be based solely upon
modelling to the mannequin.*

General principles
of fitting a jacket

A basic pattern carefully draped on
the mannequin usually fits with little
or no alteration. However, on a subject
whose posture varies from that of
the dress form, the results will only
be able to be duplicated by fitting
on the body. The same applies to
flat pattern cutting: calculations and
measurements derived from the bust,
waist and hip size will provide a basic
working foundation for obtaining the
general outline of the paper pattern in
accordance with the figure, but only
practical knowledge and experience in
fit, by checking the jacket on a model,
will achieve a precise pattern.

PROCEDURE FOR
FITTING A JACKET

1. Finding the correct front and back
balance

2. Sleeve balance, obtaining the correct
pitch

3. Waist suppression

4. The location of the bust point

5. The location of the neck point

6. Postural stance

Opposite page: Fig.10.1 Nicholas
Oakwell Runway suit; the balance of the
suit in perfect harmony with the wearer.
Right: Fig. 10.2 The vertical and
horizontal balance lines on the body:
centre line (C.F.), centre back (C.B.), bust
level, and true waist level.

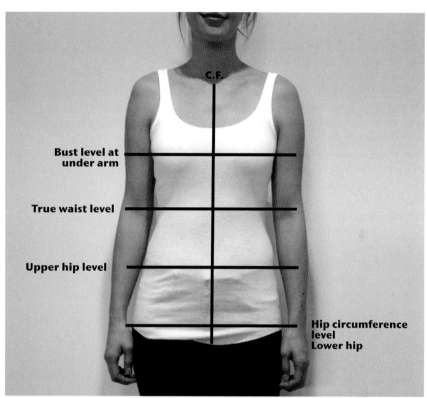

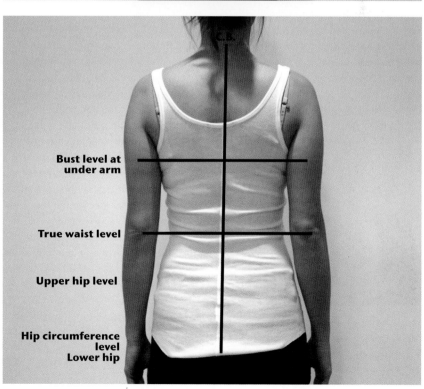

These are the basic elements that need to be questioned when observing the fit of a jacket; but understanding these skills can take years of trial and error for an apprentice or student. This chapter describes how to spot discrepancies on the jacket in relation to the body, with descriptions of what to look out for, and how to transfer the relevant adjustments to the pattern. The subject matter of fitting is so complex that it is impossible to include every possible alteration a cutter will encounter in the fitting room, in one chapter, as it is the subject matter of a book title in its own right. That said, it defines some of the more common problems that can affect the fit of a jacket, and tips of how to scrutinize them, which is another step to obtaining beautiful patterns, and an essential part of the process.

The purpose of fitting is to provide a master pattern from which to create other designs, for the flat pattern cutting method. Every correction, no matter how small, which perfects this pattern, is important, because any flaw in the master pattern is then transmitted to every design drafted from it.

Knowing where to place the vertical and horizontal grain on the body eliminates much of the guesswork. The centre line and centre back are the vertical balance line levels, and must hang perpendicular to the floor. The horizontal lines are the hip circumference

Fig. 10.3 The Forward fitting, which is a semi-finished fitting; everything is made up apart from the collar and sleeves. They are hand basted for a final check before the "Finish".

Fig. 10.4 The toile fitting of Nicholas Oakwell Runway suit.

level, upper hip, true waist level, and bust level. The bust level crosses over the bust points, ½" below the underarm and over the shoulder blades.

During all fittings the subject should stand in front of a mirror, so the cutter can see the results, without having to step away and look at the jacket. Watching the progress of the fitting also encourages the subject to keep their head upright, and face forward. All fitting should be done with the jacket right side out, and should only be done on one side. All changes should be transferred to the pattern immediately after the fitting.

There are two possible fitting procedures, and both have their advantages: the first one involves baste fittings in the actual cloth; the second is a toile fitting, cut in calico or muslin.

Baste fittings are used by bespoke tailors on Savile Row, for more classic styles. The jacket is cut in the actual cloth, with inches of inlay. It is a shell fitting of the jacket, with a canvas, and the pieces are hand basted together

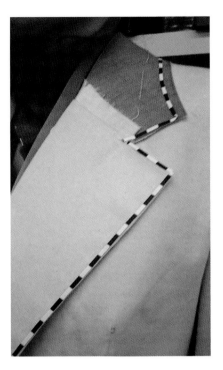

Fig. 10.5 Design tape is used in toile fittings to plot precise style lines.

with white stitches. All the adjustments are marked in chalk during the fitting, and altered directly onto the garment; made possible by the added inlay. The advantage of using the real suiting is that the fit is 100% accurate for the properties of the fabric.

There are four stages of baste fittings in bespoke tailoring:

1. The plain baste – a shell fitting, with canvas, no pockets.

2. The pocket baste – a shell fitting, with canvas, and all pockets machined.

3. The forward fitting – the forepart is completely made up, with finished facings, to include the back, side seam, and shoulder seams. Only the collar and sleeves are basted. It is a semi-finished fitting.

4. Finish – the jacket is completely finished off. Some alterations may still be recommended at this stage.

Toile fittings are used in ready-to-wear, or haute couture, for testing the pattern in dummy fabric, if the style is complex. The jacket is cut in a cream cotton fabric known as calico or muslin. The advantage of fitting in this way for ladies' jackets is that the seams can be ripped open, and re-pinned, or draped to fit; or even slashed through and more fabric pinned in, to dramatically change the proportion. Alterations can be pinned in at the seams and darts, in the way of tucks, without harming the surface of the fabric. Pencil lines can be drawn on to mark details, or design tape can be used to plot precise style lines. The design tape sticks to the calico.

The problem with a toile fitting is that the calico does not always truly represent the qualities of the selected cloth. To rectify this (budget permitting), it helps to toile in the real fabric, or something close to it, but this can be expensive. A toile fitting can also be combined with a baste fitting; so initially the pattern is tested with a calico toile, then after stages of fit, cut in the real fabric and prepared for a baste fitting as well. This is the intelligent method of practice, for a young cutter.

Three or four toile fittings are recommended to perfect a pattern, depending on the complexity; sometimes fewer are required. The process is to cut out the shape, fit, alter the pattern, cut a new toile, and fit again, until satisfied.

Finding the balance of a jacket

The general hang of a jacket is referred to as the 'balance'. The issue of balance is the most significant principle in cutting. Balance implies the relation of the jacket with the form of the wearer. It is the principle of construction that decides whether the garment is suited to the figure, whether its forces are acting in harmony, with all parts arranged in unison.

In tailored jackets, balance is generally defined as the length of the back in relation to the forepart, at the front of the jacket. A jacket that is perfectly balanced in relation to a proportionate figure will be hopelessly out of balance when placed upon a figure of stooping or erect attitude.

What makes the subject of balance complicated is that it must diverge with different figures and posture; but also the balance varies with different styles of jacket. A close fitting, tapered jacket needs a longer back balance than one of a semi-fitting, straight style, and a relatively longer front balance is preferred for an overcoat.

So far, as fashion influencing balance, the same principles apply to both ladies' and men's tailored jackets. In the case of ladies' jackets with many seams, balance marks (also known as notches) are marked at the waist and hip and other parts, to be able to govern and control each panelled section.

Correct balance

Stand to the side of a fit model wearing the jacket to judge the balance. The images below depicts perfect front and back balance, indicated with a balance level line in white, at the hem. The fronts should be about ¾"/1" longer than the back, depending on

Fig. 10.6 The correct level of balance, showing front and back hem line in correct alignment.

Fig. 10.7 The balance level at the hemline will tilt upwards at the front hem, if the front balance is too short. This is indicated with the white line, as an incorrect level guideline.

Fig. 10.8 The balance level at the hemline will appear too long in the front at the hem, if the front balance is too long.

the style of course. Any more and the front balance is too long.

Short front balance

When the front balance is too short, the fronts of the jacket lift up, making the jacket uncomfortable to the wearer. Put simply, the front rises higher than the back from the side angle, as indicated by the new balance level line in Fig. 10.7. An alteration can be made to the pattern by adding height to the shoulder, or slashing through the waist line of the pattern and adding length – in effect, dropping the front to lengthen the balance. The amount to lengthen the front is purely based on judgment in the fitting, and checking the side angle of the jacket.

Long front balance

A long front balance produces a garment, which falls away in the front and hangs away in the back. The front balance from the side appears long from the side angle, as indicated in the adjusted balance level of Fig. 10.8. The reverse of the adjustment explained for a short front balance can be applied to rectify the problem, by picking up the front shoulders, or slashing through the pattern and removing the required amount. This will in effect take up and shorten the front balance.

Long back balance

A long back balance causes closeness in the fit on the hips and a loose fit at the top of the back. The back neck and shoulder may be raised, to shorten the back balance. A short back balance causes the jacket to stand away from the hip and to gape at the top neck. A piece may be added to the pattern across the back shoulders and back neck to lengthen the back balance.

As a final explanation, balance may be said to be the harmonious arrangement between the various parts of the jacket with the figure it covers; this applies to all other garments and sleeves.

Fig. 10.9 The basted sleeve from the side should hang vertically in line with the straight grain of the jacket body.

Fig. 10.10 The basted sleeve should suspend in line with the mark stitches on the pocket flap, without drag lines distorting its appearance.

Sleeve balance

The correct hang of a sleeve defines its comfort and appearance. It is the pitching of the sleeve that decides the balance. Finding the pitch points can be tricky to an in-experienced tailor, student, or home dressmaker. The sleeve should fall without drag marks in the front or the back of the sleeve, and should suspend in the centre of the front hip pockets and from the side view drape vertically on the straight grain.

If the sleeve hangs too forward, lowering the front pitch point and raising the back pitch point by the same amount will drop the sleeve, to incline towards the back. If the sleeve is too far back, raising the front pitch point and lowering the back pitch point will angle the sleeve more forward. It is advisable to baste the sleeves by hand first to ascertain the correct sleeve pitch points and correct distribution of sleeve ease and fullness, before machining.

Waist suppression

Waist suppression is the shaping applied to the waist on jackets. It is essentially the distribution of width at the waist; more importantly, it proves that each panel is inter-dependent. The marriage between each panel is a matter of co-ordination, which can be achieved through the addition of balance notches on the waist.

Depending on the style of jacket, significant suppression tapers in at the waist to create an hourglass silhouette; reduced suppression will hang straight, creating a looser fit. As a rule, the bust and hips are larger than the waist; when cutting a flat pattern for a jacket, it is made large enough through the bust and hip, then tapered to fit hollows at the waist.

Incorrect distribution of suppression will throw the balance out, affecting the shoulder blades, hip, and button wrap width; extra fitting and darts in the forepart often make a jacket closer fitting. However, if the extra allowance is not added into the pattern, the jacket will appear to be large enough on paper, but the front edges will

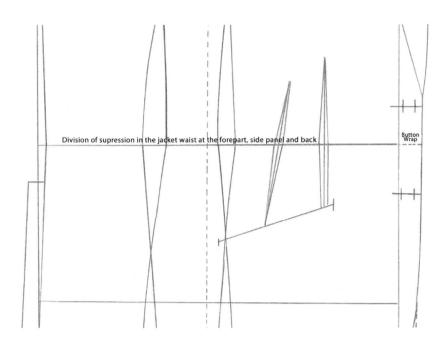

Division of suppression in the jacket waist at the forepart, side panel and back

Button Wrap

Fig. 10.11 General division of arranging suppression at the waist.

not close. Equally, incorrect balance will cancel out the suppression at the waist; if there is correct suppression for the figure at the centre back, but the back balance is too short, the coat will not fit in the waist.

If there is correct suppression in the jacket waist measurement, and the front button wrap closes to the correct overlap by 1½", but the centre back requires further definition by taking in the seam, then the front wrap should

be let out to compensate for the value it will be nipped in by at the centre back. Therefore, if the centre back waist needs to be taken in on the pattern ¼", let out the front edge by ¼". If this action is not completed, in the next fitting the jacket will not have enough button wrap to close and will be ¼" smaller in the half jacket waist measurement. This will create unsightly draglines in the front button area on the jacket, as the wrap is straining to close, due to a tight jacket waist.

The waist is a crucial divisional point. The upper and lower sections of the jacket are equally reliant, and to repeat what was mentioned previously – if they are not considered and cut in harmony with each other, and fitted in agreement with the figure, problems will arise throughout the technical process.

Thankfully, if enough width and allowance are added into the pattern at the waist, the suppression can be decided during the fitting stages, and can be pinned in as desired, divided equally between each panel. It is significantly more complicated to let the jacket out, if it is cut too small in

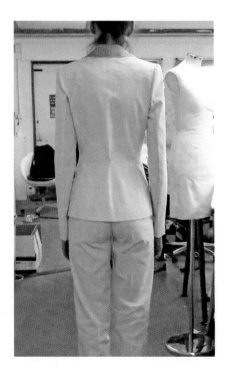

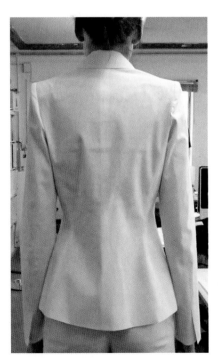

Fig. 10.12 (i) The centre back needs further waist definition and reduced flare over the seat area of the buttocks. (ii) The amount the centre back seam needs to be nipped in. (iii) The front wrap is correct; therefore, the front edges will need to be let out on the pattern to accommodate the new suppression: ¼".

Fig. 10.13 Marking the front edge with a chalk mark allows the cutter to check the jacket waist measure and calculate the final suppression.

Fig. 10.14 The bust position is marked with chalk or pins directly onto the jacket being fitted.

the first initial fitting. Some cutters will choose to cut the waist loose in the flat paper pattern and notably nip in the waist, during the toile fits. In ready-to-wear and traditional bespoke tailoring, an alterations tailor will often execute the final waist definition on the suit jacket in the final fitting. This is why a tailor will mark the front edge with chalk at the point of overlap, to check the button wrap extension, calculate the waist suppression and record a half jacket waist measurement.

The location of the bust point

In the cutting of ladies' jackets, the importance of the bust point determines the visual effect of the garment. It is useful to mark its position during fit stages, so it is in balance with the wearer, and then transferred on to the pattern.

If the bust point is positioned incorrectly it can create uncomplimentary silhouettes to the proportion of the bust line on the jacket; if the bust point sits too far away from the centre front, towards the underarm, it creates the illusion of a wide chest. It is like a barrel in appearance, when compared to the waist and hip proportion, which

is unflattering for the female form. Moving the bust point position, to be closer to the front and away from the

side body, can amend this. The first front dart should be re-positioned to square 90° vertically from the new point. The neck dart should also be moved so that the end of the dart is level with the new bust point.

The same applies to a bust point that has been positioned too low, visually dictating that the wearer has a dropped bust – brutally unattractive. To fix, simply raise the point to be higher, and amend in the pattern.

In a flat pattern the bust point will be difficult to navigate exactly, and is plotted as an initial guideline in the divisional grid system, based on measurements taken from the size chart or customer. The point must be checked in a fitting. This also concerns patterns obtained through draping: the bust point has been taken from the mannequin, which again would need to be checked on a fit model for accuracy.

Incorrect Bust Point Position too far towards the underarm

Fig. 10.15 The bust point is positioned too far to the underarm of the jacket, creating a wide bust silhouette, which is unflattering for the form.

The location of the neck point

The location of the neck and shoulder point, which is also known as 'straightening' and 'crookening', is determined by the diameter of the neck, and prominence of bust; but it can also be influenced by the style of jacket, the posture or stance of the wearer and the attitude and general proportion of the wearer.

To uneven the front neck point: 'crookening' (Fig. 10.17)

The word 'crooken' is colloquial speech from traditional tailors, used predominantly on Savile Row. The word evolved from the term 'crooked' to describe a level or straight neck point on a jacket that needs to be un-levelled, to fit the body.

A shoulder that has been cut too straight and level sits too close into the neck, and is too short through the length of the front, causing the hem to swing too far into the centre front. In the image below, the balance level lines are indicated on the toile of a jacket, for a

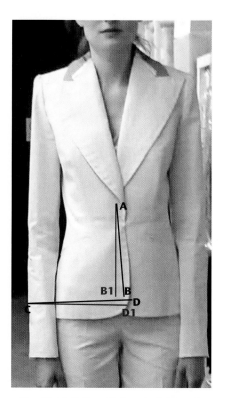

Fig. 10.16 Toile with too straight neck and shoulder position, causing the hem of the forepart to lift up.

shoulder that has been cut too straight.

Line A to B is indicated at the button wrap; notice the angle of the front edge overlap. This line should hang at a 90° angle, and be vertically straight to be in line with the centre line on the body.

Line C to D is represented at the hem; the angle of the hemline tilts up at the front edge, to nothing at the side. This is clearly a front neck point issue, which has been cut too straight, and the problem can be fixed by carrying out the alteration to uneven the shoulder angle at the neck point – 'crookening'. This changes the angle of the shoulder at the neck point to sit further away from the neck, and have more length; to nothing at the shoulder ends. This drops the fronts only at the centre line, giving the appearance of a shoulder angle that is not level.

A new red line – A to B1, and C to D1 – shows the correct angle that needs to be obtained at the front edge, and hem in the centre line; the following amendment to the pattern will achieve this.

The amendment to correct an over straightened neck point is to add length into the centre front only; remember the sides are at a good balance level. The amount the jacket needs to be 'crookened': 3/8″. The original block is indicated with a black line, and the alteration is marked with red dotted lines.

A

Positioned 3/8″ higher than point 14, and 3/8″ horizontally away from point 14.

B

3/8″ wider from point 24, to retain the same shoulder length measurement. If this action were not carried out, it would shorten the shoulder from the intended width.

A and B

The approximate shoulder length, equal to points 14 and 24. The front armhole is re-drawn back into the underarm at point 37.

C

Lapel point, which is re-marked 3/8″ narrower and higher at the peak to nothing at the button position; this is to retain the original lapel proportions.

D, E and F

The new neck dart position 3/8″ back from the original position.

G

The new position of the break line, marked 3/8″ inside of the original break and ruled to nothing at the button position.

This adjustment is used to lengthen the balance of the fronts. The original block can be used to pivot the neck and shoulder point on the paper; the front length will drop from the neck and be in correct alignment.

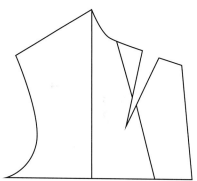

The basic block before neck alteration

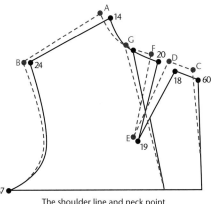

The shoulder line and neck point with crookening alteration

Fig. 10.17 To crooken a shoulder line and neck position.

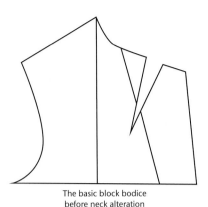

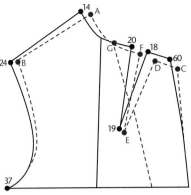

The basic block bodice
before neck alteration

The shoulder line and neck point
with straightening applied

Fig. 10.19 A toile with long front edges. The length has been pinched out of the lapels
to raise the front length to be level and shorter.

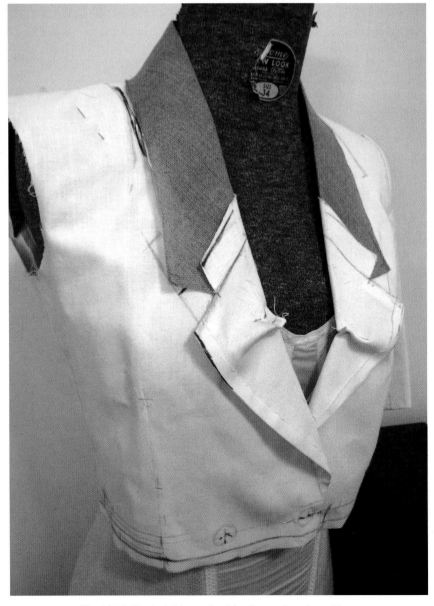

Fig. 10.18 To straighten a shoulder line and neck position,
pinch in the lapel until the hem rises to the correct balance.

Straightening alteration (Fig. 10.9)

A shoulder that has been cut too crooked is positioned too far away from the base of the neck. In other words, the collar will not sit close into the subject's neck because the neck point is too wide, and the shoulder angle needs to be straightened. Consequently, it causes the lapel to lengthen, to gape and stand away from the chest, and the hem of the front coat to swing away from the button point, and the hem level. The extra length can be shortened with a straightening alteration, which straightens the shoulder, neck point and armhole. The addition of a dart in the break line of the lapel and a bridle tape, stitched along the roll line, which is drawn in tight at the chest, will also reduce the length of the lapel. Fig. 10.8 shows a toile with shoulders that need to be straightened; the extra length has been pinned out of the lapel; this is an ideal way to judge the value to straighten the neck by.

The black dots indicate the original lines from the basic block and the red dotted lines indicate the adjusted pattern points, showing where the pattern has been pivoted on pattern paper and re-marked.

To straighten the neck point, firstly judge the amount to be reduced by pinching in the excess at the lapel break line. This example uses the value of $3/8"$.

A
Positioned $3/8"$ lower than point 14 and $3/8"$ horizontally into the neckline.

B
$3/8"$ narrower from point 24.

A and B
The approximate shoulder length, equal to points 14 and 24. The front armscye is re-drawn back into the underarm at point 37.

C
The lapel point, which is re-marked $3/8"$ wider and lower at the peak to nothing at the button position.

D, E and F

The new dart position ³⁄₈″ forward of the original position.

G

The new position of the break line, marked ³⁄₈″ from the original break and ruled to nothing at the button position.

This small adjustment is a trick used to shorten the balance of the fronts: by pivoting the neck and shoulder point, the length of the fronts will shorten and be in correct alignment.

The style of coat will also influence the neck point. If the coat is to button high into the neck, it will take a less crooked shoulder than if it is to button to the waist. A double-breasted style of jacket requires a straighter shoulder and neck point, as do overcoats. These are all options to consider, when deliberating the question of the neck point and shoulder position in jacket cutting.

Postural stance

A person's body is not symmetrical. In daily practice in bespoke tailoring, figures vary in attitude from the regular stance position used for ready-to-wear jackets. The regular, the tall, the short, and the corpulent may classify figures, with posture that is erect, stooping, and shoulders that are straight, sloping, and down on one side. The attitude and general proportion of the figure must be studied for bespoke jackets and are essential for the correct location of the neck and shoulder, so that the garment will be in balance with the figure.

It is also an important skill to identify postural discrepancies for ready-to-wear fittings; sometimes the model in a fitting will have figure irregularities that will distort the jacket. This is normal, as not even a model's body is perfectly symmetrical, but having this knowledge can help to solve fit issues that will arise.

In the mass population postural stance has slowly evolved to be more forward in stance, due to the increased use of computers, and sitting at desks;

the levels of this stance vary in attitude to tilt from the neck, hip or waist.

To adjust a pattern for the leaning forward stances the length of the centre back to the armscye needs to increase; and the length from the nape of the neck at the centre back to the bust line (points 0 to 1 on the back pattern only) should be shortened. This can be observed when trying on the jacket. This posture will cause the jacket to be long in the fronts. The forepart pattern should be shorter at the armscye, comparatively to the back pattern, which is lengthened.

The measurement to adjust depends on the level at which the tilt in posture occurs: the waist, hip or neck.

In contrast, figures can tilt into overly erect stances; leaning back from the waist and the hip, from using gymnasiums to correct posture. Most runway models will stand overly erect, and amendments to the pattern will need to change, to accommodate this stance.

This is the opposite fitting problem to the forward leaning stance. The length of the centre back to the armscye should be shortened to accommodate this. Also the length from the nape of the neck at the centre back to the bust level line (points 0 to 1 on the back pattern only) should be increased, a variation that will be especially noticeable in trying on a jacket, as this posture makes the jacket tilt up in the front, and spring out at the lower front edge, when observed from a side view.

A final note

When beginning a fitting, it is imperative to study the entire jacket, from front, back and side views, and carry out a careful analysis of all flaws, before ripping a seam. To learn to fit successfully, observe the figure keenly and study the relationships between its contours, just as a sculptor would do. An awareness of grain must be identified, in order to know where and when to adjust it, and learning to follow unwanted wrinkles and bulges to their origin, in order to know

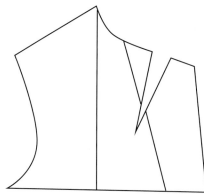

Regular S.B neck point

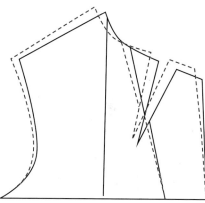

Crookened S.B neck point

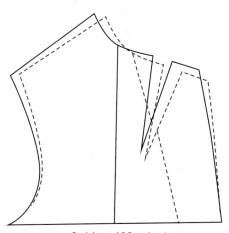

Straightened S.B neck point

Fig. 10.20 The regular S.B. shoulder, the crookened S.B. shoulder, and the straightened S.B. shoulder; indicated with red dotted lines.

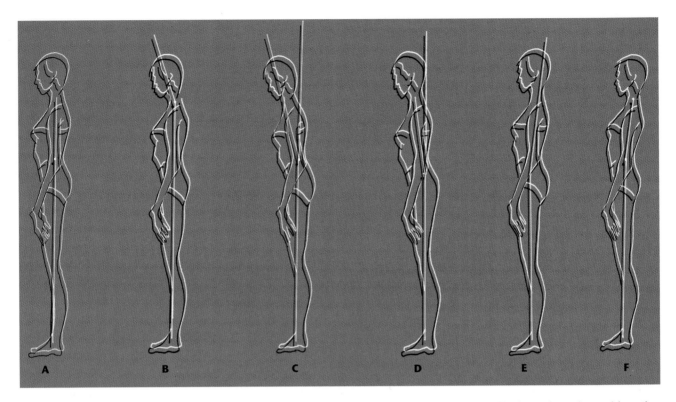

Fig. 10.21 The postural stance chart. a) Correct posture b) The figure leans forward at the neck c) The figure leans forward from the waist. d) The figure leans forward from the hip e) The overly erect posture – leans back from the hip f) The overly erect posture – leans back from the waist

whether they are caused by figure irregularity, mistakes in pattern shape, or posture.

Fitting that requires the re-pinning of seams on the figure is in fact draping in its most complex form. Since the body is never motionless, and it is harder to pin the fabric securely in position, it takes skill and precise handling to pin accurately, without pricking the subject.

In addition to basic handling skills, the fitting requires an understanding of pattern shapes. The curves in a pattern edge do not necessarily mean that a curved seam will appear in the jacket, but may denote flare, or a part of the body that requires ease to smooth over a rounded part of the body. To fit without an understanding of this relationship between pattern shape and pattern contour and to work simply on the pattern, is to assume the body is flat. In an attempt to fix a problem, or wrinkle line, the inexperienced cutter may unwittingly create a new one. It is this understanding of pattern shapes and grain that achieves mastery of fitting.

The ability to meet the fitting demands in a fashion house, and understanding the varying figures and posture stance, cannot be taught easily, and the pressure can be daunting for a young cutter. Yet, a well-fitted jacket can be accomplished, by checking patterns with toiles or bastes, and using common sense in fittings. It is important to implement an intelligent procedure based on knowledge, shrewd observation, and a methodical understanding gained through experience, devoting practice, patience, and perseverance.

Glossary

Atelier 'Atelier' is the French word for workshop. It is the workshop of couturiers or tailors, who craft patterns and produce the garments in-house, with master and apprentice craftspersons. They are normally regulated by royal European guilds that endorse traditional skills.

Balance The arrangement of a garment hanging on the body in perfect harmony, without drag lines, or disorder in the fit.

Balance levels Landmark points on the body – true waist, bust line, hip circumference level, and upper hip sections – for interpreting correct balance in fittings.

Balance notches Balance notches are marks added to the pattern as language for the tailor or sample machinist, which indicate balance levels on the body. They match together when sewing, and help the tailor to scrutinize balance in the fitting.

Baste The term 'baste' is used to describe the white hand stiches used in bespoke tailoring. Bastes are loose stitches, applied with basting thread; the thread snaps easily for the purpose of ripping out, as they are a temporary, not permanent stitch.

Bespoke tailoring Specific to a customer's needs and specifications, executed by a tailor. The distinguishing points are that the customer has complete control over the cloth, style, design details, and the fit is personal to the measurements of the wearer. Carried out through a series of fittings, it is very expensive and demands the highest quality of fabric, construction and fit. Bespoke tailoring is specific to suits; one suit can take several months to fit and make by hand.

Bias grain Bias grain lines are marked at a 45° angle to the selvedge/warp threads on the fabric. It is an ideal grain line to use for draped garments, or for stretching purposes in tailoring.

Break/roll line The break line on a tailored jacket is the line where the lapel folds back into the body.

Bust point The location of the centre of each breast, directly over the nipple area.

Button extension The button extension is added to the centre line of a jacket to accommodate button fastenings and depends on the style of jacket (S.B. or D.B.), and size of the buttons selected.

Button wrap The total wrap-over width on double-breasted or single-breasted fronts, when the top side of the forepart buttons over the under side of the forepart.

Centre back The vertical line that follows the spinal column and is used for drafting patterns for the back; abbreviated to C.B.

Centre line/centre front The vertical line used for drafting or draping patterns for the front part of the body; it follows a line that is directly in front of the spinal column. It is abbreviated to C.F., for centre front.

Chest canvas Woven horsehair, which is woven tighter, and feels harder to the touch than hair cloth; used to cover the bust area on the hair cloth internal canvas.

Collar canvas Collar canvas is an internal structure used to sandwich between the top collar and under collar; it is hand pad stitched to the collar fabric.

Collar fall The 'fall' is the section of the collar which folds and falls on the shoulders.

Collar melton A fabric similar to felt in appearance, which is pad stitched to collar canvas to form the under collar of a traditional bespoke collar construction.

Collar stand The 'stand' applies to the height the collar sits into the neck before it folds over.

Cut on fold To 'cut on the fold' is to place a line of the pattern on the vertical fold line of the fabric; the centre back of the tailored top collar is cut without a centre back seam, so it is cut with a fold line at the centre.

Double-breasted (D.B.) This refers to the button extension to the centre line of the jacket. 'Double' denotes two rows of buttons.

Double jet pocket A pocket with two exposed single jets cut in self-fabric, to match the cloth cut for the body of the jacket.

Draping Modelling pre-cut pieces of calico or muslin to the mannequin, to the desired style, with the use of pins. (*See also* Modelling).

Ease Patterns are not be made to the exact size of the body, as it would restrict movement and be uncomfortable to the wearer. There are two kinds of ease: the first is fitting ease, which applies to the number

of inches included into the pattern to make it wearable; the second is construction ease. This is the amount the pattern is expanded to create the desired fullness for a given design aesthetic. On jackets this is included in the sleeve head and the back shoulder seam. (*See also* Fullness.)

Facing The facing is a pattern piece that is used to finish the edges of a garment; normally machined on, bagged-out, and folded to sit on the inside. On a jacket, the facing is sewn to the front edge of the forepart, from the notch lapel to the front hem.

False forearm This refers to the displacement of the under seam, positioned further into the underarm. (*See also* Three-quarter sleeve.)

Fast fashion An approach to fashion employed by mass-market or high-street stores, whereby trends featured on the runway are quickly re-interpreted, imitated, and manufactured cheaply, to be placed in stores in large numbers.

Felling Felling is a tight hand stitch used to join seams in tailoring that have been basted together. When the seam has been hand felled, the baste stitches can be pulled out.

Fifty/fifty sleeve A sleeve type in which the under sleeve and top sleeve are distributed exactly evenly.

Fit model A person used by a designer in the industry to test the fit and look of the sample garments produced from a pattern. The model's size will adhere to the target size of the pattern.

Flat pattern cutting The pattern making technique drafted on paper in two dimensions.

Fullness In bespoke tailoring, fullness refers to the extra width added into a sleeve to create a roll at the sleeve head.

Fusing Bonded interlining that can be pressed to certain parts of a garment to retain its shape and add structure.

Gorge The seam that joins the collar to the lapel.

Grading A term used in ready-to-wear flat pattern cutting to describe the process of re-sizing a block to increase or decrease the size code.

Hair cloth Woven horsehair, which is softer than chest canvas; used as an internal structure inside a tailored jacket to cover the full length of the forepart front.

Haute couture 'Haute couture' is the French phrase for 'high sewing'. The term refers to custom designed clothes made by hand from start to finish by the most skilled couturiers, with extremely close attention to detail. These clothes are very expensive and of the highest quality and finish, often made for the elite in society. The amount of time, skill and art that is required means that one piece can take several months to finish.

In-breast pocket Internal chest pockets, which run across the facing and lining inside the jacket.

Inlay Inlay is a larger width, normally several inches, added to net sewing lines, or in addition to the $\frac{3}{8}$" seam allowance; a large inlay will be left on the hem for the purpose of lengthening.

Interlining This is a term used to describe internal fabrics that are used to add structure; whether it is canvas, fusing (which is applied with a heat press), linen, or silesia.

Jet and flap pocket A pocket with one exposed upper jet with a flap concealing the pocket opening, which is underneath.

Jigger button An internal button, used to support the overlapped fronts of a double-breasted extension.

Ligne Button diameter measurement.

Lining An internal finish that is inserted in tailored jackets to hide the seam allowances, fraying edges, and interlinings; normally cut in a shiny silk or Bemburg.

Modelling Draping styles of garment on the form from pre-cut pieces of calico and muslin. Any style of garment can be modelled on a mannequin.

Net/net sewing lines These are the sewing lines of the pattern, without any seam allowance or inlay. The patterns are drafted as 'net', and traced off as a copy, with seam allowance added to the net sewing lines.

Notched collar/lapel A notched lapel is the most traditional informal collar shape, identified with two notches.

Outer breast welt pocket A single rectangular pocket positioned on the left side of the jacket, above the breast.

Pagoda shoulder A shoulder proportion first made popular in the 1970s by Tommy Nutter, Savile Row tailor. The shoulder ends raise high, in comparison to the neck, and are filled out with layers of wadding, hand basted to the shoulder pads.

Patch pocket A patch pocket is a piece of cloth, cut in self-fabric that is applied onto the fronts of the hips, either by hand or machine.

Peak collar/lapel A peak lapel is a formal lapel, traditionally reserved for tuxedo styles or double-breasted fastenings on jackets. It is pointed in appearance and can be covered with silk.

Ready-to-wear Ready-to-wear is the term for factory made clothing, in standardized size codes, intended to be worn without considerable alteration, with the intention to fit most people.

Roll The term 'roll' is used to describe extra width, which is incorporated into a pattern for the purpose of rolling. Roll is added to the lapel edge of the jacket facing pattern, and the edge of the top collar for the purpose of reducing tightness; the ends of a collar or lapel will turn up if there is not enough roll incorporated into the pattern.

Seam allowance This is an allowance added to the net sewing lines for the purpose of construction. A usual seam allowance is $\frac{3}{8}$".

Self Or 'self fabric': means to cut the pattern piece in the same fabric/suiting as the main body fabric.

Selvedge The selvedge of the cloth is a self-finished edge, which prevents the warp and weft threads from unravelling. In woven fabric the selvedge runs parallel, vertically, to the warp threads, which run the entire length of the fabric. The textile mill it has been woven at, with the name woven into its selvedge edge, identifies the vertical warp grain on wool suitings.

Shawl collar A style of lapel in which the top collar is grown-on to the lapel of the facing pattern.

Silesia A form of cotton used for pocket bags, and to add internal structure inside the lapel of a jacket.

Single-breasted (S.B.) Is a reference to the size of the button extension to the centre line of a jacket. Single implies one column of buttons.

Slash 'Slash' is a term used to describe the action of cutting through a line with scissors.

Sleeve roll Sleeve roll is added to the crown of the top sleeve, to add a roll at the sleeve circumference. It is intended to fill out the extra ease/fullness included in the pattern.

Spread 'Spread' is a term used in dart manipulation. 'Slash and spread' refers to the technique in which a dart is cut, closed and spread open in a new location on the body.

Square a line To 'square a line' is to obtain perfect 90° angles both vertically and horizontally.

Straight grain Grain lines are what make a pattern work, when chopped in cloth. Just as the body has horizontal and vertical lines, so does the fabric. Pattern drafting must match the lines of the body, to the lines of the cloth. The straight grain is a 90° angle, marked vertically on each pattern piece. For a tailored jacket the straight grain line on the pattern is directly parallel to the vertical selvedge on the woven fabric/cloth.

Suitings Fabrics used to make suits; therefore appropriate for jackets and trousers for traditional tailoring.

Technical drawing Also known as a flat sketch; this is a black and white front and back sketch used to communicate designs for presentation and production. The garment is drawn flat, off the body, with construction details and technical information.

Three-quarter sleeve The three-quarter sleeve is another name for the false forearm. It is given this name because of the displacement of the under seam, which changes the proportion of the top sleeve to be three times bigger than the under sleeve.

Toile/muslin A test version of the pattern cut in muslin fabric or calico, to trial the pattern and fit.

To 'true' a line Is to draw over a line to achieve a smooth running of lines that seam together in a pattern.

Woven fabric/cloth Woven fabric starts with vertical threads, known as the warp threads, held parallel to each other on a loom. Horizontal threads, known as the weft threads, are woven into the vertical threads, at a perfect right angle to each other. The direction of the threads indicates the direction of its vertical and horizontal grain lines.

List of Suppliers

United States

Tailoring and pattern making supplies
Bear Paper and Trim
www.bearpaperandtrim.com

B. Black & Sons
www.bblackandsons.com

Material Concepts
www.materialconcepts.com/products/
sewn-products-supplies/marker-
pattern-making

Steinlauf and Stoller Inc.
www.steinlaufstoller.com

Scissors (tailoring and pattern cutting)
Wiss
www.wisstool.com

Dress stands
Siegal & Stockman
www.siegal-stockman.com

Wolf Form Company Inc.
www.wolfform.com

United Kingdom

Pattern making tools
Morplan
www.morplan.com

MacCulloch & Wallis
www.macculloch-wallis.co.uk

Tailoring supplies
Burnstein & Banleys
www.theliningcompany.co.uk

Richard James Weldon
www.richardjamesweldon.com

Dress stands
Kennett & Lindsell
www.kennettlindsell.com

Scissors
William Whitely & Sons Ltd.
www.whitely.co.uk

Europe

Dress stands
Siegel & Stockman (France)
www.siegel-stockman.com

Zimmerman Busten (Switzerland)
www.buesten.ch

Index